HOMERIC RENAISSANCE
The Odyssey *of George Chapman*

HOMER'S ODYSSES.
Translated according to ỹ Greeke.
By. Geo: Chapman
At mihi ỹ viuo detraxerit Inuida Turba
Post obitum duplici fænore reddet Honos.

Solus sapit

hic homo.

Reliqui vero.

Vmbræ mouentur.

Pallas

Vlysse.

Imprinted at London by
Rich: Field, for Nath-
aniell Butter.

HOMERIC RENAISSANCE

The Odyssey *of George Chapman*

by George deF. Lord

Archon Books
1972

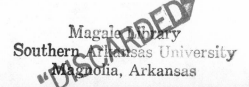

First published 1956 by
The Yale University Press
Reprinted 1972 with permission in an unaltered
and unabridged edition as an Archon Book by
The Shoe String Press, Inc.
Hamden, Connecticut 06514

[*Yale Studies in English*, Volume 131]

ISBN 0-208-01130-7
Library of Congress catalog card number 70-179566

Printed in the United States of America

FOR RUTH

CONTENTS

PREFACE

FROM the time they appeared Chapman's translations of Homer received widespread attention from poets, critics, and scholars. While there has been much comment of a general nature on their style and some analysis of particular features, no study both comprehensive and particular enough to do justice to the subject has so far appeared. The remarks of Pope, Lamb, Coleridge, and Swinburne, as well as recent articles on their ethical character by scholars like Chapman's distinguished editor, Miss Phyllis Bartlett, have been extremely valuable. Yet Chapman's translations make large claims not only as interpretations of Homer but as English epics. This is especially true of his *Odyssey*, a poem which demands a full study of ethical structure and poetic texture in relation to Homer and within the framework of Renaissance classicism.

This book was begun six years ago as a Ph.D. thesis at Yale. I first conceived my task as a twofold enquiry into the ethical nature of Chapman's *Odyssey* and its value as an English epic poem. In order to evaluate Chapman's interpretation, I found myself drawn much farther into a study of Homer's *Odyssey* than I had anticipated. This study resulted in my publishing an article on the *Odyssey* itself which is listed in the bibliography.

This book is also concerned with Homer and I hope will prove of interest to classical scholars as well as English scholars. I have tried to make full use of Homeric studies, within my limitations as an amateur. My chief regret on this score is that W. B. Stanford's fascinating study of *The Ulysses Theme*, an admirable synthesis of classical learning and critical perception, has appeared too late for me to make more than incidental use of it. I am also disappointed that the much-needed new edition of Chapman's *Homer* by Allardyce Nichol will not be published until some months after this book goes to press.

A word of explanation is needed about the texts of Chapman's *Homer* from which I have quoted and also about the prose translations of original passages from Homer which I have supplied. The Chapman text is *The Whole Works of Homer* (1616). Except for making lower-case 's' and 'i', 'j', 'u' and 'v' consistent with modern practice, I have retained the original spelling. Chapman's chaotic punctuation has been modernized. In the footnotes I cite Chapman's versions as *Odysses* or *Iliads* (their actual titles) in order to distinguish them from citations of Homer in the briefest manner. The page numbers refer to *The Whole Works*, the line numbers to Hooper's useful nineteenth-century editions which are cited in the bibliography. In my own prose translation I have made much use of Miller's Loeb Library version except where it seemed unnecessarily archaic or unidiomatic.

Although Chapman called his poem the *Odysses* he usually alluded to the hero as Ulysses. He was not, however, rigorously consistent in this inconsistency but used the name Odyssaeus when it suited his purposes. I would claim the same privilege in discussing several reincarnations of the Homeric hero.

I am greatly indebted to Basil Blackwell for permission to quote from Stanford's *The Ulysses Theme*, to the Princeton University Press for permission to quote from Erich Auerbach's *Mimesis*, to Prentice Hall for permission to quote Maynard Mack's comments on Augustan poetry (listed in the bibliography), to *The Sewanee Review* for permission to quote myself, to the *Review of English Studies* and *Studies in Philology* for permission to quote Phyllis Bartlett and Donald Smalley respectively, and to the Modern Language Association for permission to quote from Miss Bartlett's edition of Chapman's poems.

PREFACE

I am indebted to Douglas M. Knight, Sears R. Jayne, Paul M. Pickrel, William Frost, H. C. Fay, and Leslie A. Rutledge for the privilege of reading their doctoral theses (listed in the bibliography).

Many friends and colleagues at Yale have given much time and attention to the manuscript at various stages, and I wish to thank Charles T. Prouty, Eugene M. Waith, Douglas M. Knight (now President of Lawrence College), and Stuart Small of the Department of Classics for useful criticism of the thesis. Cleanth Brooks and Laurence Michel have made helpful suggestions about a later version. In particular I wish to thank Davis P. Harding for his careful reading of the chapters on Chapman's style and for his valuable recommendations about their organization, and Talbot Donaldson for his detailed comments on my own style. Bernard Knox has done me a great favour in supplying the point of view of the classical scholar. I owe him as much for certain pungent objections as I do for his friendly encouragement.

To Louis L. Martz, who has had his eye on this essay from its beginning, I can only suggest my thanks by saying that he could not have been more generous of his time and thought if the book had been his own.

Final revisions of this manuscript were completed on time borrowed from another project made possible by the generous assistance of a Morse fellowship from Yale. Benjamin C. Nangle has given generously of his time in scrutinizing the final proof.

The staff of the Yale University Library have been unfailingly co-operative at all times. I also wish to thank members of the New York Public Library, especially in the Rare Book collection, the Library of the University of London, the British Museum, the Library of Congress, and the Elizabethan Club at Yale for various services rendered.

Many thanks are also due to my wife who has patiently read and re-read each metamorphosis of the manuscript and made invaluable and tactful suggestions on my own style and logic.

Finally I would like to express my profound gratitude to the staff of Chatto & Windus Ltd and to Professor C. Day Lewis and Mrs Norah Smallwood in particular for their invaluable assistance.

G. deF. L.

TRUMBULL COLLEGE
YALE UNIVERSITY
16.9.55

CHAPTER I

Translation and Interpretation

'THE archetypal Ulysses offered a wider foundation for later development than any other figure of Greek mythology, thanks to Homer's far-reaching conception of his character and exploits.' This statement, which W. B. Stanford makes at the beginning of his excellent new book, *The Ulysses Theme*,[1] may serve both as an encouragement and a warning to interpreters of Homer's most complex hero. The extraordinary fascination which Odysseus has exercised on western civilization from Homer through James Joyce has found expression in an equally extraordinary range of interpretations. The unsurpassed versatility of Homer's Ὀδυσσεὺς πολύτροπος is demonstrated, for example, in the metamorphoses he has undergone in such figures as Pindar's plausible cheat, the cynical tempter of Neoptolemus in *Philoctetes*, the sinister rogue Sinon describes in the *Aeneid*, Plutarch's Stoic, Dante's politician, Shakespeare's statesman, Tennyson's insatiate adventurer, or Joyce's bourgeois Dubliner, to mention some of the better-known ones. All these reincarnations have something of Homer's hero in them, yet how contradictory is the composite portrait they present! The vehemence with which Odysseus' supporters and detractors have fought suggests how strong and personal an interest he has elicited from a hundred generations of men. Such vehemence comes as no surprise, however, to anyone who has followed the critical battles over Falstaff or Hamlet, for Odysseus stands high among those great characters of literature with whom we feel we must come to terms, perhaps because they seem to embody so much of our own selves, good and bad.

Yet any attempt to come to terms with Odysseus and

show him as he really is in Homer is bound to be, at best, only a partial success. Whatever a poet, translator, or critic presents as Odysseus will inevitably reflect his particular predilections and the pressures and interests of the period in which he lives. Stanford concludes his study of Odysseus' post-Homeric history with a statement of this fact:

With one exception every portrait of Ulysses described in the previous chapters has been incomplete. Homer alone presented the whole man—the wise king, the loving husband and father, the eloquent and resourceful *politique*, the courageous wanderer, the goddess-beloved hero, the yearning exile, the deviser of many ruses and disguises, the triumphant avenger, the grandson of Autolycus and the favourite of Athene. Subsequent writers in tradition usually selected one, or a related group, of these roles to suit their personal inclinations or artistic purposes.[2]

Even if the new portrait should manage to represent and synthesize all these facets of Homer's 'polytropic' hero—as Chapman's translation, I believe, comes close to doing—the portrait will still be coloured in the manner of the age which produced it. We can only see a classic through our own eyes, however much our vision is broadened by anthropology, history, and philology, and the best we can do even with a poem like the *Odyssey*, which has spoken so compellingly to all ages, is to find the closest and fullest equivalents in our own experience for the experiences which it presents. This is shown clearly in comparing different translations and nowhere more clearly than by a comparison of the two most famous English versions: only a century after Chapman's fiery Elizabethan epic Pope's version appeared in the cool, rational accents of the Augustan Age. Whatever standards of faithfulness to his original guide the translator, he cannot, nor should he try to, avoid his own idiom, and idiom is plainly one of the most influential delineators of character. Bentley's objection to Pope's *Iliad* can be made with equal truth against all translations. To some extent misrepresentation is inseparable from translation, as the well-known Italian saying holds, and if we want Homer's *Odyssey* we will not find it in Chapman, Hobbes, Butcher, Lawrence, Rouse or Rieu, or any other, however much or little each may contribute to our understanding of the original. Yet there may be consolation in the fact that we cannot find Homer's *Odyssey*, as his contemporaries experienced it, in Homer either.

Must we then give up the attempt to evaluate different translations and take refuge in the relativistic view that

ἄλλος γάρ τ' ἄλλοισιν ἀνὴρ ἐπιτέρπεται ἔργοις

—'different men take pleasure in different things'? The answer, I believe, is that while each version will necessarily be a limited one, the best will be that version which finds the nearest equivalent for Homer's comprehensive vision.

According to this standard Chapman's extremely original translation stands very high, chiefly because it comprehends within one vital figure more of Homer's tantalizing hero than any other translation or reinterpretation with which I am acquainted. Chapman was faithful to the essence of Homer's conception, I believe, in presenting Odysseus' career as a moral evolution and succeeded thereby in reconciling the schismatic views of previous interpretations. The far-reaching importance of this new interpretation has not been fully understood by Chapman's critics. The second great virtue of this translation, in my opinion, is a poetic style flexible enough to represent the many varieties of experience in the original, where the familiar and the fabulous, the noble and the humble, intermingle.

We are all likely to approach a well-loved and familiar poem like the *Odyssey* with the firmest convictions about its meaning. In my own case certain preconceptions which I had held for a long time made it very difficult at first to understand what Chapman was doing. From my own experience I also know how difficult it is to entertain an interpretation as original as Chapman's without feeling that something very great and very dear is being threatened or misrepresented. Frequently, in the course of this book, I will be obliged to advance my own interpretation of Homer's *Odyssey* in order to evaluate Chapman's, and though I have tried to ground my ideas firmly in Homer's text and in Homeric scholarship, many readers may find them even more disturbing than what I take to be Chapman's. Since I have stated my basic interpretation of the *Odyssey* elsewhere, and since it emerges in the process of discussing Chapman, it would seem doubly repetitious to attempt a summary here.[3] As an amateur classicist I approach Homer with trepidation and with the awareness that no interpretation of this great poem can pretend to exclusive validity.

II

A recent critic has observed that Chapman 'probably believed that he was inspired by the soul of Homer'.[4] Although the observation referred primarily to Chapman's vision of Homer in 'The Teares of Peace', there is much evidence besides to indicate that the first English translator of all Homer's works believed himself to possess a special insight into their meaning. In his dedication of the *Odyssey* Chapman promised his patron no less a gift than 'Homer, three thousand yeares dead, now reviv'd'.[5] His notes, especially in the *Iliad*, resound with scathing criticisms of earlier translators and scholars, while his introductory comments to the different translations reflect a jealous and proprietary attitude devoid of humility except when he contemplates the greatness of his original.

Chapman's claim to a peculiar insight into Homer's meaning has usually met with amusement or indifference among his critics. Their attention has been concentrated on what have been taken as the eccentricities of his style or on his frequent departures from Homer's literal sense, often with the implicit idea of showing the preposterousness of

16

such a claim. Important recent studies have been devoted to showing the ways in which Chapman allegedly read into Homer alien ideas and philosophies in order to express his private conceptions of Odysseus. Thus Donald Smalley claims that in the *Odyssey* Chapman found 'his own destined task of presenting to the modern world Homer's creation of the faultless man',[6] while Miss Phyllis Bartlett declares that 'Chapman's Ulysses is first and foremost a pious man'[7] and that Chapman has made him perfect 'through an injection in his veins of a natural stoicism'.[8]

Such assertions raise issues of central importance about Chapman's translation. Is his Ulysses in fact pious and stoical? In what ways are Chapman's alterations of and additions to Homer's literal sense departures from the meaning of Homer's *Odyssey* and his conception of the hero's character? While a good deal has been written about certain aspects of Chapman's *Homer*, no study of the whole structure and meaning of his *Odyssey* and its relation to the original has yet been made. Without such a comprehensive approach, conclusions based on a small selection of passages may be highly misleading. Such is the case with Miss Bartlett's and Mr. Smalley's observations on Chapman's Ulysses, valuable as these articles may be in other respects. Until one has grasped Chapman's whole view of the design of the poem the argument that he made Ulysses ultra-pious or stoical may seem convincing. The province I have taken for this essay, accordingly, is the total meaning of Chapman's *Odyssey*. We will examine his prefatory remarks and notes, his additions and changes in the literal meaning, and the character of his poetry in order to determine the meaning of his translation as accurately as possible. In the process we will compare the original passages and draw on Homeric scholarship to decide whether or not Chapman's interpretation was faithful to Homer's poem.

An evaluation of the style of a poetic translation must necessarily wait upon such conclusions about its whole view of the original. We cannot judge the success of Chapman's style until we know what the central conceptions were which he was trying to express, and ultimately, of course, style is inseparable from meaning. Even though a series of passages in the translation may be individually most un-Homeric in many respects—even though, for example, some of Ulysses' speeches may be reflective, analytical, self-revealing, full of moral comment, witty, ironical, inter-larded with original symbols, in tempo and sound and various other ways most unlike the corresponding lines in the Greek—we cannot determine their fidelity until we have examined them in the context of the whole translation and the interpretation which animates it. While insisting on an 'organic' approach to Chapman's poem, I wish to em-phasize at the outset that there are instances of quaintness and obscurity of expression that can be recognized at once as inappropriate by any standards. Except for obvious instances of this sort, 'fidelity' will entail much more than literalness.

'Fidelity' involves two principal relations between trans-lation and original—that of theme and that of style. The first half of this book is devoted to a serious examination of Chapman's claim to a vision of the *Odyssey's* true meaning. The second half of the book is concerned with the poetry in which he embodied this vision. The logical point of de-parture for such a study, then, is to be found in the most recent statements of the nature of this vision.

Miss Bartlett and Mr. Smalley have contributed a great deal to our understanding of Chapman in stressing the strong ethical character of his *Odyssey*, but I think they misconceive the true nature and function of his ethical emphasis in ascribing a stoical firmness to his hero throughout the poem. Taking as a main clue to Ulysses' character F. L. Schoell's well-known study in which he shows the influence on Chapman's tragic heroes of the Stoicism of Epictetus and Plutarch, they both conclude that Chapman's Ulysses was moulded in the same pattern. 'So it was', Smalley asserts, 'that Homer came to reveal his mysteries, which had been shrouded so long in darkness, by indicating his adherence to a philosophy which Chapman had suggested in his first extant poem ("The Shadow of Night") and by making Odysseus bear a considerable resemblance to Clermont d'Ambois in *The Revenge of Bussy d'Ambois*'.[9] Miss Bartlett makes the same identification even more emphatically:

An examination of Ulysses' character as it emerges in the translation brings Chapman's ' Homericall labours ' into focus with his tragedies and poetic compositions. Chapman, like the Stoics, found in Homer's Ulysses the incarnation of manly virtues ; and in his enthusiasm for this discovery, endowed him with so many more than he originally had, that he emerges as good a stoical hero as the renowned Clermont d'Ambois, a pre-eminent exemplification of the 'good life' as defined in Chapman's poems of Epictetan origin.[10]

Ulysses' alleged Stoicism is the substance of Miss Bartlett's argument, but Smalley goes on to find in the hero's career an allegory of Chapman's Platonic doctrine of 'Learning' which he set forth in 'The Teares of Peace'. 'Learning', in Chapman's words, is

> To have skill to throwe
> Reignes on your bodies powres, that nothing knowe ;
> And fill the soules powres so with act and art,
> That she can curb the bodies angrie part :
> All perturbations, all affects that stray
> From their one object, which is to obay
> Her Soveraigne Empire.[11]

Ulysses' alleged Stoicism, in Smalley's view, subserves this purpose, the acquisition of 'Learning':

In Odysseus, Chapman sees the 'absolute man' in the process of 'acquisition', struggling in the stormy sea of mundane existence to reach the peace of heaven and the next life. Chapman's Ulysses is 'absolute', then, not because he has secured perfect 'Learning', but because he is perfect in his manner of 'acquisition', a model that other men may follow in their own sailing of life's troubled waters.[12]

This view of the evolutionary character of Chapman's hero is valuable and more enlightening than Miss Bartlett's conception of him as the perfect Stoic who passes through a series of crises with equanimity. But Chapman's Ulysses, as we shall see, is anything but perfect in his manner of learning from experience. Self-willed and rash in the extreme, it is only when he has been overwhelmed by adversity that he begins to make any real growth towards this kind of wisdom. In defence of his position Smalley quotes a note in which Chapman defines the subject of the *Odyssey*: 'The information or fashion of an absolute man and necessarie (or fatal) passage through many afflictions (according with the most sacred Letter) to his naturall haven and countrey is the whole argument and scope of this inimitable and miraculous Poeme'.[13] This is cited as evidence for the proposition that Chapman saw Odysseus as a faultless man. Smalley interprets the note to mean that Chapman saw Odysseus as 'perfect in his manner of acquisition', progressing resolutely toward his 'naturall haven', never making the same mistake twice, but always learning from each adventure how to avoid future perils and temptations. The true meaning of Chapman's comment may be understood, however, only in terms of another important note, where some of 'the many afflictions' through which the hero must pass are specified. This note explains a distinction which Chapman has interpolated in line 97 of Book I between the opposing pulls of Ulysses' 'judgment' and his 'affections', as he languishes unhappily in his seventh year on Calypso's island. The passage will be discussed at length later on, but that part of the note which applies to Chapman's conception of the entire poem should be quoted here:

This is thus translated the rather to expresse and approve the Allegorie driven through the whole Odysses, deciphering the intangling of the Wisest in his affections and the torments that breede in every pious minde: to be thereby hindred to arrive so directly as he desires at the proper and onely true naturall countrie of every worthy man, whose haven is heaven and the next life, to which this life is but a sea, in continuall aesture and vexation.

(p. 3)

Chapman's identification of the cause of the hero's 'afflictions' as his 'affections' or passions could not be more clear or emphatic. This emphasis on his passionate and irrational behaviour at this stage is fatal to the theory that Chapman saw him as a Stoic, and equally fatal to the thesis that Chapman made of him the 'faultless man', perfect in the acquisition of 'Learning'. The note suggests that, far from endowing Ulysses with more virtues than he originally had, Chapman made a particular effort to stress his moral imperfections at this point in the story. This insistence on Ulysses' unruly and passionate nature is not an isolated example, but, as I shall show, is reflected at many points in the translation. The ethical bias of Chapman's *Odyssey* does not inhere in any attempt to make Ulysses a morally-perfect hero, but rather in the explicit emphasis which Chapman gives to the values which Ulysses must recognize before he can attain happiness. Once we have grasped the full implications of this view we must then decide whether it has a basis in Homer, or whether this is something extraneous and imposed by Chapman on the original. We shall find the conception of Ulysses as a character beset with human faults, which he gradually overcomes with the help of the gods and his own increasing self-control, a novel one in the history of Homeric criticism and a vastly more interesting conception than the accidental adventures of the faultless man. Then if we find warrant for such an interpretation in

Homer, Chapman's claim to a unique insight will no longer be preposterous.

Chapman's reference to 'allegories driven through the whole Odysses' also raises important questions about the way in which these central meanings are presented both in his translation and in Homer. Centuries of allegorical exegesis of Homer have brought deserved discredit on the approach. It will be a major part of our task to determine the nature of Chapman's allegorical approach and the extent to which it is justified by the original. Allegorical interpretation of the *Odyssey* from the Stoics through some of Chapman's contemporaries is marked by grave distortions and over-simplifications of the poem. Has Chapman avoided these dangers?

III

F. L. Schoell has shown Chapman's extraordinary debt in his tragedies and original poems to certain important Renaissance editions of the classics. Time and again whole speeches are revealed as verbatim translations from the text or commentaries of these books. The degree of this influence, especially in Chapman's debt to editions of the Stoics in his original work, has led some of Schoell's successors to infer corresponding influences in his *Odyssey*. Miss Bartlett makes such a conclusion:

For the past thirty years scholars have been increasingly interested in Chapman's debt to the Stoics. Professor F. L. Schoell, who proved that Chapman knew Epictetus through the Latin version of Wolfius (1563, 1593), observed that the years 1610-1612 were the period in Chapman's life when he 'n'a pas su résister à l'attrait du beau stoïcisme d'Épictète, tout parfumé de sagesse antique, et pourtant, par quelques côtés, si proche du christianisme'. This period may well be extended through 1615, for the translation of the *Odyssey* shows clearly the fascination that stoical doctrine continued to hold for him.[14]

Schoell had proved the influence of Epictetus on Chapman's poems and plays by comparing them exhaustively with the *Discourses* and *Encheiridion* in the editions of Wolfius.[15] Many long passages in Chapman were shown to be taken directly from these books. Miss Bartlett does not, however, indicate a single borrowing of this sort in the *Odyssey*. I have compared all Chapman's interpolations and alterations having the faintest aura of Stoicism about them with Epictetus and with the commentary of Wolfius without finding any traces of borrowing or even of recognizable influence. Considering the independence with which Chapman approached the task of translating the *Odyssey*, may we not assume that if he had wished to make a Stoic version his translation would show in some degree the kind of specific indebtedness which we find throughout *The Revenge of Bussy d'Ambois*? Unquestionably the self-restraint which Ulysses gradually develops toward the end of his experience has certain affinities with elements in the Stoic philosophy as represented by the *Discourses*, *Encheiridion*, and by Plutarch's *Moralia*, but Ulysses' self-restraint is nothing like the Stoic's detachment from the world, but a pre-requisite to his attaining the rewards which he seeks in the world—his wife, his home, and his kingdom.

Chapman's Ulysses is not the product of any particular philosophical or religious view. By the time Chapman translated the *Odyssey*, Epictetus' philosophy, 'si proche du christianisme', had mingled with neo-platonic, Platonic, humanistic and Christian ideas in a characteristic Renaissance synthesis. Chapman must have made a conscious effort not to interpret Homer in terms of any particular creed, for there are no borrowings from any other philosophical sources like those which Schoell demonstrates so fully in the original dramatic work. Wherever Chapman departed from Homer's meaning I have sought such borrowings in the books with which he has shown to be so familiar—Xylander's *Plutarch*,[16] Ficino's *Plato*[17] and his *Commentary* on

23

Plato's *Symposium*,[18] Natalis Comes' *Mythologiae*[19] and Erasmus' *Adagia*[20]—but I have not found a single unequivocal example like the dozens which appear in the poems and plays. While Chapman showed himself unusually independent of philosophical sources in the *Odyssey*, there are two important works of continental humanists which he used constantly, the *Homer* of Johannes Spondanus (Jean de Sponde)[21] and the Greek-Latin *Lexicon* of Johannes Scapula.[22] Spondanus prints alongside the Greek the word-for-word Latin translation in hexameters of Andreas Divus and he also includes extensive commentaries which are, in the orthodox Renaissance way, often concerned with the moral implications of the poems. Frequently these are pious half-truths of a kind all too common in the history of Homeric interpretation, which see Homer's characters and incidents in the simple blacks and whites of moral exempla, but now and then there are flashes of real insight. Chapman used Spondanus' commentaries with discrimination, although, as Schoell has suggested, his debt to this volume was very great:

> Le nom de Spondanus, empressons-nous de l'ajouter, a été plusieurs fois cité à propos des commentaires homériques de Chapman: par T. Warton d'abord, puis par Regel, Lohff et J. E. Sandys.
>
> Et il eût été véritablement surprenant qu'ils ne le citassent pas, car Chapman a vingt, trente fois le nom de Spondanus au bout de la plume. Mais, chose curieuse, personne encore, à notre connaissance, ne s'est avisé d'examiner de près le volumineux *Homère* de Jean de Sponde [Johannes Spondanus] et de rechercher ce que Chapman doit au juste, pour sa traduction aux éclaircissements de Sponde, pour ses *Commentaires* aux *Commentaires* de Sponde, pour ses épîtres homériques et sa 'critique homérique' aux *Prolégomènes* homériques de Sponde.[23]

Nor, one might add, has anyone investigated the relation between Chapman's vocabulary and the Latin translation in Spondanus. Schoell's demonstration of the influence of Spon-

danus on the actual text of Chapman's *Odyssey* is limited
to one long and very illuminating speech of Nausicaa in
Book VI. Wherever there was a possible borrowing I
have examined both the Latin translation and the commentaries, and this search has been highly rewarding. Much
of Chapman's Latinate diction is derived from this text,
while many important passages in his translation incorporate
ideas and even whole sentences from the commentaries,
especially where Spondanus' remarks conform to Chapman's general interpretation of the poem.

The *Lexicon* of Johannes Scapula also had a dual influence
on Chapman's *Odyssey*. Stylistically, it is responsible for
some of Chapman's compound epithets, which are often
grotesque and sometimes especially so because of the lexico-
grapher's faulty etymology. In larger matters of interpretation, Chapman occasionally finds in Scapula authority,
not always dependable, to be sure, for giving explicit moral
interpretation to a passage. Despite Schoell's remark that
'on peut affirmer que Chapman n'a, pour ainsi dire, pas
traduit un seul vers grec sans vérifier le sens d'un ou de
plusieurs mots dans son dictionnaire',[24] the borrowings from
Scapula are by no means as common as those from Spondanus. Finally, it should be noted that the influence of these
books, while wide, is in the main local, for we cannot
ascribe to them fundamental influences on Chapman's conception of the *Odyssey*. He used them to implement a view
which the evidence shows he formed independently of any
special source.

IV

Chapman's distinctive style as a translator of Homer has
received much more attention over the years than the equally
distinctive ways in which he interpreted the themes of
Homer's epics. With varying degrees of enthusiasm Chapman's critics have singled out the originality of his manner
for discussion. Pope found his translations 'something like

what one might imagine Homer himself would have written before he arrived at years of discretion'.[25] The nineteenth-century critic, R. H. Horne, while deploring 'the licentious spirit of English translations . . . purporting to be from Homer', likewise testified to the Homeric quality of Chapman's version, which he found to be 'a paraphrase by a kindred spirit' and which he preferred to Pope's 'paraphrase in his own spirit'.[26] Havelock Ellis thought Chapman had embodied the character of the age in his 'slowly-evolved translation of Homer . . . with its unflagging energy and spirit' and made it 'the crowning achievement of Elizabethan Humanism'.[27] The emphasis on the individuality of Chapman's style occurs over and over again, but a curious fact about these and other critical remarks is that they are directed at Chapman's translations collectively, as though the differences between them were insignificant from the viewpoint of style. In fact, however, his *Odyssey* is as different from his version in fourteeners of the *Iliad* as it is from other versions of the *Odyssey*, yet there is a pronounced tendency among the critics to make generalizations about the style of Chapman's *Homer*, as though this style were uniform throughout. Thus Matthew Arnold based all his opinions of Chapman's *Homer* on the *Iliad*, where he was least likely to find the virtues he admired, and he condemned Chapman's 'ballad-manner' as though unaware that Chapman abandoned this verse-form in subsequent translations.[28] Hallett Smith continues the curious practice in his excellent new book, *Elizabethan Poetry*, when he fails to make any critical distinction between the *Iliad* and the *Odyssey*.[29] The glowing exception among Chapman's critics is Coleridge, who had little use for the *Iliad*, but found the *Odyssey* 'as truly an original poem as the *Faerie Queene*'.[30]

Originality may seem a dubious asset in the translation of a great and ancient epic poem, and one may detect a note of disapproval in most critical remarks on this score. This qualifying note probably arises from an uneasy feeling that

26

originality and faithfulness to Homer are incompatible. For a long time there was a widespread conviction among scholars that the excellence of a translation depended on its literalness. This view reached its fullest expression in Chapman's nineteenth-century critic, H. M. Regel:

Wir verstehen heute unter einer treuen Übersetzung eines fremden Dichters eine solche, die ihn Zeile für Zeile, ja sogar möglichst wörtlich, und dabei in demselben Metrum wie im Original wiedergiebt, und halten diese Übersetzungsmethode für die einzig zulässige und anwendbare. Nicht so Chapman, dem es, wie den meisten älteren Übersetzern, hauptsächlich darauf ankam, den Inhalt seines Autors wiederzugeben, zwar den richtigen Sinn seiner Verse, aber nicht gerade mit denselben Worten; er wollte nur denselben Eindruck wieder bei seinen Lesern hervorbringen, den das Original auf *ihn* gemacht hatte.[31]

Here Regel, in supposing that there are English or German words which are 'the same as' Greek words and that they can reproduce the effect of the original language, is committing what might be called the fallacy of interlingual identities. The assumption is that the real meaning of the passage, for all practical purposes, inheres in the denotations of words, and that series of words whose denotations are similar to those of the original, in the same metre as the original, will reproduce the meaning of the original. This assumption over looks entirelythe distinctive idiom of each language and tends to regard words as building blocks rather than living cells whose meanings are interdependent. The fallacy of this kind of fidelity was exposed in F. W. Newman's amusing illustration, where he translates what is evidently a mock Homeric passage,

ὅστις ἐπετράφθη τέμενος πίστει βασιλῆος,
φημί τοι, οὗτος ἀνὴρ οὔτ' ἄρ τρέμει οὔτε φοβεῖται·
δὴ μάλα γάρ ῥα ἑὰς κρατέοι κεν ἐσαιὲν ἀρούρας,

by 'Whoso hath been entrusted with a demesne under pledge with the king; (I tell you,) this man neither trembleth (you see) nor feareth; for (look ye!) he (verily) may hold (you see) his lands for ever'.[32] It is clear how unfaithful a translation can be which insists on being faithful to the untranslatable particles of Homeric Greek. In its milder forms, however, the same policy of literalness can beguile us into attributing fidelity to a translation which imitates some mechanical features of the original. The false assumption, I think, lies behind Matthew Arnold's argument for English hexameters:

Applied to Homer, this metre affords to the translator the immense support of keeping him more nearly than any other metre to Homer's movement; and, since a poet's movement makes so large a part of his general effect, and to reproduce this general effect is at once the translator's indispensable business and so difficult for him, it is a great thing to have this part of your model's general effect already given you in your metre, instead of having to get it entirely for yourself.[33]

Arnold, as well as Regel, shows an unjustified confidence in the power of superficial resemblances to convey a significant part of the total experience of a poem into another language. Dactyllic hexameters are adapted to the structure of Homer's Greek and completely alien to the rhetoric, rhythms, and accents of English. If there are fundamental resemblances between translation and original, the same metre may, in Arnold's words, help to 'reproduce' the 'general effect' of the original, provided that the metre used is as natural to the new language as to the old. On this score it may be noted that Chapman is least Homeric when he is doggedly imitating Homer's compound epithets, which are as grotesque in English as they are natural in Greek. The 'general effect' of the *Odyssey* is due to the interaction of many elements which we designate by the words 'plot', 'theme', 'rhetoric', 'tone', 'rhythm', 'metaphor', or 'symbol'. Until the translator comprehends the living organism composed of these elements, his translation, however literal, will be spurious. Diction has always been a major stumbling-block to translating Homer or Virgil. Ezra Pound has made an illuminating point on this score in a letter to W. H. D. Rouse about his translation of Book II of the *Odyssey*:

NO, NO, Doc: Here you are backslidin' on all your highly re-spectable principles and slinging in licherary langwidg and puttin' your sentences all out of whack.

'Odysseus' boy jumped out of bed as rednailed, etc. appeared thru the dawn mist', or whatever; and if he reached for his six-shooter before puttin' on his boots, *that* is a point to be made, as highly illustrative of the era. A guards officer wdn't. But I reckon in Idaho in the 80's Blue Dick or Curly might have. And for his feet, they ought to be well-kept, or elegant or patrician, otherwise they slide into book-talk.

Tain't what a man says, but wot he *means* that the traducer has got to bring over. The *implication* of the word.

As fer them feet [presumably Telemachus' 'lissom feet' in Rouse], the blighter had been usin' cold cream, the bloomin' Bloomsbury knutt.[34]

Chapman was fully aware that no amount of literal fidelity would capture the meaning of Homer. His criteria of translation are mostly set forth in his preface to the *Iliad*, where he scoffs at those who

affect
Their word-for-word traductions (where they lose
The free grace of their naturall Dialect
And shame their Authors with a forced Glose.)[35]

He recognized the crucial principle that a certain licence was needed because of fundamental differences between Greek and English:

For even as different a production
Aske Greeke and English, since, as they in sounds
And letters shunne one forme and vision,
So have their sense and elegancie bounds

In their distinguisht natures, and require
  Onely a judgment to make both consent
In sense and elocution, and aspire
  As well to reach the spirit that was spent
In his example, as with arte to pierce
  His Grammar and etymologie of words.[36]

The translator has a double responsibility. He must be faithful to the meaning of the original, but he must also be faithful to the nature of his own language. If he writes of Telemachus' 'lissom feet', he has failed in both responsibilities. 'The line and rhythm of the ideal poetic translation, the ideal reproduction, ought after all to be as indigenous as its language.'[37] If the translation is not a poem it fails to imitate the most important aspect of the original. Chapman recognized this, and he possessed, furthermore, an essential vision of the profound relevance to himself and his age of the poem he was translating. We cannot evaluate the original style of Chapman's *Odyssey* until we have grasped this vision and tested it by the essential meanings of Homer's poem. Only then can we judge whether or not his highly individualized speeches, varied pace and tone, changing rhythms, rhetorical inversions, and metaphorical language violate the spirit and meaning of the original, or, on the other hand, whether Chapman created with the resources native to his language a poem faithful to Homer because of its originality.

NOTES TO CHAPTER I

1. (Oxford, Basil Blackwell, 1954), p. 7.

2. *Ibid.* p. 211.

3. 'The *Odyssey* and the Western World', *Sewanee Review*, 62 (1954), 406-27.

4. Janet Spens, 'Chapman's Ethical Thought', *Essays and Studies by Members of the English Association*, 11 (1925), 150.

5. 'Epistle Dedicatorie', *Homer's Odysses. Translated according to ye Greeke By Geo: Chapman* (London, 1615?), F 1ʳ.

6. 'The Ethical Bias of Chapman's *Homer*', *SP*, 36 (1939), 182.

7. 'The Heroes of Chapman's *Homer*', *RES*, 17 (1941), 270.

8. 'Chapman's Revisions in his *Iliads*', *ELH*, 2 (1935), 107.

9. 'The Ethical Bias of Chapman's *Homer*', p. 171.

10. 'The Heroes of Chapman's *Homer*', p. 269.

11. *The Poems of George Chapman*, ed. Phyllis Brooks Bartlett (New York, MLA; London, Oxford University Press, 1941), p. 184, ll. 504–510.

12. 'The Ethical Bias of Chapman's *Homer*', p. 183.

13. *Odysses*, I, 1 n., p. 1.

14. 'The Heroes of Chapman's *Homer*', p. 271. Cf. F. L. Schoell, *Études sur l'humanisme continental en Angleterre* (Paris, Champion, 1926), p. 107. Schoell does not mention, nor have I been able to find, any 1593 edition of Wolfius. Miss Bartlett is evidently referring to the edition of 1595.

15. *Encheiridion. Item, Cebetis Thebani Tabula de vita humana prudenter instituenda . . . Omnia H. Wolfie interprete* (Cologne, 1595). I have used this edition. First edition: Cologne, 1563.

16. *Plutarchi Chaeronensis quae exstant omnia. Cum latina interpretatione Hermanni Cruserii: Gulielmi Xylandri, et doctorum virorum notis . . .* (Frankfort, 1599). I have used this edition.

17. *Divini Platonis Opera omnia quae exstant. Marsilio Ficino interprete* (Frankfort, 1602). I have used this edition. First edition: Florence, 1482.

18. *Marsilio Ficino's Commentary on Plato's Symposium: the text and a translation, with an introduction,* by Sears Reynolds Jayne (Columbia, University of Missouri Press, 1944). I have used this edition.

19. Schoell (p. 26) shows that although Comes' book was first published in 1551, it was not until 1581 that its widespread European popularity began, when two editions appeared, one in Venice and one in Frankfort. I have used the edition of Arnold Sittart (Paris, 1583), who, Schoell says, 'se contenta de "pirater" l'édition tres améliorée de Wechel (Paris, 1581) non sans se vanter, toutefois, d'avoir émendé le texte et les citations'. Sittart merely added his own *Mythologiae Musarum Libellus*, and the book is otherwise substantially the same as the first edition.

20. *Adagiorum Chiliades quatuor cum sesquicenturia . . . Henrici Stephani animadversiones* (Geneva, 1558). I have used this edition. First edition: Venice, 1508.

21. I have used the Geneva, 1606 edition, the full title of which appears

in the bibliography. No differences except for spelling have been noted between this and a microfilm copy of the first edition (Bâle, 1583).

22. The full title of this work is given in the bibliography. I have used the Bâle, 1615 edition, the earliest one available at Yale. Schoell (p. 149 n.) points out that all later editions are substantially the same as the first edition (Bâle, 1580): 'Il va sans dire que les éditeurs successifs du lexique l'ont quelque peu corrigé et remanié. Mais, en substance, les éditions de 1820 sont celle de 1580.'

23. Schoell, p. 163.

24. *Ibid.* p. 157.

25. *The Iliad of Homer Translated by Mr. Pope* (London, 1715), I, F 2^r.

26. 'Remarks on Translation', *Classical Museum*, 1 (1844), 400.

27. *Chapman with Illustrative Passages* (Bloomsbury, The Nonesuch Press, 1934), p. 42.

28. *On Translating Homer* (London, 1861), pp. 42-50. W. H. D. Rouse has pointed to Arnold's apparent ignorance of Chapman's *Odyssey* in his edition of Arnold's essay (London, John Murray, 1905), pp. 11-12: 'The conceits which Matthew Arnold finds fault with are to be found, true enough, but far fewer in his *Odysseys* than in his *Iliads*, which alone Matthew Arnold appears to have read'.

29. *Elizabethan Poetry: A Study in Conventions, Meaning and Expression* (Cambridge, Harvard University Press, 1952), pp. 303-12.

30. S. T. Coleridge, 'Notes on Chapman's *Homer*', *Notes and Lectures upon Shakespeare and some of the Old Poets and Dramatists*, ed. Mrs. H. N. Coleridge (London, 1849), p. 231.

31. 'Über George Chapman's Homerübersetzung', *Englische Studien*, 5 (1882), 36.

32. 'Homeric Translation in Theory and Practice. A Reply to Matthew Arnold, Esq., Professor of Poetry, Oxford, by Francis W. Newman', in *Essays by Matthew Arnold* (London, Oxford University Press, 1914), pp. 354-5.

33. *On Translating Homer*, pp. 76-7.

34. In *Hudson Review*, 3 (1950), 60-1.

35. *Poems*, p. 392, ll. 37-40.

36. *Ibid.* p. 393, ll. 17-26.

37. Douglas M. Knight, *Pope and the Heroic Tradition: A Critical Study of his Iliad* (New Haven, Yale University Press; London, Oxford University Press, 1951), p. 3.

CHAPTER II

The Allegorical Background

C HAPMAN'S *Odyssey*—the first complete English translation—is also the first real attempt to reconcile the
moral significance which scholars and critics for 2,000 years
had found in Homer's poem with a true appreciation of its
dynamic structure. Chapman began with the traditional
view of the *Odyssey* as moral allegory, but he departed
radically from the tradition in conceiving of the allegory as
evolutionary and complex instead of static and schematic.
He felt, as we have seen, that he had a unique insight into
Homer, and thus his introductory discussion and his comments on individual passages positively vibrate with an
excited sense of discovery. Unlike some earlier and some
contemporary English translators of the classics, who proclaimed to a man the virtuous influences to be found in
their authors—even the more scandalous parts of Ovid or
the *Golden Ass*—Chapman's testimony to the moral significance of Homer was no lip service to a contemporary
fashion, but a profound conviction. The depth of this conviction is not to be judged from Chapman's comments only
but from the text of his translation, where the reader can
judge for himself how reasonable and faithful was his understanding of Homer.

When Chapman wrote to his patron, the Earl of Somerset, that the *Odyssey* was not a mere fantasy or fiction 'but
the most material and doctrinal illations of Truth; both for
all manly information of Manners in the young; all pre-
sumption of Justice, and even Christian pietie, in the most
grave and high governed', he was expressing a view in full
accord with contemporary judgments of the function of all
serious poetry.[1] Spenser referred to similar sanctions in

C   33

stating the purpose of *The Faerie Queene* to be 'to fashion a gentleman . . . in vertuous and gentle discipline'.[2] Spenser's view of Homeric characters as moral *exempla*, of Agamemnon and Ulysses as 'a good governour and a vertuous man', was also, as Professor Bush remarks, 'Renaissance orthodoxy'.[3]

Equally orthodox was Chapman's view that these 'most material and doctrinall illations of truth' were cryptically expressed by his author in allegory and that the allegory was a necessary means of concealing these mysteries from the eyes of the 'vulgar'. If the story seems an impossible fiction —'if the Bodie (being the letter, or historie) seemes fictive, and beyond Possibilitie to bring into Act', he writes to Lord Somerset, the inner reality shadowed forth by it is to be plumbed—'the sense then and Allegorie (which is the Soule) is to be sought: which intends a more eminent expressure of *Vertue*, for her lovelinesse, and of *Vice* for her uglinesse, in their severall effects, going beyond the life, then any Art within life can possibly delineate'.[4] Such a belief that fables contained truths of a higher order than 'true-to-life' realism was likewise held by some of Chapman's greatest contemporaries. Thus Sidney says that Aesop's 'pretty allegories, stealing under the formall tale of Beastes, make many, more beastly than Beastes, begin to heare the sound of vertue from these dumbe speakers',[5] and Spenser speaks in the same vein of 'good discipline . . . clowdily enwrapped in Allegoricall devises'.[6] Even Chapman's discovery of inducements to 'Christian Pietie' in Homer has a much more extravagant precedent in Arthur Golding's attempt, in a dedicatory epistle to the *Metamorphoses*, to reconcile the Ovidian cosmogony with that of Moses.

II

If we turn our attention now to the historical precedents for Renaissance allegorizing, we shall find that Chapman and his contemporaries—Sidney, Spenser, Golding, Ascham, and many others, fall into an unbroken tradition extending 2,000 years back to classical times. No classical writer except Virgil was subjected so fully to allegorical interpretations as Homer. The origin of this type of interpretation with Theagenes and Anaxagoras in the sixth century B.C. is described by the literary historian, J. W. H. Atkins, as a reaction against denunciations of Homer by philosophers because of his allegedly impious and immoral fables. Atkins implies that the defence of Homer by this method was a somewhat casuistical one: '. . . philosophy, which had led the attack, provided also the main line of defence. Already among philosophers the idea had obtained currency that the earlier poets in their myths had concealed profound wisdom in enigmatic and symbolic fashion; and that by means of an allegorical interpretation it was possible to arrive at the real significance of the myths concerned.'[7] Another reason for the development of allegorical interpretation in ancient times is given by Comparetti: 'Allegory was applied by the ancients to mythology generally and to the language of the poets particularly, as these latter formed, in the absence of a religious code, the only written authority for the common faith. . . . For those who were anxious to find documentary authority for the common beliefs, no other writer could have the weight of Homer, whether on account of his pre-historic antiquity or the marvellous power of his genius or the character and national importance of his poems. . . .'[8] Thus many of the ancients, like many English writers of the sixteenth century, sought to justify their love of poetry on the grounds that it was morally instructive. In the case of Homer, however, their motives were more positive, since 'the Bible of the Greeks' embodied, with Hesiod, the principal written record of their relations with the gods and of their heroic past. Homer was so much part of their spiritual identity that they were impelled to reconcile everything in his poems with their ideas of morality and decency.

35

Early in the Christian era the practice of allegorical interpretation received a new impetus from methods of scriptural
exegesis which were extended as well to classical literature.
As Lathrop says, 'the spirit of this reconciliation of profane
literature with sacred is as ancient as the effort to amalgamate the two which was made in the great formative era
of Christian civilization by the learned fathers of the fifth
century'.[9] Typical of medieval practice is Fulgentius' *Con-
tinentia Vergiliana*, an extended allegorical interpretation of
the *Aeneid*.

Allegorical interpretations of Homer—whether by the
ancients or by men of the Renaissance—are characterized by
a monotonous sameness of approach. The oft-repeated idea
that poetry was the conveyor of moral truths seemed to
anaesthetize the aesthetic sensitivity of allegorical interpreters.
Their eyes saw only the moral abstractions and were blind
to the poetry and to the subtleties of Homer's characterization. For at least 1,600 years allegorical interpreters
of the *Odyssey* tended to repeat *ad nauseam* the half-truth
that Odysseus is a model of virtue, until that half-truth har-
dened into a dogma. The dogma imposed on its practi-
tioners the task of justifying the hero's conduct on every
occasion.

The allegorists did not, of course, monopolize Homer
unchallenged throughout this period. The character of
Odysseus was constantly subjected to reinterpretation, much
of it unfavourable, in poetry and drama. The history of his
reincarnations is summarized by Stanford as follows:

Homer was large-minded enough to comprehend a unity in
apparent diversity, a structural consistency within an external
changefulness, in the character of Ulysses. But few later authors
were as comprehending. Instead, in the post-Homeric tradition,
Odysseus' complex personality becomes broken up into various
simple types—the *politique*, the romantic amorist, the sophisticated villain, the sensualist, the philosophical traveller, and others.

36

Not till James Joyce wrote his *Ulysses* was a successful effort made to re-create Homer's polytropic hero in full.[10]

In my opinion, of course, Chapman's translation accomplished a successful re-creation long before Joyce. Otherwise this seems to be a just description of a tendency to over-simplify Homer's hero, a tendency as pronounced in the work of the allegorists as anywhere else.

The earliest complete allegorical treatise on Homer that has survived substantially intact is the *Allegoriae Homericae* of a certain Herakleitos whom H. J. Rose places in the reign of Augustus. Herakleitos' view of the *Odyssey* is a commonplace of literary history: 'In general, the wandering of Ulysses, if one would see it truly, will be found to be an allegory: presenting Ulysses as the product of all virtue, [Homer] has philosophized throughout, since he detested the vices which feed on human life'.[11] Herakleitos lists among these vices the hedonism of the Lotophagoi and the savagery of the Cyclops. He interprets the Circe episode thus: ' . . . the potion of Circe is the vessel of voluptuousness, and when the licentious drink it, they lead, during their temporary satiety, the very wretched lives of pigs. Hence Ulysses' comrades, being a foolish lot, were overcome by gluttony, but the wisdom of Ulysses defeated the luxury of Circe.'[12] The substance of this interpretation goes back at least as far as Socrates, according to Xenophon,[13] and can be found in writers as far apart in time and temperament as Horace[14] and Roger Ascham.[15] It is, no doubt, an adequate general statement of the theme of the Circe episode, although tending to oversimplify it.

When, however, the identification of Ulysses with triumphant virtue is extended beyond a few encounters which bear it out and is erected into a monolithic principle it obliterates the meaning of the *Odyssey*, disregards the significance of each separate episode, and reduces the whole poem to a flat, repetitive series of moral *exempla*. The damage such an approach could do is evident in that popular Renaissance compendium of myths, Natalis Comes' *Mythologiae*. With relentless monotony Comes flattens every incident in the *Odyssey* under his one ruling idea until they all represent a single abstraction. Since the *Mythologiae* was typical of Renaissance doctrine on the *Odyssey*, I shall take the liberty of quoting at some length:

Now let us consider why this [the story of Ulysses] has been fashioned thus. First let me say that anyone who diligently consults his memory about Ulysses will understand that these fables represent the whole span of a man's life and that they contain admirable precepts which have as their object the patterning of our souls in every vicissitude of fortune according to wisdom. For who is Ulysses if not wisdom, which passes unscathed and triumphant through every danger? And who, accordingly, are Ulysses' companions if not the perturbations of our souls? Why has he lost many of them in battle with the Cicones beneath the mountain at Ismarus? Why were some devoured by the Laestrygonians? Why were others consumed by the Cyclops? Why were still more swallowed whole by those direst monsters Scylla and Charybdis? The answer is that they were either overwhelmed by wrath or grief, or broken by adversity, and they were frightened and lost heart, so that they were incapable of reaching that region of the upright, as it were, their native land.[16]

In stressing the universal significance of Odysseus, his wisdom, the 'perturbations' and 'affections' which dominate his companions, and in identifying Ithaca as the *piorum locus*, Comes may well have set Chapman an example. Comes, however, applies his interpretations with no regard for the full meaning of individual episodes or of the poem as a whole. Once he has lit on a general principle he forces it on everything, regardless of the context. It is absurd, for example, to blame the deaths of the sailors whom Ulysses led into the Cyclops' cave on some moral deficiency in these poor wretches.

III

It is equally hard for me to believe that Odysseus should be regarded as Homer's incarnation of all the virtues. It seems to me that any reader, free from the dogma of tradition, should be able to see that the hero's behaviour on many occasions is far from exemplary by any standards. If one reads with care Chapman's general statements about the *Odyssey* in his dedicatory epistle and notes he will be struck by an extraordinary and extremely significant departure from the crystallized traditional view. Some of Chapman's statements, as we have seen, seem to agree perfectly both with the views of his contemporaries and with those of the allegorical interpreters who wrote over a period of 2,000 years. His testimony to the presence in the *Odyssey* of 'illations of Truth' for the instruction of young and old in manners and Christian piety and his injunction to the Earl of Somerset to look behind the body of fable for the soul of allegory are, at first sight, a pious nod in the direction of convention. But the earnestness with which Chapman held this belief and the courage and originality which marked his departure from tradition and convention in the pursuit of it permeate every passage of his translation and his auxiliary comments as well.

Chapman did what no extant scholar, critic, writer of commentaries, allegorical interpreter or translator contemporary, medieval, or ancient, had ever done. He reconciled what many of them had held to be Homer's moral idealism with instances of Odysseus' immoral behaviour which they ignored, suppressed, or distorted to fit their preconceptions about the poem. In doing so, Chapman felt with some reason that he had rediscovered his beloved Homer. The vision of Homer which he describes in 'The Teares of Peace' is evidence, as Donald Smalley remarks, of 'an almost religious attitude' toward his original.[17] Chapman often proclaimed his unique insight into Homer in the

39

polemic tones of contemporary fashion, most prominently in a note to the *Iliad* where he tells how such translators as Laurentius Valla, Eobanus Hessus, and Hugues Salel have missed the true meaning which he alone has understood: 'Against . . . all these plebian opinions, that a man is bound to write to every vulgar reader's understanding, you see the great master of all elocution hath written so darkly that almost three thousand sunnes have not discovered him, no more in five hundred other places than here'.[18] Because of this 'darkness', which is probably Chapman's name for the oblique and concrete qualities of the poems, Chapman considered his highest duty as a translator to be the revelation of Homer's concealed mysteries. It is in this way that the great epic poet must be restored to life, and Chapman accordingly advises the Earl of Somerset in his dedication to the *Odyssey* to esteem 'not as the least of your New-yeares Presents'

> *Homer* (three thousand yeares dead) now revived,
> Even from that dull Death, that in life he lived;
> When none conceited him . . .

Fidelity to his trust entailed, Chapman felt, occasional additions to the literal sense whenever the meaning was obscured by the 'darkness' of Homer's style. In a note to the *Iliad* he asks his reader waspishly, 'What fault is it in me to furnish and adorne my verse (being his translator) with translating and adding the truth and fulness of his conceit, it being as like to passe my reader as his, and therefore necessarie?'[19] The starting-point for a discussion of Chapman's specific views of the *Odyssey's* moral theme is a distinction between Homer's two epics which he makes in the dedicatory epistle: 'And that your Lordship may in his [Homer's] Face, take view of his Mind: the first word of his Iliads is μῆνιν, *wrath*: the first word of his Odysses, ἄνδρα, *Man*: contracting in either word his each workes Proposition. In one, *Predominant Perturbation*; in the other, *over-ruling Wisedome*: in one, the Bodies fervour and fashion of outward Fortitude, to all possible height of Heroicall Action; in the other, the Minds inward, constant, and unconquered Empire; unbroken, unaltered, with any most insolent, and tyrannous infliction.' The themes of the *Iliad* and the *Odyssey* are thus complementary, according to Chapman. Where the passion of Achilles overcomes restraints in the one, the wisdom of Odysseus triumphs over 'perturbation' in the other. The distinction is carried out through the antithesis of body and mind. This statement appears to have misled some recent critics who have written on the ethical elements in the *Odyssey*. 'Over-ruling *Wisdome*' and 'the minds inward, constant, and unconquer'd Empire' are not, as they suggest, qualities which Chapman felt characterized Ulysses throughout, but qualities on which his successful return home and his rehabilitation of Ithaca and his household depend. Thus Phyllis Bartlett ascribes to Chapman, on the basis of this statement, a view of Ulysses as a model of stoical virtue: 'By every right Ulysses should have been perfectly patient and stoical—as renaissance critics had assumed him to be—and so, when oft-times his powers of endurance fail him, Chapman in friendly fashion bolsters him up'.[20] Unquestionably Ulysses is patient and enduring through many adventures, in Homer as in Chapman, but there is little evidence which will show under close scrutiny that Chapman felt committed to making him 'perfectly patient and stoical' in every stage of his experience.

Chapman, in fact, saw Ulysses as an emergent, dynamic character, one beset by passions that constantly threatened to destroy him, but struggling through repeated failures toward an ideal which he very gradually discovered in the process. Far from idealizing Homer's hero in the traditional manner, Chapman sometimes took pains to emphasize his faults.

Chapman's first note to the *Odyssey* shows his conception of Ulysses as a character evolving toward an ideal of man: 'The information or fashion of an absolute man and neces-

sarie (or fatal) passage through many afflictions (according
with the most sacred Letter) to his naturall haven and
countrey is the whole argument and scope of this inimitable
and miraculous Poeme' (I, 1, p. 1). 'Information' here means
'the formation or moulding of mind or character'. 'Fashion'
has a similar sense—'the action or process of making'.
Both words denote growth towards 'the absolute man' and
not a static and uniform perfection. The remainder of the
note confirms this interpretation. Chapman emphasizes
Ulysses' evolution towards moral excellence by adopting,
with a significant alteration, Scapula's definition of the
epithet Homer applies to him in the first line of the poem—
πολύτροπος. The word normally defined as 'of many shifts'
or 'versatile' Chapman translates by the longish phrase
which I have italicized:

> The Man (O Muse) informe, *that many a way,*
> *Wound with his wisedome to his wished stay.*
>
> (I, 1-2, p. 1)

In his note Chapman then justifies his translation by altering
Scapula's definition, of which the pertinent part is 'cuius ingenium velut in varias partes vertitur': 'And therefore is the
epithete πολύτροπον given him in the first verse: πολύτροπος
signifying *Homo cuius ingenium velut per multas & varias vias,*
vertitur in veram'. Throughout Chapman's translation 'stay'
denotes whatever is fixed, permanent, and true in contrast to the flux of passion and impulse. In the opening
lines of his translation Chapman thus makes Ithaca the
goal of a spiritual pilgrimage as well as the terminus of a
voyage.

The radical difference between Chapman's conception of
Odysseus' story and that of Comes and other allegorists lies
in his conviction that, after the fall of Troy, Odysseus was
deeply divided within himself, torn between passion and
judgment. Chapman thereby transferred Odysseus' problems from the external arena in which Comes and Hera-

kleitos and others had placed it—where, as absolute virtue, he was contending with the folly and greed of his men—to the inner arena of his own character. The sailors remain a part, but a minor one, of the problems he must deal with, while, as Chapman saw it, Odysseus' principal mission was the conquest of himself. The result was a more complex and much more interesting character than the allegorists had presented, and also, of course, a more dramatic story than their views had made possible.

In his enthusiasm for the conflict which he discovered in his hero, Chapman sometimes pushed his own view too far. Occasionally he imposed a moralistic view on the Homeric situation where little or no support could be found in the original context and occasionally he over-emphasized the moral element to the exclusion of other factors in a highly complex situation. Yet often his insistence on Odysseus' inward *psychomachia*, though it may appear at first blush absurd, turns out to be rather plausible. Chapman's treatment of Odysseus' plight on Calypso's island at the beginning of the poem is a good illustration. In Book I Athene introduces his case to the council of Olympians, telling how Calypso holds

> this homelesse-driven
> Still mourning with her, evermore profuse
> Of soft and winning speeches, that abuse
> And make so languishingly, and possest
> With so remisse a mind, her loved guest
> Manage the action of his way for home.
> Where he (though in affection overcome)
> In judgment yet more longs to shew his hopes
> His countries smoke leap from her chimney tops,
> And death askes in her armes.
>
> (I, 94-103, pp. 3-4)

Chapman here makes Odysseus' plight in his seventh year on Calypso's island an explicit moral dilemma in which 'judgment' and 'affection' are so opposed and so nicely

43

balanced that he cannot endure staying and cannot bear to leave. The 'remissness' ascribed to Odysseus does not seem justified, at this point in the story, by Homer: 'It is his daughter [Calypso] who keeps back that wretched, sorrowing man, and constantly enchants him with soft and winning words so that he may forget Ithaca. But Odysseus, in his longing to see even the smoke leaping up from his country, wishes to die.'[21] Plainly Odysseus is more than ready, at this point, to leave Calypso and Ogygia for Ithaca and Penelope. What Chapman has done, as his note explains, is to develop the implications of 'the soft and winning words' with which Calypso plies Odysseus, taking them as a hint from Homer that the nymph has not compelled, but rather seduced him into staying in inglorious ease:

This is thus translated the rather to expresse and approve the Allegorie driven through the whole Odysses, deciphering the intangling of the Wisest in his affections and the torments that breede in every pious minde: to be thereby hindred to arrive so directly as he desires at the proper and onely true naturall countrie of every worthy man, whose haven is heaven and the next life, to which this life is but a sea, in continuall aesture and vexation. The words occasioning all this are μαλακοῖς λόγοις: μαλακός signifying, *qui languide, & animo remisso rem aliquam gerit*; which being the effect of Calypso's sweete words in Ulysses, is here applied passively to his owne sufferance of their operation.

(I, 97 n., p. 3)

Odysseus may be the 'Wisest', but his wisdom, as Chapman emphasizes, is not always operative nor always in control. At this crisis of his adventures Chapman sees him as a figure of heroic potentiality who is all the more representative because he is entangled in the desires of the flesh.

By this psychological treatment Chapman manages to relate Odysseus' plight to the theme of Jove's speech which opens this council of the Olympians. Using Aegisthus as a notorious example Jove has just expatiated on man's curious practice of doing what he knows is evil and what he knows will ultimately add to his share of sorrow. This prominent speech, with its emphasis on man's power to distinguish good from evil, his free will, and his moral responsibility, is as much a keystone of the *Odyssey's* moral cosmogony as God's declaration of man's free will is in that of *Paradise Lost*.

> O how falsly men
> Accuse us Gods as authors of their ill,
> When, by the bane their own bad lives instill,
> They suffer all the miseries of their states,
> Past our inflictions, and beyond their fates.
> As now *Aegisthus*, past his fate, did wed
> The wife of Agamemnon, and (in dread
> To suffer death himselfe) to shunne his ill,
> Incurr'd it by the loose bent of his will,
> In slaughtering *Atrides* in retreate.
> Which, we foretold him, would so hardly set
> To his murtherous purpose, sending *Mercurie*,
> That slaughter'd *Argus*, our considerate spie,
> To give him this charge: 'Do not wed his wife,
> Nor murther him; for thou shalt buy his life
> With ransome of thine own, imposde on thee
> By his *Orestes*, when in him shall be
> *Atrides'* selfe renew'd, and but the prime
> Of youth's spring put abroad, in thirst to climb
> His haughtie Fathers throne by his high acts'.[22]

In Homer as well as Chapman Athene introduces the case of Odysseus as an apparent exception to the rule of divine justice, citing in his defence his piety and assiduous sacrifices during the Trojan War. Jove reprimands her, yet he admits that Odysseus is the wisest of mortals and lays the blame for his detention on Ogygia to the anger of Poseidon over the blinding of his son, Polyphemus. He gives permission for

Hermes to visit Calypso 'to declare our fixed resolve . . .
the return of firm-hearted Odysseus' and for Athene herself
to visit Telemachus and encourage him to upbraid the
suitors and go in search of his father. The first four Books
are devoted to the second part of this programme, the
council assembled by Telemachus and his voyage to Nestor
and Menelaus in search of information.

Book V again opens with a council on Olympus. Athene
recapitulates her complaint on behalf of Odysseus, adding,
this time, that there is no longer any reason for men to be
just and mild in their behaviour,

> Since he, that rul'd as it in right behov'd,
> That all his subjects as his children lov'd,
> Finds you so thoughtlesse of him and his birth.
> Thus, men begin to say, ye rule in earth,
> And grudge at what ye let him undergo,
> Who yet the least part of his suff'rance know:
> Thrall'd in an island, shipwrack'd in his teares,
> And in the fancies that Calypso beares,
> Bound from his birthright, all his shipping gone,
> And of his soldiers not retaining one.

(V, 17-26, p. 72)

'Shipwrack'd in his teares, | And in the fancies that Calypso
beares' is Chapman's elaboration of 'suffering great sorrows
he lies on an island, in the halls of the nymph Calypso, who
keeps him there by force'.[23] In Homer the hero is detained
by force and enchantment, as he is in Chapman, but Chapman subjectivizes the 'enchantment' and makes it plain sex
appeal as well as magic. In answer to this complaint of
Athene's Zeus now orders Hermes to Ogygia to effect
Odysseus' release, stipulating, however, that his trip to
Phaeacia must be made 'without the help of mortals or
immortals'. The four Books which follow present the consequences of this order, and thus the departure of Odysseus
from Ogygia, his voyage to Phaeacia, and his adventures

there parallel Telemachus' departure from Ithaca and his voyages to Pylos and Sparta in the first four Books.

The symmetry of these two actions invites us to compare the meanings of the divine interventions in both cases. Chapman may have recognized certain similarities in the situations of the son and the father and he may well have seen a warrant for making a problem of character out of Odysseus' plight on the pattern of Telemachus' situation when we first meet him. Both are sad: the son longing for possession of his house and his father's return: the father longing for his home and family. But their desires are ineffectual until the gods intervene. When Athene visits Telemachus and puts μένος in his breast the supernatural event duplicates Telemachus' own emergence from a youth into a man. We are not to separate the supernatural event from the psychological one, since, as E. R. Dodds has shown, Homer was unable to represent a purely psychological miracle. The μένος 'is the moral courage which will enable the boy to face the overbearing suitors'.[24] The appearance of the goddess does not mean that Telemachus gets no credit for the resolution and daring which he now begins to show, any more than his failure to show it before her intervention would free him from the charge of unmanly behaviour.

After Athene's intervention the young man who had languished for years as a virtual prisoner of his mother's would-be lovers suddenly summons an assembly and orders them, to their astonishment, to leave his court, then victuals a borrowed ship and sets out, despite their hostility, to learn all he can about his famous father. Observe how closely these events are paralleled in the opening of the main plot. After Hermes' intervention with Calypso, the father, who had languished for years as a virtual prisoner of a nymph, suddenly builds a raft and equips it with material which he finds abundantly on the island and sets out for home in spite of the terrors which he has been warned lie ahead of him. Is it strange, then, to see in Odysseus' decision to leave Ogygia a crucial development in his character? Although Odysseus fears Calypso and her supernatural powers, he has not always been her unwilling prisoner. That sybaritic life has simply palled after seven years: 'His sweet life was ebbing away while he longed mournfully to return, since the nymph no longer pleased him'.[25] As I have argued elsewhere,

The divine machinery which sets Odysseus free . . . can stand for, or, perhaps more accurately, is accompanied by, the hero's effective resolution to accept his human lot and leave Calypso's paradise. For many years he has longed to depart, yet the intervention of the gods at this moment is not simply a heavenly rescue party, a Euripidean *deus ex machina*. The elementary resources needed to build and equip the raft have been available on Calypso's island all the seven years Odysseus has been there. What he lacked for a time was the courage to commit himself once more to the strenuous dangers attendant upon such a journey, a journey which, Zeus specifies, must be made 'with guidance neither of mortal men nor of gods'.[26]

Where Chapman has gone wrong, to return to the passage with which this discussion began, is, I think, in having Athene speak of Ulysses as overcome by 'affection' at this late stage in his development. By this time he has long ceased to respond to Calypso's 'soft and winning words'. This does not, in my opinion, affect the validity of Chapman's basic interpretation. The Calypso adventure is not only important in itself and as a crucial moment in Odysseus' career, but as a leading example of Chapman's conception of his hero and of the way in which he went about explicating 'the Allegorie driven through the whole Odysses'.

Chapman's general idea of the allegory in Homer's *Odyssey*, as we have seen, is that it presents subtly and obliquely Odysseus' struggle for mastery over himself as well as his battle with natural forces and such enemies as his wife's suitors. Chapman's conviction that he possessed a unique insight into the *Odyssey*, affirmed with all the arrogance usual to Elizabethan prefaces, is none the less justified if one considers that apparently no extant writer before him had it, and only one, to my knowledge, has shared it since.

This exception is D. J. Snider, whose evangelical commentary on the *Odyssey* published in 1895 has evidently met with undeserved neglect.[27] For all its facile manner and homiletic style, Snider's essay is a challenging one and takes a fundamental view of the *Odyssey* so like Chapman's that it helps to illuminate the moral themes which the great Elizabethan translator found in Homer. Like Chapman, and unlike the cut-and-dried allegorical interpreters of the *Odyssey*, Snider sees the poem not as a schematic *psychomachia* in which the hero personifies Virtue, but primarily as an interior struggle between Odysseus' reason and his passions:

But now that Troy is destroyed, how will Ulysses return to institutional life, which he has destroyed in Troy, in himself, and, through his absence, in Ithaca?

The Return must in the first place be within himself, he must get rid of the destructive spirit begotten of war. For this purpose he has the grand training told in his adventures; he must put down the monsters of Fableland, Polyphemus, Circe, Charybdis; he must endure the long servitude under Calypso; he must see Phaeacia. When he is internally ready, he can go forth and destroy the suitors, destroy them without becoming destructive himself, which was his outcome at Troy. For the destruction of Troy left him quite as negative as the suitors, of which condition he is to rid himself ere he can rid Ithaca of the suitors. This destruction becomes a great positive act, now he restores Family and State, and brings peace and harmony.

(p. 520)

Chapman, as we shall see, also found in the hero's wanderings a process of spiritual regeneration and of re-indoctrination in the institutions and values of society as an inner preparation for the restoration of Ithaca. Snider, as far as I know, is the only critic of Homer in the allegorical tradition whose view is as flexible as Chapman's in the sense that he is not blinded by the moral elements of the poem from seeing the moral defects which the hero must overcome.

IV

In our own time the term allegory has acquired such a wide range of meanings that it is essential, before discussing Chapman's translation in detail, to arrive at an acceptable definition. It should be noted, incidentally, that Chapman and his contemporaries used the term to represent only the inner meaning of the fable, the moral signification, that part of a metaphor which I. A. Richards calls the 'tenor', as we may see from the introductory remark already quoted that 'if the Bodie (being the letter, or Historie) seemes fictive . . . the sense then and allegorie . . . is to be sought . . .'.

While writers contemporary with us all agree that allegory is a relationship between the seen and the unseen or the material and the immaterial, their views on the nature of the relationship differ very widely. Some are willing to consider as allegories works in which the vehicle is complex and carries details beyond those needed to represent the immaterial. Others confine the term to a simple relation between abstractions and the images which represent them. The latter allow no details to the vehicle which have no evident correspondence to some part of the tenor. The chief spokesman for this second view is C. S. Lewis: '. . . you . . . start with an immaterial fact, such as the passions which you actually experience, and can then invent *visibilia* to express them. If you are hesitating between an angry retort and a soft answer, you can express your state of mind by inventing a person called *Ira* with a torch and letting her contend with another person called *Patientia*. This is allegory. . . .'[28] According to this view, the *visibilia* contain no details but those that can be instantly referred to the immaterial fact. The personifications have no existence apart from the abstractions they represent. They have the least possible reality as characters because they obey absolutely and always the immaterial fact which they were created to represent. *Ira* is always angry, whatever the circumstances, and *Patientia* always patient. The motives for their behaviour are never explained, but merely imposed, as it were, at the instant of their birth by their names and physical accoutrements.

By this definition there is nothing allegorical about Chapman's translation except for some incidental personifications and nothing allegorical in Homer's poem beyond certain names which identify the leading qualities of a few characters like Arete, Alcinous, Antinous, Odysseus, Calypso, and so forth.[29] All of these have qualities in excess of those their names represent, which make them the complex creatures which we recognize as human beings. Alcinous is sometimes foolish, Antinous sometimes reasonable, and so forth.

What Lewis defines as 'symbolism' comes nearer to describing Chapman's allegory: 'If our passions, being immaterial, can be copied by material inventions, then it is possible that our material world in its turn is the copy of an invisible world. . . . The attempt to read that something else through its sensible imitations, to see the archtype in the copy, is what I mean by symbolism or sacramentalism' (p. 45). The practice of what Lewis calls 'symbolism' is the occupation, one would think, of allegorical artists as well as allegorical interpreters. Here the 'sensible' world remains complex, and the allegorical writer can be faithful to its complexity while at the same time expressing the 'invisible world' through it. Lewis' allegorist, however, abstracts from experience only those details which are clearly equivalent to the abstractions he wants to express, so that his expressions would not be realistic.

Lewis' distinction between allegory and symbolism is misleading for another reason. 'The allegorist', he says, 'leaves the given—his own passions—to talk of that which is confessedly less real, which is a fiction. The symbolist leaves the given to find that which is more real' (p. 45). Lewis, as W. B. C. Watkins notes, 'takes the lowest common denominator of one term (allegory) to contrast with an extended sense of the other (symbolism) . . .'.[30] More than this, the distinction between degrees of reality is impracticable. The distinction should instead be drawn between kinds of reality. Despite the implications of Lewis' definitions, there is no reason why the poet's representation cannot be faithful to the reality of both worlds. If Moby Dick has a part to play in an allegory, he is none the less a whale.

Watkins' own definition is simple and practical: 'We may say that allegory is dynamic and narrative, whereas symbolism is more frequently static and lyrical; that the figures in an allegory are symbols, their action allegory'. To illustrate by a simple example, the cup which Excesse offers Guyon is a symbol; Guyon's action in hurling it to the ground is allegory.

A poem with as many kinds of reality and as fully individualized characters as the *Odyssey*, a poem that is both detailed and universal, is clearly not adaptable to Lewis' definition of allegory. Just as surely, any translation of that poem whose characters appeared primarily as *visibilia* of abstractions would be a weird representation of the original. There is nothing to prevent robust and individualized characters from being engaged simultaneously in realistic and in allegorical adventures. It would be well to remember on this score the number of times in the history of allegorical definition that emphasis has been laid on the covert nature of the abstractions being represented: allegorical abstractions, particularly in oblique poetry, are not bound to proclaim themselves at every turn. They are, as Comes says, often 'cum maximo artificio sub fabulosis corticibus occultata'.

Neither Chapman's poem nor Homer's, therefore, falls

in the category of these abstract, schematic allegories which Lewis has in mind. Thus the meaning of the allegorical representation is determined by the context to the same extent that the meaning of any image is thus determined, and is not imposed arbitrarily by a name like 'Patientia' or 'Ira'.

Although Chapman saw the career of Odysseus as a spiritual quest, he did justice, on the whole, to the complexities and contradictions in Homer's hero. While he occasionally pressed the allegory beyond any implied warrant in Homer, Ulysses emerges in his translation as the man who is all the more universal because he commands our imaginations as an individual—one whose temptations and weaknesses and longings we recognize as profoundly human because they bear the imprint of personality. *Personae* excite little sympathy—witness the Palmer in Spenser—but we can identify ourselves with Chapman's hero as we do with Homer's. Odysseus' unequalled power to arouse strong personal feelings throughout the history of Western civilization proves the comprehensiveness of Homer's characterization. While neither Chapman nor any other artist has matched the subtlety and power of Homer's creation, his hero is more like the original than any others I know, for Chapman avoided the ever-present danger of splitting Homer's many-sided hero and leaving us with a fragment, Ulysses the saint or Ulysses the rogue.

The human realism of Chapman's allegory sets it apart from all others. Yet we are bound to recognize, as Chapman did, the superhuman elements in Homer's *Odyssey* which distinguish it from works which have no mythical element, but which are equally concerned with central problems of human experience. The hero of a mythical poem may encounter dangers and trials that lie beyond normal experience. These are magnifications or idealizations of reality which do not obey and cannot be understood by natural law. Such supernatural fictions demand to be understood according to another criterion of reality than that of natural law. We find Ulysses encountering the Cyclops, the Sirens, and the Laestrygonians as well as his wife's suitors. These monstrous enemies incarnate human evils to a fantastic degree. The barbarism of Polyphemus and the voluptuous malice of the Sirens have usurped almost their entire personalities and distorted their physical forms in an unnatural fashion. These exaggerations of human qualities are the nearest things we find in Homer to Lewis' personifications, yet even they are much more complex and, psychologically, much more plausible. Certain touches such as Polyphemus' affection for his ram and the picture of the Laestrygonian princess drawing water at the spring keep us from treating them as pure *personae* or abstractions.

Homer's *Odyssey* is not a schematic allegory in the sense that *The Faerie Queene* is, or at least pretends to be. Any interpretation that treats it as such ignores its complexity and forces it into a genre where it does not belong. We must keep this point in mind in evaluating Chapman's translation. We are not obliged to judge it by the criteria of a special genre, but are free to evaluate the translation according to its power and coherence as an English poem. If the allegory seems forced and the original complexity of Homer's myth is lost, the translation has failed. As a description of this sort of failure we may take Allen Tate's definition of what he calls 'pure allegory': 'With [pure] allegory the image is not a complete, qualitative whole; it is an abstraction calculated to force the situation upon which it is imposed towards a single direction'.[31] This type of allegory, he seems to mean, blights the natural development of the imagery, eradicates all the associations of an image which would normally enrich it, arbitrarily making it a sign or an abstraction. In this 'pure' allegory, he says, 'the preponderance of meaning is wholly revealed; the characters, images, symbols, ideas, are simple, and invite restatement in a paraphrase that exhausts their meaning; they stand, not in themselves, but merely for something else' (pp. 90-1). This is the kind of allegory which he finds in *The Faerie Queene*. Although one may disagree with his evaluation of that poem on such a basis, Tate's definitions are very useful. The preferred kind of allegory he finds in *The Divine Comedy*, where it 'never rises to an insubordinate place, but consistently occupies an implicit place, from which we must derive it by main force' (p. 89). Dante's poem 'has a moral, a set of derivative ideas that seem to the reader to be relevant to practical conduct. But to say this is not to say, with most schools of modern criticism, that it is the primary significance of the work. For Dante is a poet; the didactic element is in solution with the other elements, and may be said barely to exist in itself, since it must be isolated by the violence of the reader's own will' (pp. 92-3).

If Homer's *Odyssey* is an allegory at all, it is an allegory of this type. Its characters, symbols, and ideas may 'invite restatement', but no paraphrase can possibly 'exhaust their meaning'. The didactic element of any single episode can only be 'isolated by the violence of the reader's own will'. The measure of this violence is the poverty of the paraphrase compared with the vitality of the original. Any restatement will be partial and inadequate because that great poem is primarily faithful to the intricate nature of human experience and the human mind. When Comes describes Ulysses' followers as 'animorum nostrorum motus' he makes a penetrating suggestion which helps us to understand one of their functions, but their total function in the poem is immeasurably more complicated. Part of our task, therefore, will be to decide whether Chapman's allegorical approach has oversimplified the original. For we must remember that Homer never separated the ideal and the real, nor did he think in terms of personifications and abstractions. As Roger Hinks says, in his brilliant introduction to *Myth and Allegory in Ancient Art*, 'It is only in the later period of ancient art, from the Hellenistic Age onwards, that the personification of an abstract concept was deliberately invented, and that its creator had a clear distinction in his mind between the philosophic notion and the human shape in which he sought to attire it'.[32]

V

At first glance the most striking innovation in the text of Chapman's *Odyssey* is a heightened moral tone. Behaviour is explicitly referred to moral principles which are often only implied in Homer. The most conspicuous alteration of the literal meaning of the original is found in Chapman's effort to reduce, as far as possible, the apparent discords inherent in the polytheistic system of Homer in order to produce, for Christian readers, the impression of a consistent and harmonious divine purpose and a consistent and harmonious moral law.

Chapman accordingly eliminated the *apparent* excuse by which Homer's characters attributed their own evil actions to the influence of some usually nameless deity. He was anxious to show in such cases that the responsibility for an evil choice rested squarely with the wrongdoer and to avoid at the same time any imputation of malevolence to the gods. An example is Penelope's explanation of her hesitation in welcoming Ulysses. In Homer she cites the case of Helen: 'Some god prompted her to a deed of shame; nor until then did she lay up in her mind the thought of that folly, that dreadful folly, which first brought grief upon us as well'.[33] The objectifying of evil human motives by attributing them to some anonymous θεός or δαίμων is characteristic of Homeric psychology. E. R. Dodds gives us a valuable reminder that it is never the poet but always his characters who regard human behaviour in this way, that this kind of divine machinery '"duplicates" a psychic intervention', presenting it in a concrete pictorial form, since only in this way could it be made vivid to the imagination of the hearers. 'The Homeric poets', he continues, 'were without the refinements of language which would have been needed

to "put across" adequately a purely psychological miracle.'³⁴
We are doubtless mistaken, therefore, if we read Penelope's
remarks as meaning that Providence deliberately destroyed
Helen's power of choice and compelled her to sin, especially
since Penelope here shows confidence in her power to resist
such impulses. Chapman consequently recast the passage in
a way consistent with his own view of the poem:

> But God impell'd her to a shamelesse deede,
> Because she had not in her selfe decreed,
> Before th'attempt, that such acts still were shent
> As simply in themselves, as in th'event.
>
> (XXIII, 339-42, p. 356)

Helen's sin is thus presented as a divine punishment for her
indifference to an absolute moral law: only after she had
lapsed into the pragmatic heresy of judging the deed by the
anticipated outcome, rather than by the laws of God, could
she be led to sin. Helen's case is made consistent with the case
of Aegisthus as Zeus has spoken of it, and Chapman avoids
the anomaly of making the gods arbitrary agents of evil.

Toward this end of making the *Odyssey's* polytheism
conform more nearly to Christian monotheism Chapman
on several occasions substitutes the devil for the anonymous
daemons to whom Homer's characters ascribe evil influences. In Book XII Ulysses tells how he tried to argue his men
out of their determination to land at Thrinacia, having been
warned by Teiresias of the fatal consequences of killing the
sacred cattle of the Sun, and how, nevertheless, his companions yielded to the persuasions of Eurylochus to sail no
farther. The hero then remarks to his audience, 'Then
indeed I knew that some god was surely plotting evil'.³⁵
Chapman translates:

> and then knew I
> That past all doubt, the divell did apply
> His slaughterous works.
>
> (XII, 426-8, p. 188)

Δαίμων, which Chapman renders as 'divell', only acquired that meaning long after Homer. Spondanus translates it here 'daemon' (p. 175), but Scapula's lexicon, which Chapman used assiduously, emphasizes the fact that in Homer it means 'god'.[36] Chapman translates the same word in the same way when it occurs in the description of the flat calm that fell on the sea as Ulysses drew near the Sirens: 'Then presently the wind ceased, and there was a breathless calm, and a god lulled the waves to sleep'.[37] Chapman renders the final clause thus:

> The *Sirens* divell charm'd all.
>
> (XII, 252, p. 185)

The Devil makes one other appearance in a gnomic couplet added to one of Penelope's speeches in Book XVIII:

> Whom God gives over, they themselves forsake;
> Their greefes their joyes, their God their devill make.
>
> (XVIII, 403-4, p. 203)

Here, as elsewhere, Chapman's translation is guided by the twin principles of individual moral responsibility and divine justice.

In all such cases, however obviously they may alter the literal meaning of the original, we may find Chapman justified by Zeus's central statement in Book I that the gods do not tempt and mislead men into wickedness or torment them for pleasure, but that men aggravate the natural difficulties of their lot by flouting the divine law.

In the same spirit Chapman consistently alters the honorific epithets which Homer attaches to the names of evil characters as well as good ones. The latest editor of the *Odyssey* explains these anomalies on the grounds of metrical convenience or oversight.[38] Where Homer calls the murderous adulterer Aegisthus ἀμύμων, 'faultless', Chapman substitutes 'faultful'.[39] ἀντίθεον Πολύφημον, 'godlike Polyphemus', becomes 'God-foe Polypheme'.[40] This change may be objected to as a violent alteration of Homer's meaning on the grounds that Polyphemus is, after all, Poseidon's son and the Cyclopes *are* godlike in their toil-free lives and indifference to the higher deities. Yet Chapman's alteration, for his readers, seems justified by the gratuitous cruelty, cannibalism, and social isolation in which they lived, all of which distinguish them radically from the Olympians as they are usually depicted in the *Odyssey*. In the same fashion Homer's ἀντίθεοι μνηστῆρες, 'godlike wooers', is changed into 'th'ungodly wooing guests'[41]; his μνηστῆρες ἀγήνορες, 'heroic' or 'proud wooers', into 'the rude wooers'.[42] In such cases a doggedly literal translation would only make nonsense for English readers.

A similar change involves the intensification of moral disapprobation where it is somewhat ambiguously expressed in a Greek word. A typical example is ἀτασθαλία—'blind folly, presumptuous sin, recklessness'. This key word is applied to Penelope's suitors and to the sailors who ate the cattle of the Sun to explain the fatal punishments which they incurred. Where Ulysses tells Eurycleia that the dead suitors 'by their ἀτασθαλία brought on themselves a shameful death' (XXII, 416), Chapman emphasizes the wickedness, rather than the foolishness, of their behaviour:

> Their lives directly ill were therefore cause
> That *Death* in these sterne formes soe deeply drawes.
>
> (XXII, 536-7, p. 344)

Here it should also be mentioned that Chapman has chosen to emphasize the note of retributive justice at the cost of Homer's more humane attitude. In the original, Eurycleia exults over the dead suitors, but Odysseus reprimands her.[43] As W. B. Stanford says,

This, if ever, is the time for Odysseus to boast and exult, and for Homer to write a triumphal song equal to those of Moses and Deborah after the defeat of the enemies of the Lord. But that is not Homer's, or Odysseus's, way. Instead, when Eurycleia is about to raise a cry of triumph, Odysseus prevents her: 'Rejoice only in your heart, woman, and restrain yourself; raise no triumphal shout. It is wrong to boast over slain men. It was destiny and their own stubborn deeds that laid these men low. They showed no reverence for mankind, good or bad, who ever came to them. Therefore by their own wanton folly they met a shameful fate.' This is a remarkably dispassionate pronouncement for a Homeric hero in his moment of success. It contrasts vividly with the vaunts of victorious champions in the *Iliad*. Odysseus completely ignores his own achievement. He sees himself only as the instrument of destiny in punishing harshness, inhumanity, and folly. It is partly the feeling of *Non nobis, Domine*; but there is a difference. The emphasis here is less theistic than humanistic: men reap what they sow.[44]

This modesty, I might add, is something new and quite different from the way Odysseus behaved after he had blinded and escaped from Polyphemus. Here Chapman is rigorous: he makes Eurycleia exclaim with horror, while Ulysses urges her to rejoice because 'it is no pietie to bemone the proud' (XXII, 529, p. 344).

In another case where the moral evil and folly of the sailors' act of disobedience tend to merge with each other in ἀτασθαλία Chapman emphasizes both the irrational and immoral aspects by recognizing each meaning of the word separately:

O men unwise,
They perisht by their owne impieties.

(I, 11-12, p. 1)

Chapman likewise makes many corresponding expressions in Homer more explicitly moral. δαΐφρων 'Οδυσσεύς—the prudent Ulysses—is distinguished from the wicked Aegisthus in the translation by 'his more pious mind' (I, 81, p. 3). Some such distinction seems to be implied in the original, where Zeus ascribes ἀτασθαλία to Aegisthus (I, 32-43), and commends Odysseus as περὶ νόον βροτῶν—'beyond mortals in wisdom' (I, 66), but Chapman goes beyond

Homer in attributing the hero's ultimate success specifically to piety and not to prudence alone. The net effect of all these departures from the strict sense of the original is to make more evident the central ethical principles which Chapman saw in the poem.

VI

A still more important device which Chapman employs to gain this end is the development of certain basic motifs of Homer's poem into symbols highly charged with moral content. Innumerable references to appetite or eating and also to the sea are woven into the very texture of the Greek epic. Chapman has developed these into explicit symbolic patterns of passions in constant conflict with reason. This conflict, as we have seen, embodies Chapman's conception of one of the *Odyssey's* central themes. The prerequisites to man's welfare, as he sees it, are the virtues of temperance and self-control.

The prime effect of Chapman's patterns of moral symbols is to widen the application of Homer's moral standards and to develop implicit into explicit judgments. In Homer the standards are embodied to a large extent in a handful of typical cases, and we are left to draw our own conclusions about actions on which Homer is silent. The major offences on which Homer passes overt judgments are Aegisthus' marriage with Clytemnestra and murder of Agamemnon, the suitors' wooing of Penelope and illicit consumption of Ulysses' substance, and the slaughter of the cattle of the Sun. The moral injunction most widely stressed in the *Odyssey* is charity to strangers, and some of the suitors are doubly condemned because their lawlessness is aggravated by meanness: they refuse to share the food they steal from their king with hungry beggars like the king himself.

The motifs of eating and the sea which Chapman has moralized engage some of the most deeply felt and familiar human experiences in Homer's poem—hunger, homelessness, and terror of the sea's violence. In Homer the suitors' gluttonous consumption of Ulysses' sheep and cattle is explicitly condemned only as the unlawful use of another's goods. By implication, at least, this gorging is also disapproved of as a callous waste of food. But temperance in eating and drinking is not in itself emphasized as a virtue in Homer. As a rule not only the suitors, but Ulysses and his sailors and the Pylian, Spartan and Phaeacian courts partake of copious feasts that often last all day. The suitors' banquets are implicitly criticized in Homer for other reasons than gluttony. The meals of the good characters are usually preceded by sacrifices and libations described in some detail, while the lawless princelings in Penelope's house seem to fall to without these preliminary rites. This is clearly evident in the implied contrast between the turbulent banquets in Ithaca and the ritual solemnities in which Telemachus first finds the entire community of Pylos engaged: 'Here the townsfolk were offering sacrifice to the dark-haired Earthshaker on the shore of the sea. There were nine companies and five hundred sat in each, and in each they held nine bulls ready for sacrifice.'[45] Homer stresses the importance of such sacraments by this comment on Eumaeus: 'Nor did the swineherd forget the immortals, for he had an understanding heart, but as a first offering he cast into the fire bristles from the head of the white-tusked boar, and made prayers to all the gods that wise Odysseus might return to his own house'.[46]

The suitors' feasts are also implicitly condemned for being ill-mannered and disorderly when contrasted with the grace and dignity of normal meals. Except for the last sentence, the following passage is a formula which appears four times in the course of the poem:

Then a handmaid brought water for the hands in a fair pitcher of gold and poured it into a silver basin for them to wash, and drew up a polished table beside them. And the grave housewife brought bread and set it before them, and abundant delicacies, giving freely of her store. And a carver passed platters of meat of all kinds, and set golden goblets by them, while a herald walked constantly to and fro, pouring them wine.[47]

When Telemachus entertains Athene in disguise, he has his table set as far as possible from the suitors, 'Lest the stranger, vexed by the uproar, should dislike the meal, seeing the arrogant company he was in'.[48] The suitors are so boisterous that Telemachus must ask them to refrain from 'brawling'. Unlike the elegant preparations for this meal, the grossest details preliminary to the suitors' meals are stressed as in this typical passage: 'And when they had come to the stately house they laid their cloaks on the chairs and high seats, and men fell to slaying great sheep and fat goats and fatted swine and a heifer of the herd, and so made ready the meal'.[49] As Gilbert Murray says, the suitors' feasts 'seem like the massacres of a slaughterhouse followed by the gorging of pirates'.[50]

Chapman's development of gluttony into a moral symbol for intemperance of all sorts introduces an undertone of asceticism that has no exact counterpart in Homer. The effect is to widen the implications of Teiresias' warning in the specific case of the sacred cattle into a general principle of conduct. Chapman's version of this passage follows the original closely:

> If both thine owne affections, and thy friends,
> Thou wilt containe, when thy accesse ascends
> The three-forckt Iland, having scap't the seas,
> (Where ye shall find, fed on the flowrie leas
> Fat flocks, and Oxen which the Sunn doth owne,
> To whom are all things as well heard as showne,
> And never dare one head of those to slay,
> But hold unharmefull on your wished way)
> Though through enough affliction, yet secure,
> Your Fates shall land ye.
> (XI, 131-40, p. 163)

From the very beginning of the poem Chapman shows

Ulysses' sailors as under the domination of the grosser passions and desires which man must control under penalty of death, spiritual as well as physical. Where Homer, in the exordium, speaks of Ulysses' men as 'fools, who devoured the cattle of Helios Hyperion', Chapman says that they

> in their hungers rapine would not shunne
> The Oxen of the loftie-going Sunne.
>
> (I, 13-14, p. 1)

He freely expresses his contempt for their appetite-dominated lives by alterations of Homer's literal sense. In Book XII, just before the oxen are killed, Ulysses explains that his men held off as long as their supplies of wine and bread lasted, λιλαιόμενοι βιότοιο, 'being eager to save their lives' (XII, 328). Chapman translates this phrase as 'those students for the gut and life', an interpretation undoubtedly suggested by Spondanus' version—'studiosi vitae' (p. 179). This is typical of certain minor instances where Chapman adopts phrases from the Latin text or commentary to express a moral judgment by images of gluttony not found in Homer.[51]

Occasionally Chapman will go even farther and interpolate comments for which there is no explicit authority in Homer. Thus he adds to Ulysses' account of rescuing his struggling and weeping companions from the land of the Lotus-eaters the observation that they

> would not leave their meate
> For heaven it selfe.
>
> (IX, 158-9, p. 130)

What ordinarily would be no more than a casual, colloquial hyperbole strikes one, on second thought, as a brilliant flash of wit in the general context of Chapman's allegorical identification of Ithaca and heaven. Not only does it illuminate the sailors' characteristic forgetfulness of their goal in the oblivion induced by eating the lotus, but it anticipates the crisis of the sacred oxen where they recklessly gamble their hope of return in exchange for food.

Chapman sees the suitors as even more culpably selling their souls for the grossest pleasures. Their gluttony is not extenuated by the sting of need. They are powerful, rich, and noble gentlemen who have wilfully abrogated their responsibilities as rational human beings and reduced themselves to the level of beasts. Worse still, their unbridled sensuality endangers the order of society for which Chapman, as a typical Elizabethan, felt the deepest reverence. Chapman accordingly develops the suitors' greed into a symbol of any destructive force in human nature, whether it threatens only the individual himself, or the order of which he is a part as well. In Homer, the suitors are admonished for violating the rights of property; in Chapman, for satisfying sensual appetites at the expense of the spirit and also for attacking the very foundations of society. Their basic fault is their unawareness of or indifference to the supernatural world, and Chapman emphasizes this trait by mocking their neglect of sacrificial rites, when he speaks of a sow

> Which must of force be offer'd to the Vow
> The Wooers made to all satiety:
> To serve which, still they did those Offrings ply.
> (XIV, 38-40, p. 211)

Here Homer has merely told of a swineherd who was 'compelled to drive a sow to the insolent wooers, that they might slay it and satisfy their desires with meat'.[52] Chapman, furthermore, makes moderation into a sacred principle, and Penelope charges the suitors with sacrilege in their intemperance:

> But they themselves let loose continuall Reines
> To our expences, making slaughter still
> Of sheepe, goats, oxen; feeding past their fill;
> And vainly lavishing our richest wine,
> All these extending past the sacred line.
> (XVII, 722-6, p. 272)

The altered emphasis in Chapman is entirely due to the last

line, which is his addition to the sense of the original.

The death of Antinous, the most evil of Penelope's ad-
mirers, is an episode of great dramatic power in Homer.
Just before the arrow pierces his throat he is glimpsed in a
characteristic pose: '[Odysseus] spoke, and aimed a bitter
arrow at Antinous. Now he was on the point of raising to
his lips a fair goblet, a two-eared cup of gold, and was even
now grasping it to drink the wine, and death was not in his
thoughts.'[53] As in the case of those sailors 'who would not
leave their meat for heaven itself', Antinous' reckless sensuality is illuminated in one flash of Chapman's mordant wit:

> He said, and off a bitter arrow thrust
> Right at *Antinous*, that strooke him just
> As he was lifting up the Bolle, to show
> That 'twixt the cup & lip much ill may grow.
> *Death* toucht not at his thoughts at Feast. . . .
>
> (XXII, 11-15, p. 333)

The understatement of the cliché, which Chapman found in
Spondanus' commentary as a solemn observation on the
deaths of the suitors, strikes the proper tone for an epitaph on
the gourmandizing Antinous.[54]

On the other hand we find Chapman correspondingly
anxious to free Ulysses of any imputation of gluttony,
since that is such an unheroic vice. Where Ulysses, disguised
as a beggar, complains that 'it [my belly] ever bids me eat
and drink, and makes me forget all that I have suffered and
commands me to eat my fill',[55] Chapman adds two lines
for this purpose:

> What ever ill
> I ever beare, it ever bids me fill.
> But this ease is but forc't, and will not last,
> Till what the mind likes be as well embrac't.
>
> (VII, 313-16, pp. 104-5)

The proper balance which Ulysses keeps between the
demands of mind and body is absolutely destroyed in the

case of Irus, a fantastic beggar who serves as a burlesque image of the suitors. Like them he is an uninvited guest in Ulysses' house who has adopted proprietary airs. Like them he assumes the prerogative of admitting strangers or turning them away, and he lords it over the other beggars just as Antinous does over the patrician element. He imitates the mocking speech and haughty manner of his social superiors, and imitates, in his gross epicureanism, their way of life: 'Now there came up a beggar of the town who made a practice of begging through Ithaca and was known for his greedy belly, eating and drinking without end. He had neither strength nor might, but in mere bulk he was big indeed to look upon.'[56] Irus apes the suitors in threatening to drive the disguised Ulysses away from his court, and the ensuing battle which they find so entertaining foreshadows the final battle in which they are all killed. Chapman develops the symbolism of the episode by transforming Irus' physical torpor into an image of his moribund spiritual condition:

> There came a commune Begger to the court,
> Who, in the city, begg'd of all resort,
> Excell'd in madnesse of the gut, drunke, eate
> Past intermission, was most hugely great;
> Yet had no fivers [fibres] in him, nor no force,
> In sight, a Man; in mind, a living Corse.
>
> (XVIII, 1-6, p. 257)

Appetite also provides Chapman with an important symbol for anarchic human impulses in the political and social order, especially in the tyrannical and arbitrary use of power by a ruler. The last sentence of Penelope's praise of her husband as a just ruler—'he did no wrong in deed or word to any man in the land, as is the way of divine kings, who hate one man and love another. But he never did wrong to anyone'[57]—is cast into this image:

> He still yet just, nor would, though [he] might, devoure,
> Nor to the worst did ever taste of powre.
>
> (IV, 923-4, p. 65)

Chapman's Athene likewise speaks of these rulers who, unlike the 'gentle, humane, just' Ulysses,

> grow
> Rude, and for ever scornfull of your rights;
> All justice ordring by their appetites.
>
> (V, 14-16, p. 72)

The most striking representation of moral nihilism, resulting in a purely relativistic system of values where each man's will becomes his law, occurs in Ulysses' famous speech to Amphinomus warning him to leave the company of the suitors while there is yet time. In the following lines Ulysses is generalizing on his own past behaviour:

> I thought me once a blessed man with men,
> And fashion'd me to all so counted then,
> Did all injustice like them, what for Lust,
> Or any pleasure, never so unjust,
> I could by powre or violence obtaine,
> And gave them both in all their powres the raigne:
> Bold of my Fathers and my Brothers still;
> While which held good my Arts seem'd never ill.
> And thus is none held simply good or bad,
> But as his will is either mist, or had.
> All goods Gods gifts man calls, how ere he gets them,
> And so takes all, what price so ere God sets them;
> Saies nought how ill they come, nor will controule
> That Ravine in him, though it cost his soule.
>
> (XVIII, 198-211, p. 279)

The whole speech will be compared in detail with the corresponding passage in Homer in the next chapter. In the present discussion we are concerned with Chapman's characteristic use of appetite symbolism in the last two lines, his extension of the consequences of intemperance from the death of the individual spirit all the way to social injustices, and his equally characteristic indictment of the pragmatic philosophy of success in

> And thus is none held simply good or bad,
> But as his will is either mist, or had.

The motif of hunger and appetite is, as we have seen, woven into the fabric of Homer's poem. In Ulysses' recalcitrant followers and in the reckless suitors this motif represents one of the chief obstacles to the hero's safe return to Ithaca and re-establishment there. The other chief obstacle is the sea, of course, where Ulysses is blown off his homeward track time and again and where he loses his ships, his men, and very nearly his own life. Together these can be taken to represent natural forces hostile to man's aspirations toward a civilized order. Chapman sometimes identifies these destructive elements in human nature with the violent aspects of the physical universe by uniting the imagery of appetite with the imagery of the sea. This union of the two chief moral symbols results in an extremely effective cross-fertilization in which the characteristic Homeric horror of the sea is transferred to moral disorder and vice versa.

The motifs merge, for instance, in Telemachus' bitter conjecture to Nestor about his father's death at the beginning of Book III:

> But his death *Jove* keepes from the world unknowne,
> The certaine fame thereof being told by none;
> If on the Continent by enemies slaine,
> Or with the waves eat of the ravenous Maine.
>
> (III, 125-8, p. 34)

There are other cases very much like this in which Chapman has attributed voracious hunger to the sea. A striking one occurs in Laertes' poignant lament for the son he thinks he has lost

> Farre away
> From friends and country destin'd to alay
> The sea-bred appetites, or, left ashore,
> To be by fowles and upland monsters tore. . . .
>
> (XXIV, 388-91, p. 369)

Such a conjunction of images prepares us to accept emotionally the intense feelings with which Chapman loads his appetite symbols, which might otherwise seem too slight for such a burden. Ungoverned appetite consequently acquires, in the course of the poem, the most sinister associations. At the same time the transfer of whatever is subhuman and bestial in human nature to the sea and associated natural forces evokes in us some of the disgust and fear with which nature often inspired these early Greeks whose security was so precarious. In the *Odyssey* there is an almost universal aversion toward the sea. Most of the characters are profoundly land-loving people—farmers and herdsmen by choice and sailors by necessity. The chief exception that comes to mind is the Phaeacians, but they are normally immune to the hazards of navigation because of their magical ships.

This will help to explain what might otherwise seem the excessive horror with which Penelope reacts to the news that Telemachus has taken ship in search of his father: 'Herald, why has my son gone? He had no need to go aboard swift ships, which serve men as horses of the deep and course over the wide waters of the sea.'[58] Chapman's translation of this speech provides a key to another of his moral symbols, where the fluidity and flux of the sea are used to represent erratic human impulses. Penelope makes an antithesis between 'wit' or reason and the sea's unstable violence, which concentrates in a single line the emotional associations which the sea evokes throughout the poem:

> Why left my sonne his mother? Why refusde
> His wit the solid shore, to trie the seas,
> And put in ships the trust of his distresse,
> That are at sea to men unbridled horse,
> And runne, past rule, their farre-engaged course
> Amidst a moisture past all meane unstaid?
>
> (IV, 942-7, p. 66)

Here are all the associations of excess, unpredictability, violence, and formlessness of which Chapman makes effective use throughout his translation. The force of this symbol is given a wider application in a passage from Chapman's 'Eugenia':

> To rise and fall for water is and winde:
> A Man all Center is, all stay, all minde,
> The bodie onely made her instrument:
> And to her ends in all acts must consent,
> Without which, order all this life hath none,
> But breeds the other lifes confusion.[59]

This quotation and the preceding one will serve to introduce another key term in Chapman's symbolism—'stay'. 'Stay' denotes fixedness, permanence, and stability. Chapman also uses it as a figure for spiritual orientation. Its intimate connection with the themes of wandering and the quest for home in the *Odyssey* is evident. Without 'stay' man is lost. Ulysses' whole destiny is thus enunciated in the opening lines of the translation:

> The Man (O Muse) informe, that many a way,
> Wound with his wisedome to his wished stay;
> That wanderd wondrous farre, when He the towne
> Of sacred *Troy* had sackt and shiverd downe.[60]

Here Chapman epitomizes his conception of the hero's career. This word also represents the highest moral virtue. It includes temperance, as in the case of the drunken Elpenor, who

> quite out of the stay
> A sober mind had given him,[61]

fell from Circe's roof, where he had been sleeping one warm night, and broke his neck. The man who has 'stay' obeys on all occasions the highest principles, as is shown by Nausicaa's praise of Ulysses:

> This man is truly manly, wise, and staid;
> In soule more rich, the more to sense decaid,

Who nor will do, nor suffer to be done,
Acts leud and abject. . . .

(VI, 315-18, p. 93)

What emerges from a consideration of Chapman's moral symbolism is the translator's concern at all times with order—moral, social and political. If the individual's loyalty to these orders fails, not only his own spirit but the very existence of civilization is threatened. This was a deep concern of the Elizabethans, but it conforms, as we shall see, to the general pattern of Homer's poem, which concerns itself first with Ulysses' struggle to bring order into his own spirit and then with his struggle to impose order on a chaotic society.

NOTES TO CHAPTER II

1. 'Epistle Dedicatorie.'

2. *The Faerie Queene*, 'A Letter of the Authors expounding his whole intention in the course of this worke . . .'.

3. *Mythology and the Renaissance Tradition in English Poetry* (Minneapolis, University of Minnesota Press; London, Oxford University Press, 1932), p. 100.

4. 'Epistle Dedicatorie.'

5. 'An Apology for Poetry', in *Elizabethan Critical Essays*, ed. G. Gregory Smith (London, Oxford University Press, 1937), 1, 167.

6. *The Faerie Queene*, 'A Letter of the Authors'.

7. *Literary Criticism in Antiquity* (Cambridge, Cambridge University Press, 1934), 1, 14.

8. Domenico Comparetti, *Vergil in the Middle Ages*, tr. E. F. M. Benecke (London and New York, 1895), p. 106. For other accounts of the classical origins of allegorical interpretation see Bush, *Mythology and the Renaissance Tradition*, p. 15; Anne B. Hersman, *Studies in Greek Allegorical Interpretation* (Chicago, Blue Sky Press, 1906), pp. 7-10; Sir J. E. Sandys, *A History of Classical Scholarship* (3rd ed., Cambridge, Cambridge University Press, 1908-21), 1, 29; E. E. Sikes, *The Greek View of Poetry* (London, Methuen, 1931), pp. 12 ff. Roger Hinks'

Myth and Allegory in Ancient Art (London, Warburg Institute, 1939), while concerned specifically with the fine arts, is most suggestive.

9. H. B. Lathrop, *Translations from the Classics into English from Caxton to Chapman, 1477–1620* (Madison, University of Wisconsin Press, 1933), p. 127.

10. *The Ulysses Theme*, p. 80.

11. *Heracliti Quaestiones Homericae* (Leipzig, 1910), ch. 50, ll. 5-9, p. 91. In the text I have referred to its more usual title. Hereafter it will be cited simply as *Herakleitos*. Translation mine.

12. *Herakleitos*, ch. 72, ll. 8-13, p. 94. Translation mine.

13. *Memorabilia*, I, iii, 7.

14. See Quintus Horatius Flaccus, *Epistulae*, ed. A. S. Wilkins (London and New York, 1899), Liber I, Epistula ii, ll. 17-26:

> Rursus, quid virtus et quid sapientia possit,
> utile proposuit nobis exemplar Ulixen,
> qui domitor Troiae multorum providus urbis
> et mores hominum inspexit latumque per aequor,
> dum sibi, dum sociis reditum parat, aspera multa
> pertulit, adversis rerum immersabilis undis.
> Sirenum voces et Circae pocula nosti:
> quae si cum sociis stultus cupidusque bibisset,
> sub domina meretrice fuisset turpis et excors,
> vixisset canis immundus vel amica luto sus.

15. See *The Scholemaster* (London, 1570), Leaf 24ʳ: 'And yet is not *Ulysses* commended, so much, nor so oft, in *Homere*, bicause he was πολύτροπος, that is, skilfull in many mens maners and facions, as bicause he was πολύμητις, that is, wise in all purposes, & ware in all places: which wisedome and warenes will not serve neither a traveler, except *Pallas* be alwayes at his elbow, that is Gods speciall grace from heaven, to keepe him in Gods feare, in all his doynges, in all his jeorneye. . . . He shall sometymes fall . . . into the lappe of some wanton and dalying Dame *Calypso*: and so suffer the danger of many a deadlie Denne, not so full of perils, to distroy the body, as full of vayne pleasures, to poyson the mynde.'

16. 'De Ulysse', *Mythologiae* (Paris, 1581), Lib. IX, Cap. i, p. 943. Translation mine.

17. 'The Ethical Bias of Chapman's *Homer*', *SP*, 36 (1939), 170.

18. *Iliads*, XIV, 343 n., p. 199.

19. *Ibid.* p. 200.

20. 'The Heroes of Chapman's *Homer*', *RES*, 17 (1941), 270-1.

21. τοῦ θυγάτηρ δύστηνον ὀδυρόμενον κατερύκει,
  αἰεὶ δὲ μαλακοῖσι καὶ αἱμυλίοισι λόγοισι
  θέλγει, ὅπως Ἰθάκης ἐπιλήσεται· αὐτὰρ Ὀδυσσεύς,
  ἱέμενος καὶ καπνὸν ἀποθρῴσκοντα νοῆσαι
  ἧς γαίης, θανέειν ἱμείρεται.   (I, 55-9)

22. Odysses, I, 50-69, pp. 2-3. Cf.:

  Ὦ πόποι, οἷον δή νυ θεοὺς βροτοὶ αἰτιόωνται.
  ἐξ ἡμέων γάρ φασι κάκ' ἔμμεναι· οἱ δὲ καὶ αὐτοὶ
  σφῇσιν ἀτασθαλίῃσιν ὑπὲρ μόρον ἄλγε' ἔχουσιν,
  ὡς καὶ νῦν Αἴγισθος ὑπὲρ μόρον Ἀτρεΐδαο
  γῆμ' ἄλοχον μνηστήν, τὸν δ' ἔκτανε νοστήσαντα,
  εἰδὼς αἰπὺν ὄλεθρον· ἐπεὶ πρό οἱ εἴπομεν ἡμεῖς,
  Ἑρμείαν πέμψαντες, εὔσκοπον ἀργειφόντην,
  μήτ' αὐτὸν κτείνειν μήτε μνάασθαι ἄκοιτιν·
  ἐκ γὰρ Ὀρέσταο τίσις ἔσσεται Ἀτρεΐδαο,
  ὁππότ' ἂν ἡβήσῃ καὶ ἧς ἱμείρεται αἴης.   (I, 32-41)

Alas, how ready mortals are to blame us gods. It is from us, they say, that evils come, but they themselves, by their own sinful folly, suffer beyond what fate has ordained. So Aegisthus, without any fatal influence, took to himself the wife of Agamemnon and slew the son of Atreus on his return, though he well knew the doom in store for him, since we warned him through keen-sighted Argus-slayer Hermes neither to woo the wife nor to slay the man, for vengeance would come for Agamemnon through Orestes when once he had reached manhood and longed for his native land.

23. ἀλλ' ὁ μὲν ἐν νήσῳ κεῖται κρατέρ' ἄλγεα πάσχων
  νύμφης ἐν μεγάροισι Καλυψοῦς, ἥ μιν ἀνάγκῃ
  ἴσχει.   (V, 13-15)

24. The Greeks and the Irrational (Berkeley and Los Angeles, University of California Press, 1951), p. 10.

25.   κατείβετο δὲ γλυκὺς αἰὼν
  νόστον ὀδυρομένῳ, ἐπεὶ οὐκέτι ἥνδανε νύμφη. (V, 152-3)

26. 'The Odyssey and the Western World', p. 413.

27. Homer's Odyssey. A Commentary (Chicago, 1895).

28. The Allegory of Love. A Study in Medieval Tradition (London, Oxford University Press, 1938), pp. 44-5.

29. 'She who is prayed to', 'Strong of mind', 'Foe of reason', 'The Hated one', 'The Concealer'.

30. Shakespeare and Spenser (Princeton, Princeton University Press, 1950), p. 115.

31. 'Three Types of Poetry', *Reactionary Essays on Poetry and Ideas* (New York and London, Scribner, 1936), p. 92.

32. *Studies of the Warburg Institute*, 6, ed. Fritz Saxl (London, 1939), 17.

33. τὴν δ' ἤ τοι ῥέξαι θεὸς ὤρορεν ἔργον ἀεικές·
τὴν δ' ἄτην οὗ πρόσθεν ἑῷ ἐγκάτθετο θυμῷ
λυγρήν, ἐξ ἧς πρῶτα καὶ ἡμέας ἵκετο πένθος. (XXIII, 222-4)

34. *The Greeks and the Irrational*, p. 14.

35. καὶ τότε δὴ γίγνωσκον ὃ δὴ κακὰ μήδετο δαίμων. (XII, 295)

36. Col. 348, δαίμων: '. . . in sa[n]cta autem Scriptura semper de spiritibus noxiis & impuris dicitur . . .'.

37. αὐτίκ' ἔπειτ' ἄνεμος μὲν ἐπαύσατο ἠδὲ γαλήνη
ἔπλετο νηνεμίη, κοίμησε δὲ κύματα δαίμων. (XII, 168-9)

38. See W. B. Stanford's comentary on the following phrases in his edition (London, Macmillan, 1948-50).

39. *Odyssey*, I, 29. *Odysses*, I, 47, p. 2.

40. *Odyssey*, I, 70. *Odysses*, I, 118, p. 4.

41. *Odyssey*, XIV, 18. *Odysses*, XIV, 28, p. 211.

42. *Odyssey*, I, 144. *Odysses*, I, 227, p. 6.

43. εὗρεν ἔπειτ' Ὀδυσῆα μετὰ κταμένοισι νέκυσσιν,
αἵματι καὶ λύθρῳ πεπαλαγμένον ὥς τε λέοντα,
ὅς ῥά τε βεβρωκὼς βοὸς ἔρχεται ἀγραύλοιο·
πᾶν δ' ἄρα οἱ στῆθός τε παρήϊά τ' ἀμφοτέρωθεν
αἱματόεντα πέλει, δεινὸς δ' εἰς ὦπα ἰδέσθαι·
ὣς Ὀδυσεὺς πεπάλακτο πόδας καὶ χεῖρας ὕπερθεν·
ἡ δ' ὡς οὖν νέκυάς τε καὶ ἄσπετον ἔσιδεν αἷμα,
ἴθυσέν ῥ' ὀλολύξαι, ἐπεὶ μέγα ἔσιδεν ἔργον·
ἀλλ' Ὀδυσεὺς κατέρυκε καὶ ἔσχεθεν ἱεμένην περ,
καί μιν φωνήσας ἔπεα πτερόεντα προσηύδα·
ἐν θυμῷ, γρηῦ, χαῖρε καὶ ἴσχεο μηδ' ὀλόλυζε·
οὐχ ὁσίη κταμένοισιν ἐπ' ἀνδράσιν εὐχετάασθαι.
τούσδε δὲ μοῖρ' ἐδάμασσε θεῶν καὶ σχέτλια ἔργα·
οὔ τινα γὰρ τίεσκον ἐπιχθονίων ἀνθρώπων,
οὐ κακὸν οὐδὲ μὲν ἐσθλόν, ὅτις σφέας εἰσαφίκοιτο·
τῷ καὶ ἀτασθαλίῃσιν ἀεικέα πότμον ἐπέσπον. (XXII, 401-16)

There she found Odysseus amid the bodies of the slain, all befouled with blood and filth, like a lion that comes from feeding on a grazing ox, a terrible sight with his blood-stained breast and head. Even so was Odysseus smeared hand and foot. But at the sight of the corpses and the welter of blood, she burst out with cries of joy at the great deed. But Odysseus rebuked her and spoke with winged words,
'Rejoice in your own heart, old woman, but restrain yourself and do

not cry aloud. It is not right to exult over the dead. The doom of the gods and their own reckless deeds have destroyed these men, for there was none on earth that they honoured, whoever, evil or good, came among them. By their own blind folly, therefore, have they brought upon themselves a shameless death.'

44. *The Ulysses Theme*, p. 35.

45. τοὶ δ' ἐπὶ θινὶ θαλάσσης ἱερὰ ῥέζον,
τaύρους παμμέλανας, ἐνοσίχθονι κυανοχαίτῃ.
ἐννέα δ' ἕδραι ἔσαν, πεντηκόσιοι δ' ἐν ἑκάστῃ
ἥατο, καὶ προὔχοντο ἑκάστοθι ἐννέα ταύρους. (III, 5-8)

46. οὐδὲ συβώτης
λήθετ' ἄρ' ἀθανάτων· φρεσὶ γὰρ κέχρητ' ἀγαθῇσιν·
ἀλλ' ὅ γ' ἀπαρχόμενος κεφαλῆς τρίχας ἐν πυρὶ βάλλεν
ἀργιόδοντος ὑός, καὶ ἐπεύχετο πᾶσι θεοῖσι
νοστῆσαι 'Οδυσῆα πολύφρονα ὅνδε δόμονδε. (XIV, 420-4)

47. χέρνιβα δ' ἀμφίπολος προχόῳ ἐπέχευε φέρουσα
καλῇ χρυσείῃ, ὑπὲρ ἀργυρέοιο λέβητος,
νίψασθαι· παρὰ δὲ ξεστὴν ἐτάνυσσε τράπεζαν.
σῖτον δ' αἰδοίη ταμίη παρέθηκε φέρουσα,
εἴδατα πόλλ' ἐπιθεῖσα, χαριζομένη παρεόντων·
δαιτρὸς δὲ κρειῶν πίνακας παρέθηκεν ἀείρας
παντοίων, παρὰ δέ σφι τίθει χρύσεια κύπελλα,
κῆρυξ δ' αὐτοῖσιν θάμ' ἐπῴχετο οἰνοχοεύων. (I, 136-43)

Cf. IV, 52-8; VII, 172-6; XV, 135-9; XVII, 91-5.

48. μὴ ξεῖνος ἀνιηθεὶς ὀρυμαγδῷ
δείπνῳ ἀδήσειεν, ὑπερφιάλοισι μετελθών. (I, 133-4)

49. αὐτὰρ ἐπεί ῥ' ἵκοντο δόμους εὖ ναιετάοντας,
χλαίνας μὲν κατέθεντο κατὰ κλισμούς τε θρόνους τε,
οἱ δ' ἱέρευον ὄϊς μεγάλους καὶ πίονας αἶγας,
ἵρευον δὲ σύας σιάλους καὶ βοῦν ἀγελαίην,
δαῖτ' ἐντυνόμενοι. (XVII, 178-82)

Cf. XVII, 532-7; XX, 248-53.

50. *The Rise of the Greek Epic* (3rd ed., Oxford, Clarendon Press, 1924), p. 67.

51. Some other examples of this practice: XIV, 365, p. 218, where Chapman translates ὕβρις by 'intemperance', following Spondanus' 'intemperantia' in XIV, 262, p. 204; XV, 446-7, p. 236, where 'beyond good counsaile' is his adaptation of the Latin mistranslation of XV, 344-5, p. 220: 'Sed gratia perniciosi ventris mala consilia habent Viri'; and XVII, 580-1, p. 269, where he also translates ὕβρει εἴξαντες by 'intemperate', following Spondanus, and invents the line:

And their inflam'd bloods bent to satiate.

52.   σὺν ἀγέμεν μνηστῆρσιν ὑπερφιάλοισιν ἀνάγκῃ,
        ὄφρ' ἱερεύσαντες κρειῶν κορεσαίατο θυμόν.   (XIV, 27-8)

53.   Ἦ καὶ ἐπ' Ἀντινόῳ ἰθύνετο πικρὸν ὀϊστόν.
        ἦ τοι ὁ καλὸν ἄλεισον ἀναιρήσεσθαι ἔμελλε,
        χρύσεον ἄμφωτον, καὶ δὴ μετὰ χερσὶν ἐνώμα,
        ὄφρα πίοι οἴνοιο· φόνος δέ οἱ οὐκ ἐνὶ θυμῷ
        μέμβλετο.   (XXII, 8-12)

54. Spondanus, p. 310, comments: 'Didymus refert Dionysium Thracem (qui fuit etiam Homeri commentator) prodidisse illud proverbium, πολλὰ μεταξὺ πέλει κύλικος καὶ χείλεος ἄκρ[ο]υ, multa cadunt inter calicem supremaque labra, hinc manasse: siquidem admovens iam labris poculum Antinous ab Ulysse interimitur. Vide Erasm. Chil. I. cent. 5. prov. I.'

55.   ἡ δὲ μάλ' αἰεὶ
        ἐσθέμεναι κέλεται καὶ πινέμεν, ἐκ δέ με πάντων
        ληθάνει ὅσσ' ἔπαθον, καὶ ἐνιπλησθῆναι ἀνώγει.   (VII, 219-21)

56.   Ἦλθε δ' ἐπὶ πτωχὸς πανδήμιος, ὃς κατὰ ἄστυ
        πτωχεύεσκ' Ἰθάκης, μετὰ δ' ἔπρεπε γαστέρι μάργῃ
        ἀζηχὲς φαγέμεν καὶ πιέμεν· οὐδέ οἱ ἦν ἲς
        οὐδὲ βίη, εἶδος δὲ μάλα μέγας ἦν ὁράασθαι.   (XVIII, 1-4)

57.   οὔτε τινὰ ῥέξας ἐξαίσιον οὔτε τι εἰπὼν
        ἐν δήμῳ· ἥ τ' ἐστὶ δίκη θείων βασιλήων·
        ἄλλον κ' ἐχθαίρῃσι βροτῶν, ἄλλον κε φιλοίη.   (IV, 690-3)
        κεῖνος δ' οὔ ποτε πάμπαν ἀτάσθαλον ἄνδρα ἐώργει.

58.   Κῆρυξ, τίπτε δέ μοι πάϊς οἴχεται; οὐδέ τί μιν χρεὼ
        νηῶν ὠκυπόρων ἐπιβαινέμεν, αἵ θ' ἁλὸς ἵπποι
        ἀνδράσι γίγνονται, περόωσι δὲ πουλὺν ἐφ' ὑγρήν.   (IV, 707-9)

59. 'Vigilia Secunda', Poems, p. 286, ll. 632-7.

60. Odysses, I, 1-4, p. 1. Cf. Odyssey, I, 1-2:

        Ἄνδρα μοι ἔννεπε, Μοῦσα, πολύτροπον, ὃς μάλα πολλὰ
        πλάγχθη, ἐπεὶ Τροίης ἱερὸν πτολίεθρον ἔπερσε.

Tell me, O Muse, of the man who was driven so very far after he had sacked the sacred city of Troy.

61. Odysses, X, 690-1, p. 159. Cf. Odyssey, X, 555:

        κατελέξατο οἰνοβαρείων.

He laid himself down heavy with wine.

CHAPTER III

Dynamic Allegory in Chapman's 'Odyssey'

THE explicit moral comments and the patterns of moral
symbolism in Chapman's translation provide a background of moral issues against which the major episodes of
the poem are enacted. They constitute a relatively simple
system, and if they alone represented Chapman's elucidation
of the allegory of the *Odyssey* one would have to admit that
the allegory was as static and obvious as the contention between Mr. Lewis's *Patientia* and *Ira*. Most of the characters immediately concerned in this pattern, it should be noticed, are
minor figures such as the suitors and Ulysses' sailors. They
are the ruck of men who fall for the grosser temptations
when moral sanctions, unsupported by physical force, are
ineffective deterrents, and they lack the faith or discipline or
imagination to deny themselves some temporary gratifica-
tion in exchange for some greater good in the future. The
major characters—Ulysses, Athene, Telemachus, Penelope,
Eumaeus, Nausicaa, and Arete, are distinguished from such
as these by some loyalty to the future or to some high principle. The suitors and Ulysses' sailors are mostly bound to
the temporal cycle of the present satisfaction of present impulses, but these other characters, being committed to high
or distant goals, are capable of hope and growth and change.
The former can mostly be said to act only in a limited sense,
because they merely repeat their characteristic actions over
and over. Ulysses' companions, with the exception of Eurylochus and poor Elpenor, are almost entirely devoid of individuality. Since they are dominated by a few basic impulses
Chapman can treat them, quite properly, as mere *personae*, as
'students of the gut and life'.

It is the other characters who give direction and movement

to the poem. Either they obey some moral principle which guides their conduct in the face of various obstacles or temptations, or they are seeking something beyond the present and above the anarchy of mere sensation and impulse. These characters, accordingly, produce the dynamic, evolutionary movement of the *Odyssey*, for they have the capacity to analyse experience and to act accordingly.

II

Chapman has underlined this principle of growth at various points in his translation, but most conspicuously, as one would expect, in the case of Ulysses. He makes clear the association between developments in the story and developments in the hero himself. The general line of growth can best be seen from three important speeches where Ulysses reflects in an unusually analytical manner on the nature of his experiences. Through all three speeches there runs a single theme—man's relation with the gods—and each marks an important step in Ulysses' growing self-knowledge, as he gradually discovers the proper limits of human power, intelligence, and freedom.

In Homer the first speech, which occurs in Book X, is a simple statement of the navigational predicament in which Ulysses and his company find themselves on Circe's island. They have lost their geographical bearings. Although they can tell direction from the sun they do not know in which quarter Ithaca lies. Ulysses is trying to convince his men of the need to ask directions, but they are reluctant to do so because of the fear of strangers which their recent encounters with Polyphemus and the Laestrygonians have given them: 'Hear my words, comrades, for all your misery. O friends, we do not know where the darkness is nor where the dawn, nor where the sun, which gives light to men, goes beneath the earth, nor where it rises. Let us now consider whether there is any device left us. As for me, I do not think

that there is.'[1] By his last two sentences Ulysses means only
that their own resources are inadequate for finding the way
home and that they must therefore take the risk of asking
the inhabitants. Chapman turns this statement of fact into an
analysis of the limitations of human knowledge and the
need for God's help:

> Now, friends,
> Affoord unpassionate eare, though ill Fate lends
> So good cause to your passion. No man knowes
> The reason whence and how the darknesse growes,
> The reason how the Morne is thus begunne,
> The reason how the Man-enlightening Sunne
> Dives under earth, the reason how againe
> He reres his golden head. Those counsailes, then,
> That passe our comprehension, we must leave
> To him that knowes their causes; and receave
> Direction from him in our acts, as farre
> As he shall please to make them regular,
> And stoope them to our reason. In our state
> What then behoves us? Can we estimate,
> With all our counsailes, where we are, or know
> (Without instruction past our owne skils) how
> (Put off from hence) to stere our course the more?
> I thinke we can not. We must then explore
> These parts for information. . . .
>
> (X, 241-59, pp. 149-50)

In this version the navigational problem serves as an image
of a much greater problem. It marks a change of view in
Ulysses who, heretofore, had often relied with calamitous
results on his own judgment and reason. The implications of
his speech are far more extensive than the practical point
with which he concludes it. This is as much a self-revealing
soliloquy as an argument: In the very process of explaining
the present difficulty the hero suddenly realizes the inadequacy of all merely human devices. As a preface to
Ulysses' encounter with Circe, who dwells on this island, it

is a strangely prophetic speech, not only because the unexpected intervention of Hermes preserves him from her
spells, but especially because through Circe he acquires the
'instruction past his own skills' to reach Ithaca. Chapman's
alterations illuminate this moment as a new phase in Ulysses'
self-knowledge and in his relations with the gods. Having
abandoned his old attitude of complete self-sufficiency the
hero is now prepared to put himself under Circe's direction
and take the trip to the underworld which is an essential
preliminary to his ultimate return to Ithaca.

The second speech, as Chapman has altered it, is even more
self-revealing and also marks a new stage in Ulysses' development. The occasion is his arrival in Ithaca, where he meets
Athene, whom he has not seen in ten years, disguised as a
shepherd. In Homer he explains his failure to recognize the
goddess as follows:

It is hard, goddess, for a mortal to know thee at sight, however
wise he may be, for thou takest whatever shape thou wilt. But
this I know well, that formerly thou wast kind to me, while we
sons of the Achaians fought in Troy. But when we had sacked
the towering city of Priam and had sailed away, and a god had
scattered the Achaians, never since then did I see thee, daughter of
Zeus, nor know thee to board my ship to ward off sorrow from
me. But ever bearing a divided heart in my breast I wandered,
until the gods freed me from evil, when, in the rich land of the
Phaeacians, thou didst encourage me and thyself lead me to the
city.[2]

The fact that he now recognizes Athene in the maiden who
helped him among the Phaeacians is, perhaps, Homer's way
of suggesting Odysseus' new insight. But the hero's gratitude
expressed in the last part of this passage is tempered by the
somewhat querulous tone in which he tells how Athene
failed to help him over such a long period. Chapman uses
this implied questioning of divine justice as the basis for an

insertion of eight lines in which Ulysses charges that his sufferings were undeserved:

> Goddesse (said he) unjust men and unwise,
> That author injuries and vanities,
> By vanities and wrongs should rather be
> Bound to this ill-abearing destiny,
> Then just and wise men. What delight hath heaven,
> That lives unhurt it selfe, to suffer given
> Up to all domage those poore few that strive
> To imitate it, and like the Deities live?
>
> (XIII, 452-9, p. 205)

This is similar to Athene's own defence of her protégé before the Olympian council which was referred to earlier:

> But that *Ithacus*
> (Thus never meriting) should suffer thus,
> I deeply suffer. His more pious mind
> Divides him from these fortunes.
>
> (I, 79-82, p. 3)

Ulysses makes his complaint in response to the difficulties which Athene has warned him he has yet to face at home. Here, as Mr. Smalley has pointed out, 'Though Athene does not reply directly to this question, Chapman renders the answer obvious in other parts of his translation. Heaven does not obviate man's difficulties. The purpose of divine grace is rather to steel man's soul to bear all ills without deviating from its proper course.'[3] It might be added that Homer also answers the question when Zeus, in response to Athene's remarks, after admitting Ulysses' wisdom and solicitous attention to sacrifices, stipulates the following conditions for his release from Calypso's island and return to Ithaca: 'Hermes, since thou art our messenger, declare now to the fair-haired nymph our fixed resolve, the return of stout-hearted Odysseus, that he may go without the conveyance either of the gods or of mortals, but after woeful suffering, on the twentieth day shall approach Scheria on a well-bound raft . . .'.[4] The return of Ulysses is not to be accomplished, therefore, by a simple act of divine intervention. Despite the approval of Zeus, the hero must confront his problems as a man, and he must solve them within the limitations of his humanity. As we shall see in the following chapter his own strength and will prove inadequate, and he reaches the Phaeacian shore with the aid of a sea-nymph and through prayers to the river-god. But this assistance is plainly to be distinguished from the sort of divine intervention which Zeus has in mind. In the present scene Chapman, by making Ulysses proclaim his virtuousness and question the justice of his sufferings, suggests further answers, as we shall see.

In Chapman the second part of this speech is an extensive development of the first sentence in the Homeric passage, in which Ulysses remarks on the difficulty of recognizing Athene because of her numerous disguises:

> But where you wonder that I know you not
> Through all your changes, that skill is not got
> By sleight or Art, since thy most hard-hit face
> Is still distinguisht by thy free-given grace;
> And therefore truly to acknowledge thee
> In thy encounters is a maistery
> In men most knowing. For to all men thou
> Tak'st severall likenesse. All men thinke they know
> Thee in their wits. But, since thy seeming view
> Appears to all, and yet thy truth to few,
> Through all thy changes to discern thee right
> Asks chief Love to thee, and inspired light.
>
> (XIII, 460-71, p. 205)

We find here again the theme of the limitations of human knowledge. But Ulysses restates it now with a different emphasis: Man cannot know divinity through his own intelligence ('sleight or Art') but only through 'free-given grace'. Without grace man, in his pride of knowledge, often thinks he knows but is deceived: 'all men thinke they know thee in their wits'. The operation of grace in man produces love and 'inspired light' wherewith he can distinguish divine truth from misleading appearances. This is another important revelation for the hero. The very fact that he has discovered Athene, however tardily, indicates a new stage in his development.

In the last and most important part of the speech Ulysses unconsciously reveals the reason for his having been so long deprived of Athene's aid. Here there is also a direct but equally unconscious refutation of his opening complaint:

> But this I surely know, that some yeares past
> I have beene often with thy presence grac'st,
> All time the sonnes of *Greece* wag'd warre at *Troy*;
> But when Fates full houre let our swords enjoy
> Our vowes in sacke of *Priams* lofty Towne,
> Our Ships all boorded, and when God had blowne
> Our Fleete in sunder, I could never see
> The seede of *Jove*, nor once distinguish thee
> Boording my Ship to take one woe from me.
> But onely in my proper spirit involv'd,
> Err'd here and there, quite slaine, till heaven dissolv'd
> Me and my ill; which chanc't not till thy grace
> By open speech confirm'd me, in a place
> Fruitfull of people, where, in person, thou
> Didst give me guide and all their City show,
> And that was the renown'd *Phaeacian* earth.
>
> (XIII, 472–87, p. 205)

Comparison with the original will show that Chapman has elaborated its meaning considerably. 'But ever bearing a divided heart in my breast I wandered, until the gods freed me from evil' becomes

> But onely in my proper spirit involv'd,
> Err'd here and there, quite slaine, till heaven dissolv'd
> Me and my ill.

84

This treats Odysseus' separation from Athene, which Homer is content to leave unexplained, as a state of spiritual isolation. Chapman merely states, I believe, what is strongly implied, however, in Homer: He treats Odysseus' δεδαϊγμένον ἦτορ —his 'divided heart'—as a subjective religious experience, and thus makes his hero more self-analytical than Homer's. Thus the complaints at the beginning of Ulysses' speech in Chapman find a more specific answer here: until the sack of Troy he had enjoyed Athene's favour; his troubles probably began when he took a leading part in the destruction of the sacred citadel referred to in the opening lines:

> The Man (O Muse) informe, that many a way
> Wound with his wisedome to his wished stay;
> That wanderd wondrous farre, when He the towne
> Of sacred *Troy* had sackt and shiverd downe. . . .[5]

There is thus a general answer and a particular one. As a general rule man's sufferings are not necessarily proportioned to his deserts. But Ulysses, furthermore, has not been as wise or just as he claims. In Chapman the connection between his actions at the fall of Troy and his subsequent separation from Athene is somewhat clearer than it is in Homer where the facts are presented without the strong implication that they are related as cause and effect. Homer does, however, mention in Book V how Odysseus and other Achaeans on the way from Troy 'sinned against Athene' and he goes on to tell how the goddess 'sent them an evil wind and long waves. There all his other noble comrades died, but the wind and wave brought him hither [to Ogygia]' (108-11). Fortunately, or unfortunately, Homer never specifies the nature of this offence. Even in Chapman Ulysses is only vaguely aware of the connection between his actions and his separation from Athene, a connection which is nevertheless revealed to the reader. Since that moment, he tells Athene, he never saw her come to his aid in trouble, as she had used to do. The intimacy

between the man and his divine patroness has been inter-
rupted by some offence on his part. The separation has cost
him years of suffering during which he has been thrown on
his own merely human resources:

> But onely in my proper spirit involv'd,
> Err'd here and there, quite slaine. . . .

In these lines Chapman enunciates the state of mind which fell
upon Ulysses after Troy. 'Proper' here means 'belonging
to oneself'. A distinction is implied thereby between the
individual human spirit and the divine spirit. The former,
by itself, is ultimately ineffectual: 'involv'd', enveloped and
entangled thus, Ulysses 'err'd', went astray both figuratively
and geographically. 'Involv'd' in the sense of 'wound'
suggests the futility of these wanderings. One should also
note the religious terminology which Chapman uses to
represent the spiritual nature of the hero's experience:
'grac'st', 'spirit', 'heav'n', and 'confirm'd'. Homer is
rarely as explicit about such inner, spiritual developments,
yet all of Chapman's version is based on the implications of
the original speech.

In the last half of the poem, after the old intimacy with
Athene is re-established, Ulysses is able to analyse his offence
in terms of principles valid for the entire *Odyssey* and
enunciated at the outset, as we have seen, by Zeus. The
chief instance of this is the hero's warning to Amphinomus,
the best of the suitors, to save himself from the coming
vengeance by quitting the company of the suitors while
there is time. In Homer it is Ulysses' most self-critical
speech, and Phyllis Bartlett calls it 'the one speech in Homer
which most nearly justifies Chapman's interpretation of
Ulysses'.[6] Though Ulysses does not mention here the
specific offences he has committed, we must remember that
he is bound, for the time being, to conceal his identity.
After some introductory remarks praising Amphinomus'
father as a just man, he says:

earth nourishes nothing feebler than man of all creatures that breathe and move. For he thinks that he will never suffer in times to come, as long as the gods make him prosperous and his knees are unbowed, but when the blessed gods decree him sorrow, he bears it reluctantly but with a steadfast heart. For the spirit of man on earth is such as the day which the father of gods and men brings upon him. I, too, once hoped to prosper, but, yielding to my might and strength, did many wicked deeds, trusting in my father and brothers. Therefore, let no man be lawless, but let him keep in silence whatever gifts the gods may give.[7]

The heart of this argument is that power is fortuitous and does not confer any exemptions from the rule of justice and fair play. It is the strongest statement for the principle of law as distinguished from the anarchy of force in Homer's poem, a principle which Homer sees as the divinely sanctioned basis of society. Chapman relates this part of the speech to Zeus's opening statement, which has been quoted earlier, that man can avoid certain catastrophes by using his reason and by acting with due regard to the consequences of his actions:

> Of all things breathing, or that creepe on earth,
> Nought is more wretched than a humane Birth.
> Bless'd men thinke never they can cursed be,
> While any power lasts to move a knee.
> But when the blest Gods make them feele that smart,
> That fled their Faith so, as they had no hart
> They beare their sufferings, and what wel they might
> Have cleerly shun'd, they then meet in despight.
> The Minde of Man flyes stil out of his way,
> Unless God guide and prompt it every day.
>
> (XVIII, 188-97, p. 279)

The final couplet emphasizes the insufficiency of intelligence alone as a guide.

In the rest of the speech, in Chapman as in Homer, Ulysses applies the preceding generalities to himself:

> I thought me once a blessed man with men,
> And fashion'd me to all so counted then,
> Did all injustice like them, what for Lust,
> Or any pleasure, never so unjust,
> I could by powre or violence obtaine,
> And gave them both in all their powres the raigne:
> Bold of my Fathers and my Brothers still;
> While which held good my Arts seem'd never ill.
> And thus is none held simply good or bad,
> But as his will is either mist, or had.
> All goods Gods gifts man calls, how ere he gets them,
> And so takes all, what price so ere God sets them;
> Saies nought how ill they come, nor will controule
> That Ravine in him, though it cost his soule.
>
> (XVIII, 198-211, p. 279)

In his former prosperity, Ulysses says, he thought himself blessed and, taking only material success as his guide, used any means to achieve his desires. The point of Chapman's translation turns on the word ὄλβιος which means both 'blessed' and 'prosperous', and it is developed in the indictment of the pragmatic philosophy of success in the couplet:

> And thus is none held simply good or bad,
> But as his will is either mist, or had.

The importance of acting according to absolute moral principles is strongly implied in both poems. The great significance of this particular speech, in Homer as well as in the translation, lies in the wrongs which Ulysses confesses. He had set up his own will as the good and used any means to achieve it. Now he is at last in a position to assert the truths which suffering has taught him. With the fulfilment of self-knowledge through an insight into his personal experiences the hero assumes a public rôle as judge and restorer of Ithacan society.

III

These self-analytical passages are landmarks in Ulysses' spiritual evolution. It is now time to turn to some of the main episodes in the translation in order to see how Chapman has embodied this general concept in the texture of the poem.

Ulysses' sojourn in Phaeacia presents an important stage in this evolution. It terminates a decade of wandering in a fabulous world. It comes at the end of countless exhausting and terrifying struggles against hostile forces of nature. It is the hero's first encounter in twenty years with normal society in peace-time. Finally, it marks a turning-point in the process by which the hero was relentlessly stripped of his fleet, his sailors, his booty, his weapons, and even his clothes. He reaches Phaeacia naked and nearly drowned; he leaves loaded with gifts, sleeping tranquilly in a magical ship which accomplishes in a single night the voyage home which he has been trying to make for ten years.

While Phaeacia is important as a setting for Ulysses' account of his adventures, his arrival and first experiences in that country provided Chapman with material rich in inner meaning. As the hero hauls himself out of the water and stumbles ashore, Chapman emphasizes the contrast between his physical exhaustion and the unconquered vitality of his spirit. At first Ulysses' fatigue, which verges on death, is described in a magnificent passage:

> Then forth he came, his both knees faltring, both
> His strong hands hanging downe, and all with froth
> His cheeks and nosthrils flowing, voice and breath
> Spent to all use, and downe he sunke to Death.
> The sea had soakt his heart through: all his vaines
> His toiles had rackt t'a labouring womans paines.
>
> (V, 608-13, p. 84)

The curious image in the last line is not in the original: 'And he let his two knees bend and his strong hands fall, for his spirit was crushed by the sea. And all his flesh was swollen, and the sea water flowed in streams up through his mouth and nostrils. So he lay breathless and speechless, scarcely strong enough to move, for terrible weariness had come upon him.'[8] From Chapman's gloss it is evident that he mistook one of the verbs in the Homeric passage for the aorist form of another.[9] Whether intentional or not, the error fits this nicely into the imagery of a succeeding passage, as we shall see.

Now Ulysses revives enough to move from the shore to a thick grove, where he covers himself with leaves and falls asleep. His decision to face in the woods the possible attacks of wild beasts rather than endure any longer 'the seas chill breath, And vegetant dewes'[10] gives Chapman a chance to have the hero state a principle which it has taken him a long time to learn. For years he had tried to outwit or circumvent the hostility of the sea. Circe, for example, had warned him of fixed and inescapable losses which he must suffer in passing Charybdis, but Ulysses rebelled none the less:

> This Neede she told me of my losse, when I
> Desir'd to know if that *Necessitie*
> (When I had scap't *Charybdis* outrages)
> My powres might not revenge, though not redresse?
> She answerd: O unhappy! art thou yet
> Enflam'd with warre, and thirst to drinke thy sweat?
> Not to the Gods give up both Armes and will?
> She deathless is, and that immortall ill
> Grave, harsh, outragious, not to be subdu'd,
> That men must suffer till they be renew'd.
> Nor lives there any virtue that can flie
> The vicious outrage of their crueltie.
> Shouldst thou put Armes on, and approch the Rocke,
> I fear sixe more must expiate the shocke.
> Sixe heads sixe men aske still.
>
> (XII, 173-87, p. 183)

90

Although Chapman has introduced here a few Christian overtones, as in 'renew'd' in the sense of 'redeemed' and in 'expiate', his translation follows the original quite closely.[11] Thus, even in Homer, Ulysses displays on this occasion a spirit admirable from one point of view, but deplorable from another. When Circe speaks to him of yielding to the gods, she is not thinking only of Scylla, as Spondanus notes:

Sed Circe respondet hoc sola patientia esse evincendum incommodum, quod a Diis infligatur, quibus resistere mortale non est datum. Ubi videtur dupliciter de Diis intelligere, videlicet de *Jove* ipso, cuius voluntate haec accidant: deinde etiam de Charybdi, vel Scylla, quas pro Deabus agnoscit.[12]

Circe clearly has in mind Ulysses' general attitude toward the gods and not merely his present hostility toward Scylla. Despite the warning the hero does not restrain himself in the crisis, for as his ship threads the strait between the monsters,

> . . . then even I forgot to shunne the harme
> *Circe* forewarnd, who willd I should not arme,
> Nor shew my selfe to *Scylla*, lest in vaine
> I ventur'd life. Yet could not I containe,
> But arm'd at all parts and two lances tooke.[13]

The principle uttered by Ulysses as he staggers ashore in Scheria shows that he has at last learned the lesson which Circe tried to teach him. He has been saved from certain death only through his submissive prayer to the god of the river which made his landing possible.[14] Now that his rebellious, self-reliant spirit has finally been chastened, Chapman marks his newly-acquired wisdom, as he leaves the shore to shelter in the woods, by adding this couplet to his reflections:

> But he that fights with heaven, or with the sea,
> To Indiscretion addes Impietie.
>
> (V, 642-3, p. 85)

By this interpolation Chapman calls the reader's attention to a major revolution in Ulysses' outlook and prepares us for his glorification of the hero as the essence of virtue in the final lines of the Book, as Ulysses lies down in his bed of leaves:

> Patient *Ulysses* joyd, that ever day
> Shewd such a shelter. In the midst he lay,
> Store of leaves heaping high on every side.
> And as in some out-field a man doth hide
> A kindld brand, to keepe the seed of fire,
> No neighbour dwelling neare, and his desire
> Serv'd with self-store he else would aske of none,
> But of his fore-spent sparks rakes th'ashes on;
> So this out-place *Ulysses* thus receives,
> And thus nak't vertues seed lies hid in leaves.
>
> (V, 658-67, p. 85)

Except for two places this translation follows the sense of the original very closely. Chapman has turned Ulysses 'the much-enduring'—πολύτλας—into the 'patient' Ulysses, and has added the last line to extend the wonderful Homeric simile into a specific image of the hero's spiritual rebirth. Here is the original for purposes of comparison: 'And the divine Odysseus, who had endured much, saw it and was glad and lay down in the midst, heaping the fallen leaves over himself. And just as a man hides a brand beneath the dark embers in an outlying farm, a man who has no neighbours, and so saves a seed of fire, that he may not have to kindle it from some other source, so Odysseus covered himself with leaves.'[15] Chapman's last line is translated almost literally from Spondanus' commentary on the simile: '. . . sic noster Ulysses, quasi semen aliquod virtutis sub istis foliis reconditur'.[16] Chapman thereby stresses the meaning of the hero's condition—he is stripped of everything but virtue: the pangs of suffering have brought forth the naked child of virtue in an extension of the image discussed earlier—

> all his vaines
> His toiles had rackt t'a labouring womans paines.

Chapman thus provides an effective but not over-obtrusive symbol of Ulysses' spiritual rebirth. We now have the essential, the 'absolute' Ulysses.

Chapman continues to develop allegorically the distinction between the hero's miserable bodily condition and his spiritual vitality through the entire sixth Book. One of the most significant places is Nausicaa's speech rebuking her companions for running away at their first sight of Ulysses: 'Stand, my maidens. Where are you fleeing at the mere sight of a man? Surely you do not think that he is an enemy? There is no living mortal who shall come to the land of the Phaeacians as an enemy, for we are very dear to the immortals.'[17] This is but the germ of the speech Chapman gives to the princess:

> Give stay both to your feet and fright;
> Why thus disperse ye, for a mans meere sight?
> Esteeme you him a *Cyclop*, that long since
> Made use to prey upon our Citizens?
> This man no moist man is (nor watrish thing,
> That's ever flitting, ever ravishing
> All it can compasse and, like it, doth range
> In rape of women, never staid in change).
> This man is truly manly, wise, and staid,
> In soule more rich, the more to sense decaid;
> Who nor will do, nor suffer to be done,
> Acts leud and abject, nor can such a one
> Greete the *Phaeacians* with a mind envious:
> Deare to the Gods they are, and he is pious.
> (VI, 307-20, pp. 92-3)

From the fifth through the eighth lines this passage translates the Homeric phrase διερὸς βροτός which simply means 'living mortal'. In his note to the passage Chapman embroiders the faulty definition of διερός in Scapula's lexicon, which is

humidus, madidus, cui humiditas inest. . . . Apud Hom. διερὸς βροτός, cui vitalis quaedam humiditas inest.[18]

Chapman glosses the phrase thus:

cui vitalis vel sensualis humiditas inest. a ῥέω, ut dicatur quasi ῥοτός, i.e. ὁ ἐν ῥοῇ ὤν, quod nihil sit magis fluxum quam homo.[19]

Spondanus' Latin version of the Homeric phrase, humidus homo,[20] agrees with Scapula's definition, and both provide Chapman with an excellent opportunity for developing extensive symbolic meanings far beyond those in the original. This particular part of the translation is grotesque, but in the context of the water symbolism which Chapman extends through his poem, as we saw in the preceding chapter, 'moist' and 'watrish' imply flux, 'humour', and instability of character. The use of 'staid' enforces these associations. Ulysses has achieved 'stay', spiritually if not geographically.

Another instance of Scapula's pervading influence is found in the four lines beginning with

This man is truly manly, wise, and staid,

as F. L. Schoell notes.[21] The lines

Who nor will do, nor suffer to be done,
Acts leud and abject

are shown to be a close translation of part of Scapula's definition of ἀνήρ, man, which stands in the same relation to another Greek word for man, ἄνθρωπος, as vir does to homo. Scapula's definition suggests the distinction:

Dicuntur etiam aliquando ἄνδρες quicunque aliquid dignum vero vel dicunt vel faciunt: & non esse ἄνδρες, qui servile quidpiam et abiectum facere sustinent.[22]

Chapman quotes part of this note without acknowledgment,[23] and takes the opportunity to make Nausicaa declare

94

within the poem the virtue of the hero, who is truly manly in contrast to the common run of men. The distinction between the two sorts of men is, however, implicit in Homer's use of ἀνήρ and ἄνθρωπος, as Geddes notes:

It is also to be noted that ἀνήρ in Iliad is not so pre-eminent, where all or most at least are ἄνδρες, while the ἀνήρ of Odyssey stands out alone, as it were, among ἄνθρωποι, which last word has an ampler range, and comes much more to the front in Odyssey as the ordinary designation of Man.[24]

Finally, Chapman pursues the distinction between Ulysses' physical decrepitude and his spiritual vitality by reading a moral meaning into Scapula's purely physiological definition, *cui vitalis vel sensualis humiditas inest*, in the line

In soule more rich, the more to sense decaid.

The speech as a whole is one of Chapman's most liberal and extreme elaborations of meanings he felt were implied in the context of the original. Chapman had a perfect right to emphasize the fact at this stage of the poem that Ulysses had become a virtuous and civilized man, but his way of doing it gives Nausicaa an extravagant degree of insight. The emphasis comes at the right time, but ineptly. Although the translation is based on mistaken authorities, it is consistent, nevertheless, with the fundamental meaning of Ulysses' experiences as Chapman sees them, and its roots extend far through the poem in Chapman's patterns of symbolism.

In this Book a corresponding alteration occurs in Chapman's treatment of the bath which Ulysses takes after his meeting with Nausicaa. Without any immediate warrant in the original he ascribes mysterious powers to the pool where the princess and her companions have been doing the laundry:

Whose waters were so pure they would not staine,
But still ran faire forth, and did more remaine,

Apt to purge staines for that purg'd staine within,
Which, by the waters pure store, was not seen.

(VI, 120-3, p. 89)

Homer merely says that 'abundant water welled up from beneath and flowed over to cleanse garments however dirty they might be'.[25] As a description of wash-water Chapman's lines are unbearably quaint and his style here is abominable, but the strange efficacy he imputes to the pool is not as far-fetched, I think, as it at first appears to be. While in Homer there is not the slightest hint of a ritual purgation, right after the bath Odysseus undergoes a miraculous rejuvenation:

With the water from the river noble Odysseus washed from his skin the brine which covered his back and broad shoulders, and from his head he wiped the scurf of the unresting sea. But when he had washed his whole body and had anointed himself with oil and had put on the clothes which the maiden had given him, then Athene the daughter of Zeus made him taller and stronger to look upon, and from his head she made the locks flow in curls like the hyacinth. Just as a skilful craftsman whom Hephaestus and Pallas have taught all kinds of artistry overlays silver with gold, and creates a work that is very graceful, so did the goddess endow his head and shoulders with added beauty. Then he went off and sat on the shore of the sea, radiant with grace and comeliness.[26]

Chapman gives to this transformation a specifically spiritual character in the phrase 'When worke sets forth   A worthy soule to bodies of such worth':

> He clensd his broad soil'd shoulders, backe and head
> Yet never tam'd. But now had fome and weed
> Knit in the faire curles, which dissolv'd, and he
> Slickt all with sweet oile, the sweet charitie
> The untoucht virgin shewd in his attire
> He cloth'd him with. Then *Pallas* put a fire,
> More than before, into his sparkling eies,
> His late soile set off with his soone fresh guise.

His locks (clensd) curld the more, and matcht (in power
To please an eye) the *Hyacinthian* flower.
And as a workman, that can well combine
Silver and gold, and make both strive to shine,
As being by *Vulcan* and *Minerva* too
Taught how farre either may be urg'd to go
In strife of eminence, when worke sets forth
A worthy soule to bodies of such worth,
No thought reproving th'act in any place,
Nor *Art* no debt to *Natures* liveliest grace:
So *Pallas* wrought in him a grace as great,
From head to shoulders, and ashore did seate
His goodly presence.

                                        (VI, 356-76, pp. 93-4)

In Homer this miraculous change in Ulysses' appearance
marks the conclusion both of his struggle with the sea and
his separation from his divine patroness. The occasion thus
dramatizes the beginning of a new phase in the hero's
career, which Chapman, without exceeding the meaning
implied in the original, endows with a specifically spiritual
meaning. Chapman's alterations and additions have brought
to us the culmination of a process of spiritual rehabilitation
through suffering and deprivation. Chapman has not vio-
lently or arbitrarily imposed these themes on Homer, for his
emphatic allegorical treatment penetrates to central themes
which Homer presents suggestively, obliquely, and subtly.

In the seventh and eighth Books our attention turns from
Ulysses' innermost experiences to his encounter with
Phaeacian civilization in all its variety and richness. This
part of his story can well be regarded as a reindoctrination
in the principles of the community. The centre of this
civilization is Queen Arete, whose name ('she who is
prayed to') suggests the devotion with which her subjects
regard her, and whose various skills and virtues comprise an
ideal portrait of woman as ruler, wife, mother, and housewife. Her importance is indicated by the fact that Nausicaa

and Pallas both advise Ulysses to make his first addresses to her rather than to Alcinous, for means to return to Ithaca. Athene describes her as follows:

> She may boast
> More honor of him [Alcinous] then the honord most
> Of any wife in earth can of her Lord,
> How many more soever Realmes affoord,
> That keepe house under husbands. Yet no more
> Her husband honors her than her blest store
> Of gracious children. All the Citie cast
> Eyes on her as a Goddesse, and give taste
> Of their affections to her in their praires,
> Still as she decks the streets; for all affaires
> Wrapt in contention she dissolves to men.
> Whom she affects, she wants no mind to deigne
> Goodnesse enough. If her heart stand inclin'd
> To your dispatch, hope all you wish to find,
> Your friends, your longing family, and all
> That can within your most affections fall.[27]

Ulysses' obeisance to this queen, who embraces all the familial, domestic, and social virtues, is filled with significance both in Homer and in Chapman. It symbolizes the hero's rededication to these values, and, of course, to Penelope, who resembles Arete in so many respects. Like the meeting with Nausicaa it forms a marked contrast with the hero's earlier encounters with the seductive goddesses Circe and Calypso. Arete, indeed, stands for the fundamental principles of civilized behaviour which were fatally violated by the crimes of Helen and Clytemnestra, to the definition and re-establishment of which the whole *Odyssey* is devoted. Homer embodies these values in his great women—Arete, Nausicaa, and Penelope—and accordingly, as D. S. Margoliouth says, 'if the germ of the *Iliad* is the Praise of Man, that of the *Odyssey* is the Praise of a Woman . . .'.[28]

Chapman follows the original more closely in this section

than in the preceding Book. The symbolic meaning of Homer is so evident here and in such close harmony with Chapman's views that there is less need for explication. Homer has suggested the ideal nature of Scheria by isolating it from the rest of the physical world. The Phaeacians have no need, therefore, for skill in war. Because of the savagery of their former neighbours, the Cyclopes, of which we are told at the beginning of Book VI, these people simply abandoned their country and moved to another land where they have almost no contact with strangers. They live in perpetual peace. Their contacts with the outside world are limited to occasional voyages in their magical ships. The gods customarily visit them without disguise. Alcinous' orchard trees bloom and bear fruit concurrently throughout the year. Homer has thus depicted a world so secure and easy that it presents the strenuous Ulysses with little temptation to delay his return. Yet the relation of Scheria to the real world is indicated by certain touches—the xenophobia of the man in the street, Nausicaa's maidenly fear of gossip, and Euryalus' insulting behaviour to Ulysses. Besides these there are many homely domestic details, such as the family wash and the spinning and grinding that are carried on in the palace.

The Phaeacians are outstanding for their cultivation of all the arts of peace: domestic economy, shipbuilding, seamanship, athletics, dancing and poetry. Their culture, as Alcinous describes it, is as varied as it is tranquil:

> Note then now
> My speech, and what my love presents to you,
> That you may tell *Heroes*, when you come
> To banquet with your Wife and Birth at home,
> (Mindfull of our worth) what deservings *Jove*
> Hath put on our parts likewise, in remove
> From Sire to Sonne, as an inherent grace
> Kinde and perpetuall. We must needs give place

To other Countreymen, and freely yeeld
We are not blamelesse in our fights of field,
Buffets, nor wrestlings; but in speede of feete,
And all the equipage that fits a fleete,
We boast us best: for table ever spred
With neighbor feasts, for garments varied,
For *Poesie, Musique, Dancing, Baths,* and *Beds.*[29]

These interests are pursued in an atmosphere of domestic, religious, and political order, which is expressed in such things as the affectionate family life of Alcinous and Arete with their daughter and many sons, the assemblies of peers of the realm, and the frequent libations and sacrifices paid individually to all the gods. In most respects the Phaeacian court contrasts strikingly with the chaotic court at Ithaca as it appears in the first two Books of the poem. The Phaeacian civilization epitomizes the values which Ulysses and Telemachus, with Athene's help, must restore to their distracted country.

As the setting in which Ulysses relates all his adventures since he sacked the temples of Troy, Scheria provides a fixed standard by which his behaviour is implicitly judged in Homer. From this perspective Ulysses reviews both the Trojan War and his subsequent wanderings through the fabulous world of the Lotophagoi, the Cyclopes, Aeolus, the Laestrygonians, Circe, Hades, the Sirens, Scylla and Charybdis, the Oxen of the Sun, and Calypso.

Chapman exploits fully the opportunities offered by the interaction of Ulysses' narrative with this setting by occasional additions which illuminate the allegorical experience in the light of all that Scheria represents. The emotional breakdown which Ulysses suffers just before he begins his long tale is especially interesting. The hero has stayed in the Phaeacian court an evening and an entire day. The time has now come to identify himself, and the most impressive introduction imaginable is to have Demodocus sing of his most famous and most brilliant military exploits—the stratagem of the wooden horse and the sack of Troy. Demodocus complies with the request, but Ulysses, instead of indulging himself pleasantly in expected feelings of pride and nostalgia evoked by the lay, is taken by surprise with very different feelings. Homer presents this unexpected emotion in one of his most moving similes:

This was the song the famous minstrel sang. But Odysseus' heart was melted, and tears wet his cheeks beneath his eyelids. And as a woman wails and flings herself about her dear husband, who has fallen in defence of his city and his people, seeking to ward off the pitiless day from his town and his children, and as she sees him dying and gasping for breath, clings to him and shrieks, while men behind her hit her back and shoulders and lead her off to slavery and toil and sorrow, while her fair cheeks are wasted with most pitiful grief, so did Odysseus let fall from beneath his eyelids tears full of pity.[30]

Homer's similes often range beyond the point of comparison, yet this one seems unusually relevant to the dramatic situation from which it arises. Odysseus, as he hears Demodocus relate his greatest conquest, weeps with pity like a woman who has lost her husband, her home, and her freedom in the defeat of her city. The simile projects the event from two diametrically opposed points of view. More than this, however, it shows Odysseus' own unexpected recognition of the harmless victims of war who are normally excluded from the hero's rather narrow vision—the nameless ones who have everything to lose and nothing to gain from the operation of the heroic ideal. Odysseus' emotions at this moment are, no doubt, complex and conflicting. He weeps partly out of pity for himself, the conqueror of Troy who is now a homeless wanderer. But we all know that such feelings are not incompatible with sympathy, any more than the pilot's exhilaration after a successful strafing mission is incompatible with pity for the poor devils he has strafed.

I believe, therefore, that one cannot over-emphasize the extent of the imaginative and emotional revolution which Homer dramatizes in this short scene. Ulysses for the first time in his life sees the other side of his military achievements and is identified sympathetically with the tragic victims of war rather than the glorious conquerors. The heroic ideal is suddenly shattered and replaced by the ideal of common humanity. Chapman, always ready to express the power of poetry to kindle the imagination, develops the first two sentences of the Homeric passage into fourteen lines:

> This the divine Expressor did so give
> Both act and passion that he made it live,
> And to *Ulysses* facts did breathe a fire
> So deadly quickning that it did inspire
> Old death with life, and renderd life so sweet
> And passionate, that all there felt it fleet;
> Which made him pitie his own crueltie
> And put into that ruth so pure an eye
> Of humane frailtie, that to see a man
> Could so revive from Death, yet no way can
> Defend from Death, his owne quicke powres it made
> Feele there deaths horrors, and he felt life fade.
> In teares his feeling braine swet, for in things
> That move past utterance, teares ope all their springs.
> Nor are there in the Powres that all life beares,
> More true interpreters of all then teares.[31]

Chapman's exalted conception of the office of great poetry is presented vigorously in this passage. Here we find the characteristic details of divine inspiration, of the power of poetry to achieve a reality more real than life, and of its power to engage the most profound emotions. As a picture of Ulysses' new emotional and psychological state it is equally noteworthy. For the first time the hero's distress is caused by the sufferings of someone else, and for the first time a great emotion overwhelms his normally analytical and calculating mind. Hereafter Ulysses will conceive of himself as primarily a member of the human race rather than as a leading member of the aristocracy of warriors.

Following this outburst, Ulysses is ready to begin his long narrative. Many of the episodes go far toward defining the lack of humanity and self-discipline which he has finally overcome, and consequently Chapman, like centuries of Homeric scholars and critics, sees them as moral allegories.

The first event which Ulysses describes contrasts strikingly with the emotional revolution which he has just experienced, and it measures the extent of this revolution. He first speaks of himself as 'known among all men for my wiles'[32] instead of using the epithet, in which he used to take such pride, of 'city-sacker'. Then, perfectly bluntly, and without attempting in any way to extenuate his actions, he begins. Chapman follows the original very closely:

> From *Ilion* ill winds cast me on the coast
> The *Cicons* hold, where I emploid mine hoast
> For *Ismarus*, a Citie built just by
> My place of landing, of which *Victory*
> Made me expugner. I depeopl'd it,
> Slue all the men and did their wives remit
> With much spoile taken, which we did divide,
> That none might need his part.[33]

Odysseus gives no specific motive for the attack on Ismarus, although the Cicones are known to have been allies of the Trojans. In omitting this fact Homer seems to have aimed at producing a pure and unmitigated act of plunder. Chapman underlines the cool brutality of the action by using abstractions of a type one commonly finds in the language of military communiqués. 'I sacked the city' becomes 'a Citie . . . of which *Victory* made me expugner'. 'I depeopled it', Chapman's interpolation, also contributes to the attitude of impersonality, as does the rhetorical equalizing of wives and booty. Both in the original and the translation the scrupulous concern for a fair division of the spoils contrasts wryly with the casual indifference to the unhappy lot of the Cicones.

The mission at Ismarus fails, eventually, because 'those damned fools disobeyed my orders'. Just a case of post-war demoralization, perhaps, although Odysseus' leadership seems to have fallen off since he turned back the panicking, home-bent troops on the beaches at Troy. My suspicion that this disastrous finale is not to be put down simply to bad discipline is strengthened by the fact that in other, fictitious raids which he describes to Eumaeus (XIV, 257-84) and to Antinous (XVII, 415-44) the consequences are equally disastrous, and Odysseus, in describing what happened, takes pains to dissociate himself from the ὕβρις which led his men to kill and plunder. It may be that in these passages he is only damning his soldiers for the impulsiveness of their attack, but he also seems to be trying to make a good impression by disclaiming piratical intentions which, especially in the case of Eumaeus, who had been enslaved by Taphian pirates, would not have endeared him to his listeners.

After the brief adventure with the Lotus-Eaters, Ulysses' insatiable curiosity leads him and a small band of men into the very cave of the Cyclops Polyphemus. The episode is a reversal of the situation at Ismarus, with the balance of power against the hero at the start and the conflict nevertheless issuing in a victory for the victims. Chapman handles the episode with the greatest skill and high-lights all the ironies in the Homeric account. Ulysses prefaces his story with a description of the unsociable, primitive, yet idyllic life of the Cyclopes:

> a race
> Of proud-liv'd loiterers, that never sow,
> Nor put a plant in earth, nor use a plow,
> But trust in God for all things, and their earth,
> (Unsowne, unplowd) gives every of-spring birth

That other lands have: wheate and barley, vines
That beare in goodly grapes delicious wines,
And *Jove* sends showres for all. No counsels there,
Nor counsellers, nor lawes, but all men beare
Their heads aloft on mountaines, and those steepe,
And on their tops too: and their houses keepe
In vaultie caves, their housholds governd all
By each mans law, imposde in severall,
Nor wife nor child awd but as he thinks good,
None for another caring.[34]

The Cyclopes live like men in the state of nature, in political anarchy and social isolation, each man's will being his law. The contrast between their way of life and that of the Phaeacians is extreme, and this contrast is emphasized by the addition of the following details, where Chapman follows Homer closely:

Nor place the neighbour *Cyclops* their delights
In brave vermilion prow-deckt ships, nor wrights
Usefull and skilfull in such works as need
Perfection to those trafficks that exceed
Their naturall confines. . . .[35]

Ulysses then tells how his landing-party disembarks on a neighbouring deserted island and feasts abundantly on wild goats and on the wine they took from the Cicones. Then the hero leaves the bulk of his forces and sets out with a picked band to discover

what men
The neighbour Ile held, if of rude disdaine,
Churlish and tyrannous, or minds bewraid
Pious and hospitable.[36]

The narrator is here, perhaps, playing on the sympathies of his audience, who have, as he knows, ineradicable memories of the brutality of the Cyclopes and of their barbarous ways.

He then describes the gift he brought:

> I tooke besides along
> A goat-skin flagon of wine, blacke and strong,
> That *Maro* did present, *Evantheus* sonne,
> And Priest to *Phoebus*, who had mansion
> In *Thracian Ismarus* (the towne I tooke).
> He gave it me, since I (with reverence strooke
> Of his grave place, his wife and childrens good)
> Freed all of violence.[37]

This is a close translation, even to 'with reverence strooke',
which translates ἀζόμενοι. This reverent behaviour toward
the 'cloth' is strangely inconsistent with the raider's otherwise untempered aggressiveness. The allusion to the attack
on Ismarus, coming on the heels of Ulysses' declared
intention of finding out whether the Cyclopes are 'churlish'
or 'hospitable', acts, both in Homer and in Chapman, as a
reminder that the hero was at the time scarcely in a sound
position to judge, and that he had no reason to expect kindness at the hands of strangers in view of the treatment
strangers had received from him. Chapman goes on to
indicate how superficial are Ulysses' civilized pretences by
making him recoil in fastidious horror at the monster's
provincialism and inhumanity. In Homer he remarks: 'my
proud spirit had a foreboding that presently a man would
come to me endowed with great strength, a savage knowing
nothing of justice or law'.[38] Chapman imparts to this an
aura of snobbery:

> [I] longd to see this heape of fortitude
> That so illiterate was and upland rude
> That lawes divine nor humane he had learned.
>
> (IX, 307-9, p. 133)

Throughout the encounter with Polyphemus Ulysses'
manner oscillates between abject humility, with earnest
invocations of the laws of hospitality, and swaggering
arrogance. A fine ironic effect is achieved in the Cyclops'

unexpected question when he discovers the little group cowering in his cave, and in Ulysses' answer: 'Strangers, who are you? Whence are you sailing over the paths of the sea? Is it on some business, or do you wander at random over the sea, risking your lives and bringing evil to men of other lands?'[39] The savage monster asks the emissaries of civilization essentially the same question that they intended to ask him. Chapman points up this strange turnabout by making Polyphemus enquire piously about the state of their souls. He ascribes a second, anachronistic sense to the Greek word ψυχαί by translating it both as 'lives' and 'soules':

> Ho guests! what are ye? Whence saile ye these seas?
> Trafficke, or rove ye, and like theeves oppresse
> Poore strange adventurers, exposing so
> Your soules to danger, and your lives to wo?
>
> (IX, 355-8, p. 134)

As we consider Ulysses' answer, in which Chapman follows Homer very closely, we may begin to wonder whether the question was as outrageous as it first seemed:

> Erring *Grecians* we
> From *Troy* were turning homewards, but by force
> Of adverse winds, in far-diverted course,
> Such unknowne waies tooke, and on rude seas tost,
> (As *Jove* decreed) are cast upon this Coast.
> Of Agamemnon (famous *Atreus* sonne)
> We boast our selves the souldiers, who hath wonne
> Renowne that reacheth heaven, to overthrow
> So great a citie, and to ruine so,
> So many nations.[40]

By the happy ambiguity of 'erring' Chapman perhaps indicates the moral as well as geographical strayings of Ulysses and his men. The answer is intended to deny the imputation of piracy (we are not pirates but soldiers), yet it unconsciously reveals, in the light of the military action

107

against the Cicones and the wrecking of the sacred Trojan citadels, that the distinction between war and piracy is sometimes very small.

This introduction is scarcely calculated to arouse Polyphemus' hospitable feelings, nor is the threatening tone of Ulysses' appeal likely to win him over:

> We suppliants are, and hospitable *Jove*
> Poures wreake on all whom praires want powre to move,
> And with their plagues together will provide
> That humble guests shall have their wants supplide.[41]

Chapman points up the inconsistency in Ulysses' behaviour by adding the word 'humble'. His assumed humility lasts only until he has escaped from Polyphemus' cave and, figuring that he is at a safe distance from the blinded monster, shouts this boast: 'Then I spoke to the Cyclops with mocking words: "Cyclops, that man was no weakling after all, whose friends you planned to devour brutally in your hollow cave. Surely your evil deeds were to fall on your own head, since you did not scruple to eat guests in your own house. Therefore Zeus and the other gods have taken vengeance on you."'[42] Chapman changes this to make Ulysses proclaim a general principle of just and humane conduct which he has himself repeatedly violated. The speech may be taken to suggest a lack of self-knowledge in the speaker:

> I staid our ores and this insultance usde:
> *Cyclop!* thou shouldst not have so much abusde
> Thy monstrous forces to oppose their least
> Against a man immartiall, and a guest,
> And eate his fellowes: thou mightst know there were
> Some ils behind (rude swaine) for thee to beare,
> That feard not to devoure thy guests, and breake
> All lawes of humanes: *Jove* sends therefore wreake,
> And all the Gods, by me.
>
> (IX, 635-43, p. 140)

In view of the way in which he introduced himself to Polyphemus, Ulysses' designation of himself as 'a man immartiall' seems a glaring inconsistency. His arrogance is heightened by the assumption that he is the agent of divine vengeance. The worst, however, is yet to come. Having narrowly escaped death for himself and his men from a great rock which the blinded monster hurls in the direction of this taunt, once the boat is at a supposedly safe distance Ulysses shouts a second insult. Chapman gives him a prefatory remark full of unconscious irony:

> But I gave way
> To that wrath which so long I held deprest,
> (By great *Necessitie* conquerd) in my brest.
>
> (IX, 670-2, p. 141)

Since his lack of self-control has just a moment before come close to destroying the whole company, it is strange that one critic should cite this as an example of Ulysses' Stoical submission to necessity![43]

Chapman continues to emphasize the moral significance of Ulysses' behaviour in this adventure by enlarging on Polyphemus' reply to the hero's second boast that Polyphemus' father, Poseidon, will be unable to restore his son's vision. The Cyclops says:

> *Augur Telemus*
> . . . said all this deed
> Should this event take, author'd by the hand
> Of one *Ulysses*, who I thought was mand
> With great and goodly personage, and bore
> A vertue answerable, and this shore
> Should shake with weight of such a conqueror;
> When now a weakling came, a dwarfie thing,
> A thing of nothing, who yet wit did bring,
> That brought supply to all, and with his wine
> Put out the flame where all my light did shine.[44]

'And bore | A vertue answerable' is Chapman's addition.

While 'vertue' here undoubtedly has for its primary meaning the obsolete sense of 'strength', its familiar moral sense is surely relevant. Thus, strangely enough, the savage monster reveals the moral shortcomings of the hero, while the shrewd hero has completely failed to understand the meaning of his adventure.

The relatively few additions which Chapman has introduced into the episode do not alter its fundamental meaning in the original. They emphasize the inadequacy of Ulysses' pseudo-civilized assumptions, which conceal from him his own savage predilections. They show with sardonic humour the inconsistency of his appeals to the sanctions of civilized principles with his acts of sacrilege and slaughter and plunder at Troy and Ismarus. It would be a great mistake, as Chapman's revelation of the episode shows, to postulate in Homer an uncritical approval of his hero's every action or to assume that carnage and crime were blandly accepted and endorsed by a 'primitive' poet who knew nothing better. In Polyphemus Homer confronts Ulysses with a fantastic image of the spirit which led him to sack the temples of Troy and to 'depeople' the town of Ismarus. When the savage-looking Odysseus emerged from the underbrush Nausicaa had asked her frightened companions the rhetorical question, 'Surely you don't think he is an enemy?' (VI, 200). Yet one is bound to wonder whether her confidence would have been justified by events if Odysseus' first stop after Troy had been Scheria instead of Ismarus. Chapman has marked the hero's victory over the Cyclopean spirit which had so aggravated his troubles in his translation of her question:

> Esteeme you him a *Cyclop*, that long since
> Made use to prey upon our citizens?
>
> (VI, 309-10, p. 93)

In Homer Ulysses' experiences with Circe contain more allegorical features than his encounter with Polyphemus.

Circe is a goddess; her potions transform Ulysses' men into beasts in form though not in mind; Ulysses is preserved by the intervention of Hermes and the gift of an antidote; and Circe is herself transformed from a dangerous sorceress to a friend, hostess, and guide of the wayfarers. In this adventure the danger is disguised, and the hero's escape from it does not depend on clever strategy. Polyphemus had an unexpected streak of tenderness toward his favourite ram, but Circe is a much more inhuman figure, beautiful, sinister, yet, if properly approached, helpful. Although Ulysses succumbed to arrogance in his conflict with Polyphemus, he survives the temptations of Circe unharmed and with new power.

This adventure has provided the most fertile field of all for allegorical interpreters of Homer. Comes summarizes his view of it in part as follows:

Atque ut summatim dicam, per hanc fabulam significare voluerunt antiqui sapientem virum in utraque fortuna opportere se moderate gubernare & ad omnes difficultates invictum consistere, cum reliqua multitudo tanquam levissima navis huc illuc fluctibus deferatur, & quocunque ventorum inconstantia impulerit: quare mutati fuerunt in beluas Ulyssis socii, cum ipse invictus ob sapientiam, quae vere est Dei munus, perstiterit.[45]

Chapman, in his general conception of the *Odyssey*, uses the basic symbol of man's moral infirmity and spiritual confusion 'like a merest cockle-shell borne here and there by the waves' which Comes uses here, but, as we have seen, he does not regard Ulysses as untroubled by such faults, while Comes always does. Herakleitos also emphasizes Ulysses' temperance in interpreting the intervention of Hermes as the victory of wisdom and self-control over the anger he felt on hearing of his comrades' fate: 'He is the counsellor who stands by Ulysses as he approaches Circe. At first the hero is inspired by passion and grief because of what he has learned and is carried away without judgment. But in a little while, as these emotions burn themselves out, he seeks to escape by the use of prudence, whence Hermes of the golden rod happens to meet him.'[46] The moly Herakleitos considers to be wisdom.[47] These examples are quite typical of traditional interpretations of the Homeric myth. Pope goes even further in the elucidation of certain details:

The flower of *Moly* is white and sweet; this denotes that the fruits of instruction are sweet, agreeable, and nourishing. *Mercury* gives this plant; this intimates that all instruction is the gift of Heaven: *Mercury* brings it not with him, but gathers it from the place where he stands, to shew that Wisdom is not confin'd to places, but that everywhere it may be found, if Heaven vouchsafes to discover it, and we are disposed to receive and follow it.[48]

Thus in all times and all places the Circe episode has been read as a moral allegory of the triumph of wisdom.

One is impelled to ask why this episode has been chosen above all the rest as a leading example of allegory. The answer is not far to seek. By its very nature this adventure requires that it be read as allegory. Taken only on the literal level simply as a fabulous experience it has little meaning. What then would be Circe's motive for transforming men into beasts? What interest would there be in Ulysses' being singled out for a purely fortuitous gift of the wonderful antidote? Where is the interest in the tale if the hero saves himself and frees his companions simply by the accidental possession of such a gift?

Chapman allies himself with a long tradition in explicitly translating the episodes as an allegory in which the hero's temperance in the face of temptations to sensuality makes him immune to the brutalization which his companions suffer.

The main feature of Chapman's treatment of the allegory in this episode is his emphasis on what he takes to be the inner realities, especially the various aspects of Ulysses' character, to which elements in the action correspond. While Hermes, in Homer, emphasizes the efficacy of the moly—'she will mix a potion for you and put drugs in your food, but even so she shall not bewitch you, for the powerful herb that I shall give you will not permit it'[49]—in Chapman he stresses just as much Ulysses' powers of resistance. Here we observe the first steps in the subjectivization of Homer's myth:

> With a festivall
> Sheele first receive thee, but will spice thy bread
> With flowrie poysons; yet unaltered
> Shall thy firme forme be, for this remedy
> Stands most approv'd gainst all her Sorcery. . . .
>
> (X, 386-90, p. 152)

As Chapman here uses it, the word 'forme' comes to mean much more than mere physical shape. It acquires some of the Renaissance associations of order as the essence of reality and truth. It becomes the essence of manliness when Hermes warns that Circe will try to destroy Ulysses,

> By stripping thee of forme, and faculties.

This translates 'that, when she has stripped thee, she may render thee a weakling and unmanned'.[50]

When Ulysses has drunk Circe's potion without being affected, she exclaims: 'No man has ever withstood this charm, once he had drunk it and it had passed the barrier of his teeth. The heart in thy breast cannot be charmed. Surely thou art Odysseus, the resourceful man, who Argeiphontes of the golden wand always told me would come from Troy in a swift black ship.'[51] Chapman shifts this tribute to the hero's intellect into a recognition of his moral fibre:

> Never drunke any this cup but he mournd
> In other likenesse, if it once had past
> The ivorie bounders of his tongue and taste.
> All but thy selfe are brutishly declind:

Thy breast holds firme yet, and unchang'd thy mind.
Thou canst be therefore none else but the man
Of many virtues *Ithacensian,*
Deepe-soul'd *Ulysses,* who I oft was told,
By that slie God that beares the rod of gold
Was to arrive here in retreat from Troy.

(X, 436-45, pp. 153-4)

Thus Homer's hero 'of many devices' becomes Chapman's 'man of many virtues ... Deepe-soul'd Ulysses'. Chapman thereby transforms the episode into a test of Ulysses' moral character.

The elaborate preparations which are now made to entertain the hero give Chapman an opportunity to emphasize, by a small but important addition, the virtues of a ritualistic approach to pleasure. Homer, when Ulysses first enters Circe's dwelling and then when he has subdued the goddess with his sword, describes how the hero was seated in a beautiful chair and 'beneath was a foot-stool'.[52] Chapman repeats the detail just as simply the first time,[53] but the second time tells how a servant

did with silkes the foot-pace consecrate.[54]

Thus the feast from which gluttony has been banished acquires a special dignity.

Even so Ulysses will not partake until he has discharged his duties to his comrades. Later he eats well and drinks deep and then sleeps with the goddess. But the issue at stake in this episode is not abstinence, of course, but temperance. Once Ulysses has made sure of his own safety and the safety of his companions he can enjoy the pleasures of Circe's table and bed. It is important to realize that here foresight is involved as much as self-control. For the first time in the course of his adventures Ulysses does not plunge blindly into the encounter, or, perhaps more precisely, for the first time he assures the security of his comrades as well as of himself before committing himself to a new adventure. As usual Homer here expresses the hero's new sagacity in terms of divine intervention, but the intervention of Hermes is, as usual, accompanied by and corresponds to inner developments. Chapman indicates Ulysses' new restraint in a quaintly-worded interpolation:

> She wisht my taste emploid; but not a word
> Would my eares taste of taste; my mind had food
> That must digest; eye meate would do me good.[55]

The translator then heightens the tone of moral responsibility in lines that strike the note of redemption in the theme of the return. Originally the hero merely says: 'Circe, what just man could bear to taste food or drink before he had set free his comrades and seen them with his own eyes?'[56] Chapman translates this thus:

> O Circe! (I replied) what man is he,
> Awd with the rights of true humanitie,
> That dares taste food or wine before he sees
> His friends redeem'd from their deformities?
>
> (X, 494-7, p. 155)

'Redeem's' translates λύσασθαι, 'set free', and Chapman apparently found this suggestion in the Latin version where the word is *redimantur*.[57]

From an analysis of these major episodes we are able to form a view of Chapman's allegorical approach reflected in the body of the translation. He shares the time-honoured view of the hero's fabulous adventures as allegorical representations of the dangers with which passions threaten both the individual and society as a whole, but in seeing Ulysses as involved in and threatened by these struggles and not placed above them by any absolute virtue, Chapman's translation is not only more dramatic than other allegorical interpretations but is in much closer harmony with Homer. This more flexible view permits great faithfulness to the spirit of the original and to the facts of human experience. Thus we see Ulysses, like most men, proof against temptations of one sort while greatly disturbed by others. In the raid on Ismarus we see him gripped by the predatory and unreflecting spirit which, the poem suggests, has brought civilization to the brink of chaos. In the encounter with Polyphemus we find the warrior's code examined satirically, and see how the hero's humility, born of peril, vanishes when the peril is gone. In the Circe episode we find Ulysses' men enslaved and degraded by sensual pleasures, pleasures which, by the exercise of moderation, their leader shows can be made to serve rather than enslave. Over this ten-year period of Ulysses' life we can see how Chapman has underlined his spiritual evolution from the prisoner of his own will and desires into one who, having conquered himself, has finally the power to conquer his nihilistic foes and restore law and order to Ithaca.

To complete this analysis of Chapman's handling of the allegory in the *Odyssey* it would be fitting to conclude with his treatment of Ulysses' final glorification by Athene. This occurs after he has killed the suitors and purged his palace in Book XXIII, and Homer here uses exactly the same simile by which the hero's earlier transformation in Phaeacia was described[58]: 'Just as a skilful craftsman whom Hephaestus and Pallas have taught all kinds of artistry overlays silver with gold, and the work he creates is very graceful, so did the goddess endow his head and shoulders with added beauty'.[59] Smalley says of this passage:

Chapman could hardly fail to recognize an ethical significance in these lines, portraying, as they do, the glorification of the 'absolute man', triumphant at last over his woes in the 'sea of life'; and indeed he did his best with his opportunity. The relationship between 'power infused' [divine wisdom] and 'acquisition' [Ulysses' wisdom] is symbolized in a striking figure.[60]

Here is Chapman's version of this passage:

> Looke how a skilfull Artizan, well seene
> In all arts metalline as having beene

Taught by *Minerva* and the God of fire,
Doth gold and silver mix so, that entire
They keepe their selfe distinction, and yet so,
That to the silver from the gold doth flow
A much more artificiall luster than his owne,
And thereby to the gold it selfe is growne
A greater glory then if wrought alone,
Both being stuck off by eithers mixtion:
So did *Minerva* hers and his combine;
He more in Her, She more in Him did shine.

(XXIII, 233-44, p. 354)

Several points might be added to Mr. Smalley's remarks on this passage. For one thing, Chapman has preserved the distinction between Ulysses' wisdom and the divine wisdom of Minerva—'They keepe their selfe distinction . . .'. This reinforces his emphasis on the fact that the hero has won 'his wished stay' partly through his own wisdom and partly through the operation of divine aid, and it marks the judgment and self-control he has so strenuously achieved through his own efforts. The simile thus preserves the balance so central to the *Odyssey* between man's moral responsibility and divine immanence in human affairs. Secondly, while the transformation does without doubt portray the 'glorification of the "absolute man"', it symbolizes more specifically, within the context of Chapman's poem, the culmination of the process whereby Ulysses is 'informed' and 'fashioned' into an 'absolute man'. This glorious transformation marks the final victory of his true form over the deforming passions which have for so long beset him. Chapman accepted and brought into the translation the suggestion so hesitantly advanced by Spondanus:

Nisi etiam Poeta velit pristinae illi Herois formae hanc a Minerva novam infundi, illa penitus latente haec tantum appareat: quod fortasse ratione non caret.[61]

117

Finally Chapman has emphasized in this transformation the themes of spiritual illumination and union with the divine in his vigorous description of the partnership of human wisdom and divine grace:

He more in Her, She more in Him did shine.

The line seems to echo the words of the Anglican Communion service: 'that we may evermore dwell in Him and He in us'.

NOTES TO CHAPTER III

1. Κέκλυτέ μευ μύθων, κακά περ πάσχοντες ἑταῖροι·
   ὦ φίλοι, οὐ γὰρ ἴδμεν ὅπῃ ζόφος οὐδ' ὅπῃ ἠώς,
   οὐδ' ὅπῃ ἠέλιος φαεσίμβροτος εἶσ' ὑπὸ γαῖαν
   οὐδ' ὅπῃ ἀννεῖται· ἀλλὰ φραζώμεθα θᾶσσον
   εἴ τις ἔτ' ἔσται μῆτις· ἐγὼ δ' οὐκ οἴομαι εἶναι.   (X, 189-93)

2. Ἀργαλέον σε, θεά, γνῶναι βροτῷ ἀντιάσαντι,
   καὶ μάλ' ἐπισταμένῳ· σὲ γὰρ αὐτὴν παντὶ ἐΐσκεις.
   τοῦτο δ' ἐγὼν εὖ οἶδ', ὅτι μοι πάρος ἠπίη ἦσθα,
   ἦος ἐνὶ Τροίῃ πολεμίζομεν υἷες Ἀχαιῶν.
   αὐτὰρ ἐπεὶ Πριάμοιο πόλιν διεπέρσαμεν αἰπήν,
   βῆμεν δ' ἐν νήεσσι, θεὸς δ' ἐκέδασσεν Ἀχαιούς,
   οὐ σέ γ' ἔπειτα ἴδον, κούρη Διός, οὐδ' ἐνόησα
   νηὸς ἐμῆς ἐπιβᾶσαν, ὅπως τί μοι ἄλγος ἀλάλκοις.
   ἀλλ' αἰεὶ φρεσὶν ᾗσιν ἔχων δεδαϊγμένον ἦτορ
   ἠλώμην, ἦός με θεοὶ κακότητος ἔλυσαν·
   πρίν γ' ὅτε Φαιήκων ἀνδρῶν ἐν πίονι δήμῳ
   θάρσυνάς τε ἔπεσσι καὶ ἐς πόλιν ἤγαγες αὐτή.   (XIII, 312-23)

3. 'The Ethical Bias of Chapman's *Homer*', *SP*, 36 (1939), 184.

4. Ἑρμεία· σὺ γὰρ αὖτε τά τ' ἄλλα περ ἄγγελός ἐσσι·
   νύμφῃ ἐϋπλοκάμῳ εἰπεῖν νημερτέα βουλήν,
   νόστον Ὀδυσσῆος ταλασίφρονος, ὥς κε νέηται
   οὔτε θεῶν πομπῇ οὔτε θνητῶν ἀνθρώπων·
   ἀλλ' ὅ γ' ἐπὶ σχεδίης πολυδέσμου πήματα πάσχων
   ἤματι εἰκοστῷ Σχερίην ἐρίβωλον ἵκοιτο.   (V, 29-34)

5. *Odysses*, I, 1-4, p. 1. Cf. *Odyssey*, I, 1-2:
   Ἄνδρα μοι ἔννεπε, Μοῦσα, πολύτροπον, ὃς μάλα πολλὰ
   πλάγχθη, ἐπεὶ Τροίης ἱερὸν πτολίεθρον ἔπερσεν.

6. 'The Heroes of Chapman's *Homer*', *RES*, 17 (1941), 271.

7. οὐδὲν ἀκιδνότερον γαῖα τρέφει ἀνθρώποιο
   πάντων ὅσσα τε γαῖαν ἔπι πνείει τε καὶ ἕρπει.

οὐ μὲν γάρ ποτέ φησι κακὸν πείσεσθαι ὀπίσσω,
ὄφρ' ἀρετὴν παρέχωσι θεοὶ καὶ γούνατ' ὀρώρῃ·
ἀλλ' ὅτε δὴ καὶ λυγρὰ θεοὶ μάκαρες τελέσωσι,
καὶ τὰ φέρει ἀεκαζόμενος τετληότι θυμῷ·
τοῖος γὰρ νόος ἐστὶν ἐπιχθονίων ἀνθρώπων
οἷον ἐπ' ἦμαρ ἄγῃσι πατὴρ ἀνδρῶν τε θεῶν τε·
καὶ γὰρ ἐγώ ποτ' ἔμελλον ἐν ἀνδράσιν ὄλβιος εἶναι,
πολλὰ δ' ἀτάσθαλ' ἔρεξα βίῃ καὶ κάρτεϊ εἴκων,
πατρί τ' ἐμῷ πίσυνος καὶ ἐμοῖσι κασιγνήτοισι.
τῷ μή τίς ποτε πάμπαν ἀνὴρ ἀθεμίστιος εἴη,
ἀλλ' ὅ γε σιγῇ δῶρα θεῶν ἔχοι, ὅττι διδοῖεν.   (XVIII, 130-42)

8.   ὁ δ' ἄρ' ἄμφω γούνατ' ἔκαμψε
χεῖράς τε στιβαράς· ἀλὶ γὰρ δέδμητο φίλον κῆρ.
ᾦδεε δὲ χρόα πάντα, θάλασσα δὲ κήκιε πολλὴ
ἂν στόμα τε ῥῖνάς θ'· ὁ δ' ἄρ' ἄπνευστος καὶ ἄναυδος
κεῖτ' ὀλιγηπελέων, κάματος δέ μιν αἰνὸς ἵκανεν.   (V, 453-7)

9. See Odysses, V, 613 n., p. 84: "Ὦ[ι]δεε of ὠδίνω a partu doleo'. Chapman read ᾦδεε as though the aorist of ὠδίνω, 'to travail in childbirth', instead of the imperfect of οἰδέω, 'to swell'. The mistaken definition is from Scapula.

10. Odysses, V, 628-9, p. 84.

11.   εἰ δ' ἄγε δή μοι τοῦτο, θεά, νημερτὲς ἐνίσπες,
εἴ πως τὴν ὀλοὴν μὲν ὑπεκπροφύγοιμι Χάρυβδιν,
τὴν δέ κ' ἀμυναίμην, ὅτε μοι σίνοιτό γ' ἑταίρους.

"Ὣς ἐφάμην, ἡ δ' αὐτίκ' ἀμείβετο δῖα θεάων·
σχέτλιε, καὶ δὴ αὖ τοι πολεμήϊα ἔργα μέμηλε
καὶ πόνος; οὐδὲ θεοῖσιν ὑπείξεαι ἀθανάτοισιν;
ἡ δέ τοι οὐ θνητή, ἀλλ' ἀθάνατον κακόν ἐστι,
δεινόν τ' ἀργαλέον τε καὶ ἄγριον οὐδὲ μαχητόν·
οὐδέ τίς ἐστ' ἀλκή· φυγέειν κάρτιστον ἀπ' αὐτῆς.
ἢν γὰρ δηθύνῃσθα κορυσσόμενος παρὰ πέτρῃ,
δείδω μή σ' ἐξαῦτις ἐφορμηθεῖσα κίχῃσι
τόσσῃσιν κεφαλῇσι, τόσους δ' ἐκ φῶτας ἕληται.   (XII, 112-23)

Come, I pray thee, goddess, tell me truly whether there is any way I might escape from terrible Charybdis and ward off that other monster when she harms my comrades.

So I spoke, and the beautiful goddess answered and said: Rash fellow! Is they heart still set on deeds of war and toil? Wilt thou not yield even to the immortal gods? She is not mortal, but an immortal bane, dread and terrible and fierce and not to be fought with. There is no defence; to flee from her is best. For if thou tarriest to arm thyself beneath the cliff, I fear that she may leap out and attack thee with all her heads and seize as many men as before.

12. 'Commentarius', p. 175.

13. *Odysses*, XII, 336-40, p. 186. Cf. *Odyssey*, XII, 226-30:

> καὶ τότε δὴ Κίρκης μὲν ἐφημοσύνης ἀλεγεινῆς
> λανθανόμην, ἐπεὶ οὔ τί μ' ἀνώγει θωρήσσεσθαι·
> αὐτὰρ ἐγὼ καταδὺς κλυτὰ τεύχεα καὶ δύο δοῦρε
> μάκρ' ἐν χερσὶν ἑλὼν εἰς ἴκρια νηὸς ἔβαινον
> πρῴρης. . . .

14. See *Odysses*, V, 596-603, p. 84:

> King of this River, heare! Whatever name
> Makes thee invokt, to thee I humbly frame
> My flight from *Neptunes* furies. Reverend is
> To all the ever-living Deities
> What erring man soever seekes their aid.
> To thy both flood and knees a man dismaid
> With varied suffrance sues. Yeeld then some rest
> To him that is thy suppliant profest.

Cf.:
> Κλῦθι, ἄναξ, ὅτις ἐσσί· πολύλλιστον δέ σ' ἱκάνω
> φεύγων ἐκ πόντοιο Ποσειδάωνος ἐνιπάς.
> αἰδοῖος μέν τ' ἐστὶ καὶ ἀθανάτοισι θεοῖσιν
> ἀνδρῶν ὅς τις ἵκηται ἀλώμενος, ὡς καὶ ἐγὼ νῦν
> σόν τε ῥόον σά τε γούναθ' ἱκάνω πολλὰ μογήσας.
> ἀλλ' ἐλέαιρε, ἄναξ· ἱκέτης δέ τοι εὔχομαι εἶναι.   (V, 445-50)

Hear me, O king, whosoever thou art. As to one much prayed to do I come to thee, seeking to escape out of the sea from the threats of Poseidon. Even in the eyes of the immortal gods that man who comes as a wanderer is reverend, just as I have come to thy stream and to thy knees, after many toils. O king, pity me, for I declare myself thy suppliant!

15.
> τὴν μὲν ἰδὼν γήθησε πολύτλας δῖος Ὀδυσσεύς,
> ἐν δ' ἄρα μέσσῃ λέκτο, χύσιν δ' ἐπεχεύατο φύλλων.
> ὡς δ' ὅτε τις δαλὸν σποδιῇ ἐνέκρυψε μελαίνῃ
> ἀγροῦ ἐπ' ἐσχατιῆς, ᾧ μὴ πάρα γείτονες ἄλλοι,
> σπέρμα πυρὸς σώζων, ἵνα μή ποθεν ἄλλοθεν αὔῃ,
> ὡς Ὀδυσεὺς φύλλοισι καλύψατο.   (V, 486-91)

16. 'Commentarius', p. 78.

17.
> Στῆτέ μοι, ἀμφίπολοι· πόσε φεύγετε φῶτα ἰδοῦσαι;
> ἦ μή πού τινα δυσμενέων φάσθ' ἔμμεναι ἀνδρῶν;
> οὐκ ἔσθ' οὗτος ἀνὴρ διερὸς βροτὸς οὐδὲ γένηται,
> ὅς κεν Φαιήκων ἀνδρῶν ἐς γαῖαν ἵκηται
> δηϊοτῆτα φέρων· μάλα γὰρ φίλοι ἀθανάτοισιν.   (VI, 199-203)

18. Scapula, column 393. Scapula's derivation of βροτός (col. 288)

DYNAMIC ALLEGORY IN CHAPMAN'S 'ODYSSEY'

from ῥέω, *flow*, is wrong. The root is √μερ, as in Lat. *mortus*. See Liddell & Scott under μορτός.

19. *Odysses*, VI, 311 n., p. 93.
20. Spondanus, p. 84: 'Non est hic vir humidus homo . . .'.
21. *Études sur l'humanisme continental en Angleterre*, p. 155.
22. Scapula, column 154.
23. *Odysses*, VI, 315 n., p. 93.
24. W. D. Geddes, *The Problem of the Homeric Poems* (London, 1878), p. 35 n.

25.   πολὺ δ᾿ ὕδωρ
καλὸν ὑπεκπρορέει μάλα περ ῥυπόωντα καθῆραι. . . .   (VI, 86-7)

26. αὐτὰρ ὁ ἐκ ποταμοῦ χρόα νίζετο δῖος Ὀδυσσεὺς
ἅλμην, ἥ οἱ νῶτα καὶ εὐρέας ἄμπεχεν ὤμους·
ἐκ κεφαλῆς δ᾿ ἔσμηχεν ἁλὸς χνόον ἀτρυγέτοιο.
αὐτὰρ ἐπεὶ δὴ πάντα λοέσσατο καὶ λίπ᾿ ἄλειψεν,
ἀμφὶ δὲ εἵματα ἕσσαθ᾿ ἅ οἱ πόρε παρθένος ἀδμής,
τὸν μὲν Ἀθηναίη θῆκεν Διὸς ἐκγεγαυῖα
μείζονά τ᾿ εἰσιδέειν καὶ πάσσονα, κὰδ δὲ κάρητος
οὔλας ἧκε κόμας, ὑακινθίνῳ ἄνθει ὁμοίας.
ὡς δ᾿ ὅτε τις χρυσὸν περιχεύεται ἀργύρῳ ἀνὴρ
ἴδρις, ὃν Ἥφαιστος δέδαεν καὶ Παλλὰς Ἀθήνη
τέχνην παντοίην, χαρίεντα δὲ ἔργα τελείει,
ὡς ἄρα τῷ κατέχευε χάριν κεφαλῇ τε καὶ ὤμοις.
ἕζετ᾿ ἔπειτ᾿ ἀπάνευθε κιὼν ἐπὶ θῖνα θαλάσσης
κάλλεϊ καὶ χάρισι στίλβων. . . .   (VI, 224-37)

27. *Odysses*, VII, 89-104, p. 100. Cf.:

                    τὴν δ᾿ Ἀλκίνοος ποιήσατ᾿ ἄκοιτιν,
καί μιν ἔτισ᾿ ὡς οὔ τις ἐπὶ χθονὶ τίεται ἄλλη,
ὅσσαι νῦν γε γυναῖκες ὑπ᾿ ἀνδράσιν οἶκον ἔχουσιν.
ὡς κείνη περὶ κῆρι τετίμηταί τε καὶ ἔστιν
ἔκ τε φίλων παίδων ἔκ τ᾿ αὐτοῦ Ἀλκινόοιο
καὶ λαῶν, οἵ μίν ῥα θεὸν ὣς εἰσορόωντες
δειδέχαται μύθοισιν, ὅτε στείχῃσ᾿ ἀνὰ ἄστυ.
οὐ μὲν γάρ τι νόου γε καὶ αὐτὴ δεύεται ἐσθλοῦ·
οἷσίν τ᾿ εὖ φρονέῃσι καὶ ἀνδράσι νείκεα λύει.
εἴ κέν τοι κείνη γε φίλα φρονέῃσ᾿ ἐνὶ θυμῷ,
ἐλπωρή τοι ἔπειτα φίλους ἰδέειν καὶ ἱκέσθαι
οἶκον ἐς ὑψόροφον καὶ σὴν ἐς πατρίδα γαῖαν.   (VII, 66-77)

Alcinous made her his wife and honoured her as no other woman on earth is honoured who directs her household under her husband's authority; so heartily is she honoured and has ever been by her children and by Alcinous himself and by the people, who look upon her as a goddess and hail her as she goes through the city. For she does not lack wisdom, and she settles the disputes of those she favours, even if they be men. If thou dost win her favour there is hope that thou wilt see thy friends and return to thy high-roofed house and unto thy native land.

In the light of this C. S. Lewis does not seem to give a fair picture of the *Odyssey*'s attitude toward women when he says, in *The Allegory of Love*, p. 4: 'In ancient literature love seldom rises above the levels of merry sensuality or domestic comfort. . . . We find the comfort and utility of a good wife acknowledged: Odysseus loves Penelope as he loves the rest of his home and possessions. . . .' Compare also the universal admiration for Penelope expressed by Eumaeus, Agamemnon, and even the worst of the suitors, Ulysses' devotion to her expressed in his refusal of Calypso's offer to immortalize him, and the romantic, yet modest and dignified figure of Nausicaa.

28. *The Homer of Aristotle* (Oxford, Oxford University Press, 1923), p. 166.

29. *Odysses*, VIII, 334-48, p. 116. Cf.:

> ἀλλ' ἄγε νῦν ἐμέθεν ξυνίει ἔπος, ὄφρα καὶ ἄλλῳ
> εἴπῃς ἡρώων, ὅτε κεν σοῖς ἐν μεγάροισι
> δαινύῃ παρὰ σῇ τ' ἀλόχῳ καὶ σοῖσι τέκεσσιν,
> ἡμετέρης ἀρετῆς μεμνημένος, οἷα καὶ ἡμῖν
> Ζεὺς ἐπὶ ἔργα τίθησι διαμπερὲς ἐξέτι πατρῶν.
> οὐ γὰρ πυγμάχοι εἰμὲν ἀμύμονες οὐδὲ παλαισταί,
> ἀλλὰ ποσὶ κραιπνῶς θέομεν καὶ νηυσὶν ἄριστοι,
> αἰεὶ δ' ἡμῖν δαίς τε φίλη κίθαρίς τε χοροί τε
> εἵματά τ' ἐξημοιβὰ λοετρά τε θερμὰ καὶ εὐναί.   (VIII, 241-9)

Come now, listen to my words, that you may tell another hero, when you are feasting with your wife and children in your halls and remember our skill, what feats Zeus has granted us from our fathers' days until now. We are not faultless boxers or wrestlers, but fast runners and the best sailors; the banquet is dear to us, and the lyre, the dance, changes of clothes, warm baths, and the couch.

30.
> Ταῦτ' ἄρ' ἀοιδὸς ἄειδε περικλυτός· αὐτὰρ Ὀδυσσεὺς
> τήκετο, δάκρυ δ' ἔδευεν ὑπὸ βλεφάροισι παρειάς.
> ὡς δὲ γυνὴ κλαίῃσι φίλον πόσιν ἀμφιπεσοῦσα,
> ὅς τε ἑῆς πρόσθεν πόλιος λαῶν τε πέσῃσιν,
> ἄστεϊ καὶ τεκέεσσιν ἀμύνων νηλεὲς ἦμαρ·
> ἡ μὲν τὸν θνῄσκοντα καὶ ἀσπαίροντα ἰδοῦσα
> ἀμφ' αὐτῷ χυμένη λίγα κωκύει· οἱ δέ τ' ὄπισθε
> κόπτοντες δούρεσσι μετάφρενον ἠδὲ καὶ ὤμους
> εἴρερον εἰσανάγουσι, πόνον τ' ἐχέμεν καὶ ὀϊζύν·
> τῆς δ' ἐλεεινοτάτῳ ἄχεϊ φθινύθουσι παρειαί·
> ὣς Ὀδυσεὺς ἐλεεινὸν ὑπ' ὀφρύσι δάκρυον εἶβεν.   (VIII, 521-31)

31. *Odysses*, VIII, 708-23, p. 124. Miss Bartlett, in 'The Heroes of Chapman's *Homer*', p. 274, seems to miss the real significance of the final couplet in this passage when she says: 'The effeminate comparison becomes far more acceptable when it has once been established that tears are the truest interpretative power which life has to offer'.

32. *Odyssey*, IX, 19-20.

33. *Odysses*, IX, 71-8, pp. 128-9. Cf.:

> Ἰλιόθεν με φέρων ἄνεμος Κικόνεσσι πέλασσεν,
> Ἰσμάρῳ· ἔνθα δ' ἐγὼ πόλιν ἔπραθον, ὤλεσα δ' αὐτούς·
> ἐκ πόλιος δ' ἀλόχους καὶ κτήματα πολλὰ λαβόντες
> δασσάμεθ', ὡς μή τίς μοι ἀτεμβόμενος κίοι ἴσης.   (IX, 39-42)

From Ilios the wind brought me to the Cicones, to Ismarus. There I sacked the city and slew the men, and we took the wives and a great deal of treasure and divided them among us, that so far as it lay in my power no man might go defrauded of an equal share.

34. *Odysses*, IX, 167-81, pp. 130-1. Cf.:

> Ἔνθεν δὲ προτέρω πλέομεν ἀκαχήμενοι ἦτορ.
> Κυκλώπων δ' ἐς γαῖαν ὑπερφιάλων ἀθεμίστων
> ἱκόμεθ', οἳ ῥα θεοῖσι πεποιθότες ἀθανάτοισιν
> οὔτε φυτεύουσιν χερσὶν φυτὸν οὔτ' ἀρόωσιν,
> ἀλλὰ τά γ' ἄσπαρτα καὶ ἀνήροτα πάντα φύονται,
> πυροὶ καὶ κριθαὶ ἠδ' ἄμπελοι, αἵ τε φέρουσιν
> οἶνον ἐρισταφυλον, καί σφιν Διὸς ὄμβρος ἀέξει.
> τοῖσιν δ' οὔτ' ἀγοραὶ βουληφόροι οὔτε θέμιστες,
> ἀλλ' οἵ γ' ὑψηλῶν ὀρέων ναίουσι κάρηνα
> ἐν σπέσσι γλαφυροῖσι, θεμιστεύει δὲ ἕκαστος
> παίδων ἠδ' ἀλόχων, οὐδ' ἀλλήλων ἀλέγουσι.   (IX, 105-15)

Then we sailed on, grieved at heart, and we came to the land of the Cyclopes, a proud and lawless folk who, trusting in the immortal gods, plant nothing with their hands, nor plough; but all these things spring up for them without sowing or ploughing—wheat and barley and vines which bear the clusters for wine, and the rain sent from Zeus makes them grow. They have neither assemblies to take council nor appointed laws, but they dwell in hollow caves, and each one is lawgiver to his children and his wives, and they care nothing for one another.

35. *Odysses*, IX, 193-7, p. 131. Cf.:

> οὐ γὰρ Κυκλώπεσσι νέες πάρα μιλτοπάρῃοι,
> οὐδ' ἄνδρες νηῶν ἔνι τέκτονες, οἵ κε κάμοιεν
> νῆας ἐϋσσέλμους, αἵ κεν τελέοιεν ἕκαστα
> ἄστε' ἐπ' ἀνθρώπων ἱκνεύμεναι.   (IX, 125-8)

For the Cyclops have at hand no ships with vermilion cheeks, nor are there shipwrights in their land who might build them well-benched ships which could carry them where they wished, passing to the cities of other men.

36. *Odysses*, IX, 253-6, p. 132. Cf.:

> αὐτὰρ ἐγὼ σὺν νηί τ' ἐμῇ καὶ ἐμοῖς ἑτάροισιν
> ἐλθὼν τῶνδ' ἀνδρῶν πειρήσομαι, οἵ τινές εἰσιν,
> ἤ ῥ' οἵ γ' ὑβρισταί τε καὶ ἄγριοι οὐδὲ δίκαιοι,
> ἦε φιλόξεινοι, καί σφιν νόος ἐστὶ θεουδής.   (IX, 173-6)

But I, with my own ship and my own comrades, will go and try those men to learn who they are and whether they are cruel and wild and unjust, or whether they love strangers and fear the gods.

37. *Odysses*, IX, 279-86, p. 133. Cf.:

> ἀτὰρ αἴγεον ἀσκὸν ἔχον μέλανος οἴνοιο,
> ἡδέος, ὅν μοι δῶκε Μάρων, Εὐάνθεος υἱός,
> ἱρεὺς Ἀπόλλωνος, ὃς Ἴσμαρον ἀμφιβεβήκει,
> οὕνεκά μιν σὺν παιδὶ περισχόμεθ' ἠδὲ γυναικὶ
> ἁζόμενοι. . . .   (IX, 196-200)

With me I had a goat-skin of the dark, sweet wine which Maro, son of Evanthes, had given me, the priest of Apollo, the god who used to watch over Ismarus. And he had given it me because we had protected him and his child and wife out of reverence.

38.
> αὐτίκα γάρ μοι ὀΐσατο θυμὸς ἀγήνωρ
> ἄνδρ' ἐπελεύσεσθαι μεγάλην ἐπιειμένον ἀλκήν,
> ἄγριον, οὔτε δίκας εὖ εἰδότα οὔτε θέμιστας.   (IX, 213-15)

39.
> Ὦ ξεῖνοι, τίνες ἐστέ; πόθεν πλεῖθ' ὑγρὰ κέλευθα;
> ἤ τι κατὰ πρῆξιν ἤ μαψιδίως ἀλάλησθε,
> οἷά τε ληϊστῆρες ὑπεὶρ ἅλα, τοί τ' ἀλόωνται
> ψυχὰς παρθέμενοι κακὸν ἀλλοδαποῖσι φέροντες;   (IX, 252-5)

The fact that Nestor asks Telemachus the same question (III, 71-4) in my opinion only shows that piracy was common, not that Homer accepted it.

40. *Odysses*, IX, 362-71, pp. 134-5. Cf.:

> Ἡμεῖς τοι Τροίηθεν ἀποπλαγχθέντες Ἀχαιοὶ
> παντοίοις ἀνέμοισιν ὑπὲρ μέγα λαῖτμα θαλάσσης,
> οἴκαδε ἱέμενοι, ἄλλην ὁδόν, ἄλλα κέλευθα
> ἤλθομεν· οὕτω που Ζεὺς ἤθελε μητίσασθαι.
> λαοὶ δ' Ἀτρεΐδεω Ἀγαμέμνονος εὐχόμεθ' εἶναι,
> τοῦ δὴ νῦν γε μέγιστον ὑπουράνιον κλέος ἐστί·
> τόσσην γὰρ διέπερσε πόλιν καὶ ἀπώλεσε λαοὺς
> πολλούς.   (IX, 259-66)

We, thou must know, are from Troy, Achaeans, driven wandering over the great gulf of the sea by all manner of winds. Seeking our home, we have come by another way, as Zeus, I suppose, was pleased to devise.

And we declare that we are the men of Agamemnon, son of Atreus, whose fame is now mightiest under heaven, so great a city did he sack and so many people did he slay.

41. *Odysses*, IX, 377-80, p. 135. Cf.:

ἀλλ' αἰδεῖο, φέριστε, θεούς· ἱκέται δέ τοί εἰμεν.
Ζεὺς δ' ἐπιτιμήτωρ ἱκετάων τε ξείνων τε,
ξείνιος, ὃς ξείνοισιν ἅμ' αἰδοίοισιν ὀπηδεῖ.   (IX, 269-71)

Nay, mightiest one, reverence the gods; we are thy suppliants; and Zeus is the avenger of suppliants and strangers—Zeus, the stranger's god—who ever attends upon reverend suppliants.

42.   καὶ τότ' ἐγὼ Κύκλωπα προσηύδων κερτομίοισι·
Κύκλωψ, οὐκ ἄρ' ἔμελλες ἀνάλκιδος ἀνδρὸς ἑταίρους
ἔδμεναι ἐν σπῆϊ γλαφυρῷ κρατερῆφι βίηφι.
καὶ λίην σέ γ' ἔμελλε κιχήσεσθαι κακὰ ἔργα,
σχέτλι', ἐπεὶ ξείνους οὐκ ἅζεο σῷ ἐνὶ οἴκῳ
ἐσθέμεναι· τῷ σε Ζεὺς τίσατο καὶ θεοὶ ἄλλοι.   (IX, 474-9)

43. See Smalley, 'The Ethical Bias of Chapman's *Homer*', p. 187.

44. *Odysses*, IX, 683-95, p. 141. Cf.:

ὅς μοι ἔφη τάδε πάντα τελευτήσεσθαι ὀπίσσω,
χειρῶν ἐξ 'Οδυσῆος ἁμαρτήσεσθαι ὀπωπῆς.
ἀλλ' αἰεί τινα φῶτα μέγαν καὶ καλὸν ἐδέγμην
ἐνθάδ' ἐλεύσεσθαι, μεγάλην ἐπιειμένον ἀλκήν·
νῦν δέ μ' ἐὼν ὀλίγος τε καὶ οὐτιδανὸς καὶ ἄκικυς
ὀφθαλμοῦ ἀλάωσεν, ἐπεί μ' ἐδαμάσσατο οἴνῳ.   (IX, 511-16)

He told me that all these things should be brought to pass in days to come and that by Odysseus' hand I should lose my sight. But I always looked for a tall and noble man to come here, but now a puny one, a man of naught and a weakling, blinded me when he had overpowered me with wine.

45. 'De Circe', *Mythologiae*, Lib. VI, Cap. vi, pp. 570-1.

46. Herakleitos, ch. 73, ll. 5-11, p. 96.

47. Herakleitos, ch. 73, ll. 5-15, p. 97.

48. *The Odyssey of Homer Translated from the Greek* (London, 1725-6), X, 361 n.

49.   τεύξει τοι κυκεῶ, βαλέει δ' ἐν φάρμακα σίτῳ·
ἀλλ' οὐδ' ὣς θέλξαι σε δυνήσεται· οὐ γὰρ ἐάσει
φάρμακον ἐσθλόν, ὅ τοι δώσω.   (X, 290-2)

50.   μή σ' ἀπογυμνωθέντα κακὸν καὶ ἀνήνορα θήῃ.   (X, 301)

51.   οὐδὲ γὰρ οὐδέ τις ἄλλος ἀνὴρ τάδε φάρμακ' ἀνέτλη,
ὅς κε πίῃ καὶ πρῶτον ἀμείψεται ἕρκος ὀδόντων·
σοὶ δέ τις ἐν στήθεσσιν ἀκήλητος νόος ἐστίν.
ἦ σύ γ' 'Οδυσσεύς ἐσσι πολύτροπος, ὅν τέ μοι αἰεὶ

φάσκεν ἐλεύσεσθαι χρυσόρραπις ἀργειφόντης,
ἐκ Τροίης ἀνιόντα θοῇ σὺν νηΐ μελαίνῃ.　　　　　(X, 327-32)

52.　　　ὑπὸ δὲ θρῆνυς ποσὶν ἦεν.　　　　　　　　(X, 315, 367)

53. *Odysses*, X, 421, p. 153: 'A foote-stoole added . . .'.

54. *Odysses*, X, 466, p. 154 (misnumbered 156).

55. *Odysses*, X, 482-4, p. 154. Cf.:

ἐσθέμεναι δ' ἐκέλευεν· ἐμῷ δ' οὐ ἤνδανε θυμῷ,
ἀλλ' ἥμην ἀλλοφρονέων, κακὰ δ' ὄσσετο θυμός.　　(X, 373-4)

Then she bade me eat, but my heart was not thus inclined. Instead I
sat with other thoughts, and my spirit boded ill.

56.　　　ὦ Κίρκη, τίς γάρ κεν ἀνήρ, ὃς ἐναίσιμος εἴη,
πρὶν τλαίη πάσσασθαι ἐδητύος ἠδὲ ποτῆτος,
πρὶν λύσασθ' ἑτάρους καὶ ἐν ὀφθαλμοῖσιν ἰδέσθαι;　(X, 383-5)

57. Spondanus, p. 142.

58. See *Odysses*, VI, 356-76, p. 94; *Odyssey*, VI, 224-37.

59.　　　ὡς δ' ὅτε τις χρυσὸν περιχεύεται ἀργύρῳ ἀνὴρ
ἴδρις, ὃν Ἥφαιστος δέδαεν καὶ Παλλὰς Ἀθήνη
τέχνην παντοίην, χαρίεντα δὲ ἔργα τελείει,
ὣς μὲν τῷ περίχευε χάριν κεφαλῇ τε καὶ ὤμοις.　(XXIII, 159-62)

60. 'The Ethical Bias of Chapman's *Homer*', p. 190.

61. Spondanus, p. 327.

CHAPTER IV

The Style

THE strangely uneven style of Chapman's *Homer* has never been better described than in Lamb's well-known remark that 'the great obstacle to Chapman's Translations being read is their unconquerable quaintness. He pours out in the same breath the most just and natural and the most violent and forced expressions.'[1] This irregularity has been indicated in much the same terms by nearly all of Chapman's critics. Matthew Arnold found his *Iliad* 'steeped in humours and fantasticality up to the very lips', yet pronounced it on the whole 'plain-spoken, fresh, vigorous, and to a certain degree, rapid'.[2] In a general survey of all Chapman's writings Swinburne defined his virtues as 'a singular force and depth of moral thought, a constant energy and intensity of expression, an occasional delicacy and perfection of fanciful or reflective beauty . . .'.[3] Yet he, too, qualified his praise with the observation that Chapman's 'subtle and resistless ingenuity can never resist the lure of any quaint or perverse illustration which may start across its path from some obscure corner at the unluckiest and unlikeliest time'.[4] Thus it would appear that the faults and virtues of Chapman's style are so opposed as to appear irreconcilable, and the critics seem almost to contradict themselves in their descriptions. After such unanimous insistence on its grotesque or obscure or tortured qualities, the recent comments of a British critic, James Smith, may come as a surprise: 'Chapman's verse . . . has a self-effacing quality which, in my opinion, is one of the most remarkable things about it. Because of this quality I would call it, not only clear, but transparent like good glass, looking through which as a medium one is not aware of looking through anything.'[5]

Although this judgment may seem to disagree with the others, one may apply all these opinions with equal justice to Chapman's *Odyssey*. It is by turns obscure and clear, forced and natural, periphrastic and compact. Its irregularity is the more remarkable because it fails in attempting to do in some places what it succeeds brilliantly in doing in others. The failures are not, therefore, indications of areas of weakness in style, but merely local instances of its breakdown. Smith accordingly qualifies his assertion of Chapman's clarity by defining his obscurity: '[It] distinguishes itself in that its limits are not a whole poem or a play, but a single line or a few consecutive lines, sometimes a single word. It can be compared, not to an atmosphere or a texture, but to a body foreign to the substance in which it is embedded. If obscurity occurs in Chapman it is of this kind; and it should be noted how insignificant it is. For it is a sign, not of a habit of mind in the author . . . but of what may perhaps be called a failure of one of the devices used to establish communication.'[6] This, I think, is a fair statement of the case in Chapman's *Odyssey*.

Taken together, these critical opinions suggest a style that is highly distinctive, and, indeed, no passage of any length from his *Odyssey* could reasonably be mistaken for the work of any other poet. In the whole body of his poetry one may occasionally find thought and image used in the manner of the metaphysicals, as T. S. Eliot does,[7] or, as Saintsbury does,[8] detect here and there accents and rhythms like Donne's. The distinctive style of the *Odyssey* does not inhere, however, in one or two particular features but in the particular way in which Chapman combines all the elements of poetry. The enjambed decasyllabic couplet, the long verse paragraphs, what a recent Milton scholar calls 'the systematic deformation of logical word-order',[9] the abundance of parenthetical and subordinate clauses, the use of anacoluthon, and the particular blend of common words with neologisms, compound epithets and Latinate words, operate together to create a highly individual style. In form Chapman is as truly original as he is in his approach to the meaning of Homer's *Odyssey*.

The inner meanings which Chapman saw in the *Odyssey* found their chief expression, as we have seen, in moral apophthegm, explicit statement, and in amplification of Homeric symbol and allegory, but they are also reflected in the austere, precipitate, lofty, and involved poetry he created for them. If, as Miss Bartlett says, he 'felt free when he translated the *Odyssey*', this freedom is found not only in his ethical interpretation, but in almost every aspect of his style as well. What he could not reproduce or imitate he sought to represent by the native resources of his own language and verse. The fixed epithet, the formula, the regular Homeric pace, go by the boards and in their places we find highly individualized speeches, occasional excursions into the low style, and passages of headlong and impetuous movement that have no counterparts in the original.

Chapman's independent attitude is extended to the example of his immediate predecessors and contemporaries as well. His *Odyssey* shows relatively little that can be traced to the influence of other great Elizabethan and Jacobean poets. In diction and verse, it owes, perhaps unfortunately, no great debt to the example of Spenser, Shakespeare, or Jonson. Its movement is, furthermore, totally different from that of Chapman's earlier work in the pentameter couplet, such as the *Shield of Achilles* or his continuation of *Hero and Leander*. His notes and critical comments reveal no conscious concern with the questions of rhetoric and prosody which so agitated the generation of poets into which he was born in 1557. In these diction and ethical ideas are his main concern. Yet rhetorical and prosodic patterns play major rôles in helping to determine the texture of the *Odyssey*.

In both rhetoric and verse Chapman's *Odyssey* is unusual. The sentences are long and complex in structure. The decasyllabic couplet is so highly enjambed that it might

almost be described as rhymed blank verse. While the enjambed couplet was no novelty in 1615, the verse of this
translation does not really resemble that of other poets who
used this form, but sounds more like some of Chapman's
own dramatic blank verse. Chapman's handling of the
couplet cannot be adequately illustrated by a few examples,
or even by a long passage. The effect is cumulative, and the
reader must grow accustomed to it gradually. At its best
this verse is supple and capable of a wide variety of effects,
ranging from the precipitous, headlong movement to the
point and balance of the closed line. Chapman can move
gracefully from one form to another, as he does in one of the
most poignant moments in the *Odyssey* when Ulysses meets
the spirit of his mother in Hades. When she has answered
his eager questions about his family and has told how she
herself died of grief for her absent son, he tries in vain to
embrace her:

> She thus, when I had great desire to prove
> My armes the circle where her soule did move;
> Thrice prov'd I; thrice, she vanisht like a sleepe
> Or fleeting shadow, which strooke much more deepe
> The wounds my woes made, and made aske her why
> She would my love to her embraces flie,
> And not vouchsafe that even in hell we might
> Pay pious Nature her unalterd right,
> And give Vexation here her cruell fill?
> Should not the Queene here, to augment the ill
> Of every sufferance (which her office is)
> Enforce the idoll to affoord me this?
>
> O Sonne (she answerd) of the race of men
> The most unhappy, our most equall Queene
> Will mocke no solide armes with empty shade,
> Nor suffer empty shades againe t'invade
> Flesh, bones, and nerves, nor will defraud the fire
> Of his last dues, that, soone as spirits expire,

And leave the white bone, are his native right,
When, like a dreame, the soule assumes her flight.
The light then of the living, with most haste
(O Sonne) contend to: this thy little taste
Of this state is enough, and all this life
Will make a tale fit to be told thy wife.
                              (XI, 259-82, pp. 165-6)

Chapman has treated the original here with characteristic freedom, adding and subtracting, as a close translation of Anticleia's reply will show:

Alas, my child, above all men ill-fated! Persephone, the daughter of Zeus, does not deceive thee, but this is the way with mortals when they die. No more do the sinews hold flesh and bone together, but the great strength of the blazing fire destroys these as soon as life leaves the white bones, and the spirit, like a dream, flits and flutters away.[10]

Chapman has used his freedom wisely in seeking an English equivalent for the Homeric passage. He stiffens slightly Anticleia's gentle remonstrance by letting her assert the justness of Persephone in the addition, 'our most equall Queene'. *Equall* then provides the cue to the rest of the sentence, where the suggestion of 'mocke', taken from Homer, is developed in 'defraud' and 'native right'. In these lines Anticleia asserts the immutability of the laws of life and death, as she does in Homer, but with a different emphasis. Homer says that the intangibleness of ghosts is 'the appointed way'—it is the δίκη of mortals when they die to be unembraceable. There is no equivalent English word for δίκη, one of the key words in Homer's cosmogony. William Chase Greene in *Moira*[11] and Werner Jaeger in *Paideia*[12] discuss its implications at length. In Homer Anticleia is simply stating the nature of things. This is the δίκη of mortals when they die, and since it is thus, there is no point in complaining. Chapman's Anticleia goes farther, and

131

not only states that this is so, but that it is just that it is so, a conception perhaps alien to the Homeric mind, which was inclined to state without comment the primary facts of existence. Chapman dramatizes his assertion of justice in several images which, without plucking out the heart of the mystery, suggest that the natural order embraces a great many incompatible claims:

> nor will defraud the fire
> Of his last dues, that, soone as spirits expire,
> And leave the white bone, are his native right. . . .

The verse itself, furthermore, dramatizes this even-handed justice in the balanced emphasis of the closed line:

> our most equall Queene
> Will mocke no solide armes with empty shade.

This balance once achieved, Chapman goes on to a more difficult balance in the run-on lines which follow, where instead of each line being divided into two related halves, the verse movement relates the parallel and contrasting hemistichs of successive lines in a flowing movement that yet retains some of the controlled quality of the closed couplet:

> nor will defraud the fire
> Of his last dues, that,
> soone as spirits expire,
> And leave the white bone,
> are his native right. . . .

The change from the closed and balanced line to this kind of paragraphing movement is very neatly managed by anadiplosis in

> Will mocke no solide armes with *empty shade*,
> Nor suffer *empty shades* againe t'invade
> Flesh, bones, and nerves. . . .

At the conclusion of the passage Chapman returns as easily

to the former pattern with a normal closed line:

> When, like a dreame, the soule assumes her flight.

Thus handled the verse provides a continuousness that is highly desirable in a translation of Homer. 'Adroitly managed', to quote Saintsbury, the enjambed decasyllabic couplet 'combines the advantages and powers of the stanza with those of the couplet, and even both with those of the blank verse paragraph to no small extent. For description it has no peer, inasmuch as it escapes the over-*vignetted* effect of the stanza, and the sharp creases, as of a picture folded and not rolled, that are inseparable from the stopped distich.'[13] When it is not adroitly managed, 'the contagion of breathlessness and "promiscuousness" seems to spread from the structure of the verse to that of the story'.[14] This is an excellent statement of the strengths and weaknesses in Chapman's versification.

Although the syntax of Anticleia's speech is relatively simple, there is a good deal of inversion, inconspicuous because deftly handled. Here it helps to make her farewell, to use a favourite adjective of C. S. Lewis, 'solempne'. Her extremely simple words of parting acquire thereby a degree of tragic passion which they would lack if left in the normal English order. By this I do not mean to suggest that inversion alone can bestow distinction on any matter whatsoever. The order here is natural in its own way, because it is the order of Anticleia's own urgent ideas:

> O Sonne (she answerd) of the race of men
> The most unhappy. . . .

This instance of hyperbaton happens also to follow, as closely as English can, the order of the Greek:

> Ὤ μοι, τέκνον ἐμόν, περὶ πάντων κάμμορε φωτῶν.
>
> (XI, 216)

This in itself is a fact of little interest. But it is evident that the construction successfully avoids the prosaic and gives

Anticleia's exclamation an emphasis proper to her state of mind, an emphasis which is also partly due to Chapman's dexterous handling of alliteration and consonance to bind the whole phrase.

The hyperbaton in the close of the passage is equally effective:

> The light then of the living, with most haste
> (O Sonne) contend to: this thy little taste
> Of this state is enough, and all this life
> Will make a tale fit to be told thy wife.

Again, in the first line and a half, Chapman's order coincides with Homer's. This order is natural here, because it dramatizes Anticleia's anxiety for the safety of her beloved son. First, 'the light' which is so remote from this world of shadows, then the sense of peril reflected in the anticipating phrase, 'with most haste', and finally the urgent imperative, 'contend to', which expresses exactly what she imagines to be the difficulty of returning to the other world. In the last two and a half lines Chapman skilfully shifts the mood to that quiet, accepting, almost humorous attitude with which the great women of the *Odyssey* in their greatest moments regard their purely personal sufferings. The scene of strong personal emotion is thereby distanced in preparation for the accounts of other spirits which Ulysses now proceeds to give in a lower key. Note how the normal syntax of the last clause contributes to the quiet conclusion of the speech.

II

With this brief introduction to Chapman's verse in the *Odyssey*, it seems best to confront boldly the two principal faults that have contributed most to his reputation for 'quaintness'—unjustified periphrasis and unnecessarily complex constructions. We have already glimpsed some more or less successful uses of periphrastic and inverted constructions, and the memory of these in the four or five pages which follow may console us with the thought that these *gaucheries* are local breakdowns of a style that is capable of excellence. They apparently stem from a loss of discrimination, or, one might even say, from a lack of sense of humour, a weakness to which such poetic horrors as Goody Blake and Harry Gill can be attributed.

The most objectionable periphrases in the *Odyssey* are those which set in motion a conflict of grotesque associations, a situation where the different suggestions of the image cannot be reconciled on any level of the image's own terms. Such is the case when Nestor, in Book III, is offended by Athene's suggestion that she and Telemachus spend the night aboard their ship.

> He (mov'd with that) provokt thus their abodes:
> Now *Jove* forbid, and all the long-liv'd Gods,
> Your leaving me, to sleepe aboord a ship,
> *As I had drunke of poore Penias whip*
> *Even to my nakednesse*, and had nor sheete
> Nor covering in my house, that warme nor sweete
> A guest, nor I my selfe, had meanes to sleepe. . . .
>
> (III, 471-7, p. 41)

The offending clause, which I have italicized, is entirely Chapman's addition: 'May Zeus and the other immortals forbid this that you should go to your swift ship from my house as from one utterly poor and without clothing, one who has not plenty of blankets and cloaks in his house on which both he and his guests may sleep softly'.[15] 'To drink of the whip' was an expression current in Chapman's day, and meant 'to get a flogging'. The fact that it was current does not mean that it is a good image, and its tortuous refinement here eliminates whatever idiomatic quality it might be felt to have had originally. 'To drink of the whip even to nakedness' is simply a horribly mixed metaphor, while such naval slang ill becomes the venerable Nestor.

He is to be sure an over-eager host, as Chapman is trying to suggest, but he is certainly not the salty old tar implied by the image. The matter is made worse by the pedantic addition of 'poore *Penia*', an obscure personification which is equally incongruous in a totally different way. *Penia* may have been suggested to Chapman by the word for 'poor' in Homer's text. This pedantry is compounded by the redundant epithet 'poore'.

When periphrasis is used to heighten or give weight to a statement the result is sometimes turgid and strange, deserving Puttenham's censorious term of '*bomphilogia*, or pompious speech'. The indispensable virtue of concreteness is often lost in the process. Thus Ulysses clothes a small matter in inept art when he explains to his Phaeacian friends his inferiority in foot-races:

> So many seas so too much have misusde
> My lims for race, and therefore have diffusde
> A dissolution through my loved knees.
>
> (VIII, 322-4, p. 116)

Such a speech might make one suspect that Chapman had read nothing greater or more recent in English poetry than Phaer's *Aeneid*. The original construction is simply: 'I have been cruelly broken amid the waves, since there were not enough provisions in my ship; therefore my limbs are unstrung'.[16] Chapman's diffuse construction and the superfluous second 'so' aggravate the windy quality of the second and third lines. The sense of the passage is perfectly clear; only the expression is complicated. In Homer people's knees are constantly being loosened under the stress of affliction, but Homer never uses a turgid expression like 'diffuse a dissolution through'. Chapman would have been better off with an English substitute for the Homeric idiom, but instead he goes on to imitate in '*loved* knees' the Homeric use of φίλος in the sense of 'one's own'. This use of the word, unrecorded by *O.E.D.*, is merely quaint in English,

and suggests the absurdities which literal translation can
achieve. Chapman is not, however, often guilty of this kind
of literalism.

A third candidate for *The Stuffed Owl* is this little description of Telemachus receiving a present from Helen:

> Thus gave she to his hands the veile, and he
> The acceptation author'd joyfully.
>
> (XV, 168-9, p. 231)

> [She gave it into his hands, and he took it gladly.]
>
> (XV, 130)

I suppose this is an attempt at elegance. At any rate it testifies
further to the annoying side of Chapman's involuted style.
This passage is execrable not only because it is wordy and
unnatural, but because this fustian stands between the reader
and a simple, incidental, concrete action. The ghost of
Holofernes has, at such moments, transmigrated into the
body of George Chapman, and dismayed us with its unmitigated vitality. It is fair to say that whatever is stilted in
Chapman's translation is usually verbose. One could easily
multiply examples, but those given represent well enough
the range of evils which the abuse of periphrasis produces.
None of these examples is taken from important speeches or
crucial narrative passages, simply because these faults tend to
occur mainly in the more routine parts of the poem, as is
natural with bathos and pomposity.

The other main fault is also one of rhetoric or syntax, a
kind of confusion caused chiefly by unnecessary departures
from the normal word-order, or by a proliferation of
dependent clauses whose antecedents are not clear, or by
both. When Peisistratus praises Menelaus' liberality, the
confusion is almost entirely due to doubts as to the proper
referents for the numerous pronouns and dependent clauses:

> Not a guest
> Shall touch at his house, but shall store his breast

With fit mind of an hospitable man,
To last as long as any daylight can
His eyes re-comfort, in such gifts as he
Will proofes make of his hearty royalty.

(XV, 69-74, p. 229)

[For a guest remembers all his days the host who shows him kindness.][17]

The fact that the first 'his' refers to Menelaus, the second and third to 'guest', and the fourth again to Menelaus, together with the 'he' in the last line but one, is likely to befuddle the reader. There is a similar uncertainty about what subject governs 'to last'. At first glance it may be 'breast', 'fit mind', or 'hospitable man'. The whole may best be described as a failure of rhetorical control, a failure to emphasize the main point in the passage. This is also due in part to the use of a pallid and vague word, 'fit', at a key place in the speech. Confusion is worse confounded in the ambiguous relationship of the final clause to the rest of the passage. Chapman's use of anacoluthon sometimes makes for obscurity, but more often the difficulty is caused by a loose floating construction of this sort.

A plethora of dependent clauses may sometimes be combined with an excessively long suspension of the main verb to create a syntactical labyrinth. Such is the case with this description of Ulysses' fears that old Eurycleia, who is washing his feet, will recognize and betray him:

Who turned him from the light,
Since sodainly he doubted her conceit
(So rightly touching at his state before)
A scar now seeing on his foot, that bore
An old note to discerne him, might descry
The absolute truth; which (witnest by her eye)
Was straite approv'd.

(XIX, 535-41, p. 300)

Here the original is almost essential as a 'trot' to decipher

138

the translation. 'But Odysseus sat down away from the hearth, and quickly turned toward the shadow, for he instantly feared that, as she touched him, she would notice the scar, and the truth would come out.'[18] Chapman's main clause, 'he doubted her conceit . . . might descry | The absolute truth', is split by four intermediate clauses. But here the suspension does not function, as is often the case in Chapman, and almost invariably so in *Paradise Lost*, really to *organize* the paragraph, for the relation of the parts is haphazard and inorganic. What we have here is the *appearance* of an integrated syntactical structure, whose parts are in fact related only in a casual, paratactical manner.

Such are the outstanding rhetorical and syntactical vices in Chapman's style. There remains one unhappy feature of Chapman's diction that is, alas, frequent enough to demand attention at this stage of the discussion—the compound epithet. These are less damaging than the bad passages we have just examined, principally because their scope is even more limited, but they do stand out. It is unquestionably a shock to come suddenly upon a line like

[They] hony-sweetnesse-giving-minds-wine fill'd.

This device Coleridge has analysed perfectly:

Excepting his quaint epithets which he affects to render literally from the Greek, a language above all others blest in the 'happy marriage of sweet words', and which in our language are mere printer's compound epithets—such as quaffed divine *joy-in-heart-of-man-infusing-wine* (the undermarked is to be one word, because one sweet mellifluous word expresses it in Homer); excepting this, it has no look, no air of a translation.[19]

These phrases are probably the result, as Coleridge says, of a misbegotten attempt to give the feeling of the original Homeric compound, but they are also no doubt related to Chapman's quest for forceful conciseness.

These monstrous phrases are sometimes related to some

falsely derived definition in the *Lexicon* of Johannes Scapula, Chapman's constant companion. Such is the case with

> The fate-borne-dogs-to-barke tooke sodaine view
> Of Odyssaeus, and upon him flew
> With open mouth.
>
> (XIV, 41-3, p. 211)

[Suddenly then the baying hounds caught sight of Ulysses, and rushed at him with loud barks.][20]

In such cases Chapman usually cites his authority in a note, as he does here:

> ὑλακόμωρος, Ad latrandum fato quodam Natus.

This is part of Scapula's definition, which is based on an assumed but unexplained mutation of omicron into omega in the second half of the compound, -μωρος, and which thereby relates the word to μόρος, 'fate'.[21] Modern lexicographers find no such mutation, but are uncertain about the precise meaning of this element. They define the compound as 'always barking'.[22] What is especially interesting about Chapman's use of Scapula in some of these cases is the literal translation of part of the Latin definition in the text of the poem itself.

A more complex example of this practice is a compound which Chapman constructs upon his own fanciful derivation of the Greek epithet:

> Her the *Phenissian great-wench-net-lai're* [layer]
> With sweet words circumvented.
>
> (XV, 557-8, p. 239)

Eumaeus employs this remarkable phrase to describe how a shifty Phoenician merchant seduced his nurse and kidnapped him as a child. The original adjective is πολυπαίπαλος,[23] and Chapman glosses it thus:

> πολυπαίπαλος: admodum vafer. Der. ex παλεύω, pertraho in retia, et παῖς, puella.

'Admodum vafer' is a correct definition and is given by Scapula. The word is actually derived from πολυ and the verb πάλλω, with παι-, which Chapman relates to παῖς, 'child' or 'maid', being the reduplicated temporal augment of the verb stem. It has no relation to παλεύω, which Chapman properly defines, following Scapula, as 'pertraho in retia'.[24] Chapman's mistaken derivation would not be so harmful, however, if he had not joined the elements in such a painfully ungrammatical phrase.

Most of Chapman's longer compound epithets are characterized by some such syntactical hodge-podge—the elements, or imagined elements, of the Homeric compound being turned into English and tumbled together without regard for grammar or good style. Here are a couple of outstanding ones:

then
> *The striv'd-for, for his worth, of worthy men,*
> *And reverenc't of the State*, Demodocus,
> Was brought in by the good Pontonous.[25]

> When *care-and-lineament-resolving* sleepe
> Had laide his temples in his golden steepe,
> His *wise-in-chast-wit-worthy-wife* did rise.[26]

III

We have now glimpsed the salient faults in the style of Chapman's *Odyssey*. Without doubt one could produce many more examples like those cited, but it is questionable whether one could find many that could not be attributed to an abuse of periphrasis or to an unnecessary complication of the normal English word-order. These faults, fortunately, are not symptomatic of a general weakness of style: when the passages fail, they fail spectacularly, but normally the style is sensitive, vigorous, and compact. The vigour and compactness are due primarily to two factors: the high proportion of verbs to other parts of speech, and the frequency of elliptical expressions. All three qualities, but especially the poem's vigour and sensitivity, may be attributed as well to Chapman's remarkable alertness to the metaphorical roots of the language.

A good example of the elliptical, compressed phrase is the question Ulysses asks Eumaeus about the manner of his enslavement:

> Or . . . set alone
> In guard of beeves, or sheepe, set th'enemy on,
> Surprisde, and shipt, transfer'd, and sold thee heere?
>
> (XV, 511-13, p. 238)

[Or, when you were alone with your sheep and cattle, did enemies take you in their ships and sell you to this man?][27]

The rapid-fire series of verbs, governed by a single subject (brachylogia), the clipped verb endings, and the alliterative beat of 's's combine in helping to give an appropriate feeling of tension and haste. Chapman is fond of these devices and uses them wherever the sense justifies a quickened tempo. The whole passage dealing with Telemachus' return to Ithaca from Sparta reflects a certain nervous intensity that suggests the danger of the wooers' ambush. In the account of the debarkation there is also a feeling of deftness and command that marks the newly won self-reliance of a young man who has just carried out his first major responsibility:

> now they stoopt the mast,
> Made to the port with oares, and anchor cast,
> Made fast the ship and then ashore they went,
> Drest supper, fil'd wine, when (their appetites spent)
> *Telemachus* commanded they should yield
> The ship to th'owner.
>
> (XV, 661-6, p. 241)

[But near the shore Telemachus' comrades furled the sail quickly, took down the mast, and rowed the ship to her mooring with their oars. Then they threw over the mooring-stones and fastened

the stern cables, and then they went ashore and prepared their
meal and mixed the flaming wine.][28]

'Fil'd wine' exemplifies the device of asyndeton which Chapman habitually uses to relate routine actions rapidly. It helps
to accelerate the narrative sequence in which the young
prince and his companion, Theoclymenus, refresh themselves in the palace before meeting Penelope:

> This said, he brought home his grief-practisd guest,
> Where both put off, both oyl'd, and did invest
> Themselves in rich robes, washt, and sate, and eate.
>
> (XVII, 113-15, p. 259)

Homer, with his more formal and formulaic manner, does
not vary the tempo of such passages in this way. As Erich
Auerbach says,

. . . no speech is so filled with anger or scorn that the particles
which express logical and grammatical connections are lacking
or out of place. This last observation is true, of course, not only
of speeches but of the presentation in general. The separate
elements of a phenomenon are most clearly placed in relation to
one another; a large number of conjunctions, adverbs, particles,
and other syntactical tools, all clearly circumscribed and deli-
cately differentiated in meaning, delimit persons, things, and
portions of incidents in respect to one another, and, at the same
time, bring them together in a continuous and ever flexible
connection; like the separate phenomena themselves, their relationships—their temporal, local, causal, final, consecutive, com-
parative, concessive, antithetical, and conditional limitations—
are brought to light in perfect fullness; so that a continuous
rhythmic procession of phenomena passes by, and never is there
a form left fragmentary or half-illuminated, never a lacuna,
never a gap, never a glimpse of unplumbed depths.[29]

Accordingly, in contrast to the abbreviations and ellipses in
Chapman's passage, Homer's ordered and leisurely descrip-

tion lingers over the ritual of the bath:

So saying, he led the sorely-tried stranger to the house. Now
when they had come to the stately house they laid their cloaks
on the chairs and high seats, and went into the polished baths
and bathed. And when the maids had washed and anointed
them with oil and had dressed them in fleecy cloaks and tunics,
they came forth from the baths and sat down on the chairs.[30]

Chapman preserves only the bare outlines of this. The
truncated phrase 'both put off' and the series of five verbs
governed by a single subject contribute to the prevailing
sense of urgency, whereas the Homeric narrative tempo is
not at all affected by the impatience which Telemachus and
Theoclymenus must feel.

Chapman does not restrict these devices of syntactical
compression to passages where speed is desirable. They are
largely responsible for the energy of this challenge addressed
by the disguised Ulysses to one of Penelope's suitors:

> I wish at any worke we two were tryed,
> In hight of spring time, when heavens lights are long,
> I, a good crook'd sithe that were sharpe and strong,
> You, such another, where the grasse grew deepe;
> Up by day breake, and both our labours keepe
> Up til slow darknes eas'd the labouring light,
> Fasting all day, and not a crum til night;
> We than should prove our either workmanship.
>
> (XVIII, 522-9, p. 286)

[Eurymachus, I wish we might have a working-contest some
day, in the spring when the days are long, at grass-mowing; I
with a curved scythe in my hand and you with another like it,
and plenty of grass so that we might test our work, fasting till
late evening.][31]

Here Chapman has gone beyond Homer's spareness in
omitting non-essential verbs and prepositions in a few places:
'I, a good crook'd sithe', 'You, such another'; and he has

144

extended the practice in the subjectless phrase, 'and both our labours keepe'. In concentrating on the essentials in this tight-lipped way, the speech suggests the effort of the actual contest. The changes of pace are deftly handled. In the midst of this tension there are two leisurely phrases that are most effective. The relatively easy movement of 'when heavens lights are long' implies the serenity of the sun, shining above this contest. The countryman's reverence for nature is also suggested in the expression 'heavens lights'. Then the enjambment of the fifth line, the repetition of 'up' in the sixth, and the trochaic inversions which stress these 'ups' help to give a kinaesthetic sense of sustained effort which is relieved in the tranquil phrase, 'til slow darknes eas'd the labouring light', with its liquid consonants and long syllables. The devices of compression are thus used with due regard for the proper tempo of the verse.

IV

The metaphorical vitality of Chapman's language in the *Odyssey* is ever-present and, on the whole, so well assimilated as to be unobtrusive. I venture to say that there is almost no passage of ten lines without a recognizable image of some sort. Yet because of their self-effacing quality these strands of metaphor do not dominate the passages. They are inseparable from the texture of Chapman's epic idiom. The earlier discussion of the more overt and striking moral symbolism of appetite and the sea may have given the reader the false impression that the style is normally self-conscious and violates that impression of simplicity and unity found in Homer. The subdued type of metaphor under discussion may be distinguished from such moral symbolism by the fact that it is not *explicitly* related to the moral conflict. The difference is in some cases only one of degree, but it will suggest the general features of the two types. The symbols, as we found, tend to proclaim them-

selves by a turn of wit, some measurable incongruity between the terms, as in 'those students for the gut and life',
or in 'the vow | The Wooers made to all satiety'. The
discrepancy between the associations of studiousness and
'gut' or between a vow and satiety calls attention to itself,
and the juxtaposition of the self-denying and the self-
indulgent instantly reminds us of the duality of human
nature, a fact which Chapman, as we have abundantly seen,
is always ready to emphasize.

The more subdued metaphor which concerns us now
functions in two ways. By keeping alive the basic motifs of
the *Odyssey*—the memory of war, the delights of peace and
the Return, the horror of wandering and homelessness, the
malignity of the sea, the precarious defences by which man
tries to save himself from it, and so forth—it provides a
continuing background against which every episode is
enacted. Its second function is to help assimilate Chapman's
symbolism by filling the gap between moralized symbol
and the narrative stream of events. These strands of extended
metaphor inevitably have some moral colouring, but it is
modulated. We are not compelled, every time we come
across a reference to the sea, to identify it with passion, nor
every time we find a harbour mentioned, to identify it with
spiritual peace. As I have tried to show, Chapman is not
doctrinaire in his use of allegory and symbol, but these
interests are accompanied by a healthy interest in phenomena themselves, whether a roast of beef or a storm at sea.
The background of extended metaphor serves constantly to
represent the day-to-day realities which are so important
a part of the original. Where Homer gets this effect
chiefly through epithets which repeatedly stress one quality
of an object—winged words, the barren sea, the black-
prowed ship, and so forth—Chapman wisely eschews a
device alien to the poetry of his age and country and
attempts an equivalent effect by a more extensive use of
metaphor.

To show the nature and effect of this practice I have chosen that phase of Ulysses' experience which lies between Hermes' intervention with Calypso and the hero's arrival at Phaeacia. In the chronology of his adventures this period follows the mythic experiences which he is to relate in Books nine, ten, eleven, and twelve, and which we have already discussed in the preceding chapter. In this phase Ulysses is no longer confronted with the fabulous temptations and perils. Instead he is faced now with purely natural forces of wind and sea and storm-beaten rock, this being the form which Poseidon's final fit of anger takes, and in the course of this struggle he discovers that exclusive reliance on his own strength has become the final obstacle to his safety. Except for the intervention of a helpful nymph, Ino Leucothea, the whole thing is presented naturalistically until the moment of rescue. There is a significant shift in the way in which Poseidon is represented: he no longer appears in the rôle of outraged father or blasphemed god, but rather as the representative of the apparently unjust and arbitrary miseries which are a part of man's fate, the blind amoral force that even Zeus must acknowledge when he agrees that the Phaeacian ship, and the sailors who fulfilled their sacred duty in conveying Ulysses to Ithaca, be destroyed. Before this force the just and the unjust must bow.

In the passage we are about to consider Chapman's extended metaphors serve to represent the nature of this kind of reality. Thus Hermes, who has brought from Olympus the command of the gods that Ulysses be sent on his way, explains to Calypso the reason he has come to her remote island:

> Jove caused my course to thee
> Against my will, for who would willingly
> *Lackey along so vast a lake of brine.*[32]

[It was Jove who bade me come hither against my will. Who of his own accord would speed over so great a space of salt-water, great past telling?]

147

Chapman has humorously emphasized Hermes' divine and supercilious indifference to the terrors of the sea. For him it is simply boring to travel over these great dull stretches where there are no cities to offer hecatombs, but orders are orders. The god contemptuously calls the sea 'a lake of brine', because that is all it is to him.

When he first sets out in his raft Ulysses has something of this divine insouciance in the face of possible dangers, but, when Poseidon hits him with a frightful storm on the eighteenth day, he plunges from over-confidence into despair:

> Woe is me!
> What was I borne to, man of miserie?
> *Feare* tels me now that all the Goddesse said
> *Truths* selfe will author, that *Fate* would be paid
> *Griefes* whole summe due from me, at sea, before
> I reacht the deare touch of my countries shore.
> With what clouds Jove heavens heightend forehead binds!
> How tyrannize the wraths of all the winds!
> *How all the tops he bottomes with the deepes,*
> *And in the bottomes all the tops he steepes.*
> *Thus dreadfull is the presence of our death.*
>
> (V, 380-90, p. 79)

[Ah me, wretched as I am! What is to befall me at last? I fear that all the goddess said was indeed true, when she declared that on the sea, before I ever reached my native land, I should fill up my measure of woes; and now it is all being brought to pass. With such clouds Jove has overcast the broad heaven, and roused up the sea, and the blasts of all the winds sweep upon me; now is my utter destruction sure.][33]

The personifications which Chapman has introduced dramatize the rigours of Ulysses' situation, identifying himself, as he does, with 'Griefe'. 'Feare' tells him that what he heard sceptically from the goddess will be brought to pass by 'Truth'. 'Truths selfe' is more impersonal and austere than

any god or goddess could be. 'Truth', then, is the reality I
mentioned earlier, that comprehends all the inexplicable
vicissitudes of man's life. In this little scene 'Truth' is the
stern, implacable officer of the law who will see to it that
'Fate' is paid the full debt owed by the man of miseries,
'Griefe'. Under the tutelage of 'Feare' Ulysses now admits
the overwhelming nature of the forces which confront him.
His awestruck horror is the opposite of the somewhat cocky
confidence with which he set out and is brilliantly evoked
in the last three lines of the quotation. In Ulysses' further
reflections upon this horror Chapman extends the vein of
storm imagery in 'sunke', 'showres' and 'undeprest':

> Thrice four times blest were they that *sunke* beneath
> Their fates at Troy, and did to nought contend
> But to renowme Atrides with their end!
> I would to God my hours of death and Fate
> That day had held the power to terminate,
> When *showres of darts my life bore undeprest*
> About divine Aeacides deceast!
>
> (V, 391-7, pp. 79-80)

[Thrice blessed those Danaans, aye, four times blessed, who died
then in the broad land of Troy, doing the pleasure of the sons of
Atreus. Would that I had died and met my fate thus on the day
when the throngs of Trojans hurled bronze-tipped spears upon
me, as I fought around the body of the dead son of Peleus.][34]

'Sunke' and 'undeprest' suggest Ulysses' change of heart
by echoing the metaphorical terms of his buoyant retort to
Calypso's warning on the eve of his departure:

> If any God shall lay
> His hand upon me, as I passe the seas,
> *Ile beare the worst of what his hand shall please,*
> *As having given me such a mind, as shall*
> *The more still rise, the more his hand lets fall.*
>
> (V, 293-7, p. 77)

[And if again some god shall smite me on the wine-dark sea, I will
endure it, having in my breast a heart that endures affliction.][35]

His old spirit revives once more, however, as he climbs back
onto his raft:

> yet he left not so
> *His drenched vessell*, for the *overthrow*
> Of her nor him, but gat at length againe
> (*Wrastling with Neptune*) hold of her; and then
> Sate in her bulke, *insulting over Death,*
> *Which* (*with the salt streame, prest to stop his breath,*
> *He 'scapt, and gave the sea againe, to give*
> *To other men.*)
>
> (V, 414-21, p. 78)

[At length, however, he came up, and spat out of his mouth the
bitter brine which flowed in streams from his head. Yet even so
he did not forget his raft, despite his evil plight, but sprang after
it amid the waves, and laid hold of it, and sat in the midst of it,
seeking to escape the doom of death.][36]

In his translation here, Chapman has raised Ulysses' self-
reliance almost to the level of *hubris*. As the storm increases
in intensity, a sea-nymph named Ino Leucothea takes pity on
him and gives him a talisman for protection, but the hero
stubbornly clings to his raft and his scepticism:

> When she is split, Ile swim; no miracle can,
> Past neare and cleare meanes, move a knowing man.
>
> (V, 472-3, p. 81)

[. . . as long as the timbers hold firm in their fastenings, so
long will I remain here and endure affliction; but when the
waves shall have shattered the raft to pieces, I will swim, seeing
that there is no better device.][37]

Now the raft is demolished, and the hero, having rested for
a moment on a spar, casts himself into the sea. Chapman, in
'prostrate', signalizes his final submission to necessity:

> Then did Ulysses mount on rib, perforce,
> Like to the rider of a running horse,
> To stay himselfe a time, while he might shift
> His drenched weedes, that were Calypsos gift.

When putting straight Leucotheas amulet
About his necke, he all his forces set
To swim, *and cast him prostrate to the seas.*

(V, 480–6, p. 81)

In this context and in view of the heightened emphasis
Chapman has given to elements of stubborn self-reliance in
Ulysses' attitude, 'prostrate' does mark a change of heart.
Having lost his raft and stripped himself of Calypso's en-
cumbering weeds, and relying now on the nymph's
apparently impracticable gift to save him from the sea which,
he now realizes, he cannot overcome by his own strength,
Ulysses leaves one phase of his experiences and enters
another. Up to now he has confided chiefly in his own pluck
and strength and cleverness. From now on he enlists the aid
of the supernatural. 'Humility' is probably too strong a
term to apply to him, for circumstances have forced him to
recognize the inadequacy of his own resources, but from
this time forth he actively seeks divine assistance. It is at this
point, significantly, that Neptune's persecution of the hero
comes to an end:

> So now feele ils enow, and struggle so,
> Till to your Jove-lov'd ilanders you row.
> But my mind sayes you will not so avoid
> This last taske too, *but be with sufferance cloid.*

(V, 490–3, pp. 81–2)

[So now, after thou hast sufferd many ills, go wandering over
the deep till thou comest among the folk fostered of Jove. Yet
even so, I think, thou shalt not mock at thy sufferings.][38]

The metaphor which Chapman has added to Neptune's
farewell anticipates that marvellous description, which we
discussed earlier, of Ulysses emerging, totally exhausted,
from the sea:

> Then forth he came, his both knees faltring, both
> His strong hands hanging downe, and all with froth

151

His cheeks and nosthrils flowing, voice and breath
Spent to all use; and downe he *sunke* to Death.
The sea had soakt his heart through; all his vaines
His toiles had rackt t' a labouring womans paines.

(V, 608-13, p. 84)

V

Ambiguity and paradox are highly characteristic features
of Chapman's imagery. Like the metaphorical patterns we
have been discussing, these are employed unobtrusively, and
they contribute to the remarkable flow and unity of the
translation in somewhat the same way that Homer's constant
epithets and formulas do. Like the metaphorical patterns
they continually suggest the principal motifs lying behind
the action of the *Odyssey*—the fall of Troy, the treachery of
the suitors, the nostalgia for missing friends and lovers—and
they bring to bear on any particular situation the perspective
of these great themes.

Ambiguity, as Chapman uses it, is primarily a means of
condensing the connotative elements of his language, just as
ellipsis serves mainly to quicken its movement or heighten
its emotional effect. These two devices, syntactical and
metaphorical, often work hand in hand, as in Penelope's
remark to her disguised husband in Book XIX:

The Gods my person, beauty, vertue to,
Long since subverted, when the Ilion wo
The Greeke designe attempted; in which went
My praise and honor. In his government
Had I deserv'd your utmost grace, but now
Sinister Deity makes dishonor woo
(In shew of grace) my ruine.

(XIX, 175-81, p. 293)

'When the Ilion wo | The Greeke designe attempted' is the
more precise and meaningful for its ambiguity. Did 'the

152

Greeke designe' 'attempt' to bring woe to Ilium, did 'the Ilion wo' 'attempt'—that is, 'test'—'the Greeke designe', or did the Greeks unconsciously 'attempt' their own woe at Troy? The uncertainty reflects not only Penelope's bitter feelings about the whole crusade, but the equivocal attitude toward the Trojan war that characterizes the *Odyssey* in general and is especially evident in the narratives of Nestor and Menelaus. As is almost invariably true, the Homeric passage is not ambiguous:

Stranger, all excellence of mine, both of beauty and form, the immortals destroyed on the day when the Argives embarked for Ilion, and my husband, Ulysses, went with them. If he might only come and watch over my life, my fame would be greater and fairer. But now I am in sorrow, so many woes has some god brought upon me. For all the princes who hold sway over the islands—Dulichium and Same and wooded Zacynthus—and those who dwell in lovely Ithaca itself, all these woo me against my will, and lay waste my house.[39]

From this we see how much detail Chapman has eliminated in the translation. In Chapman, Penelope does not mention Ulysses' name, but refers only to 'his government' in the fourth line. This anonymous reference implies that Penelope need not name him, since there is only one 'he' that matters to her. Conversely, by designating the princes of the surrounding islands only by the abstract title 'dishonor', she indicates her contemptuous indifference to their identities. The entire speech is an example of the subtlety with which Chapman has made more explicit the conflict in the *Odyssey* between some of the heroic values of the Trojan war and its own more human and catholic ideals.

A principal function served by these ambiguities is in revealing briefly the innermost character of a speaker through the almost simultaneous communication of several different impressions. This is as much the case in the des-

cription of Penelope's hesitation in welcoming Ulysses as it
was in her remarks just quoted:

> Sometimes she stood cleare
> He was her husband; sometimes the ill weare
> His person had put on transform'd him so
> That yet his stampe would hardly currant go.
>
> (XXIII, 146-9, p. 352)

This play on the various meanings of 'ill weare' is not to be
found in the original:

And now she would look with her eyes full upon his face, and
now again she would fail to know him because of the miserable
clothes he was wearing.[40]

The words refer of course to Ulysses' tatters and to the
adversities he has suffered, but in conjunction with 'currant'
they also suggest the effacing of a coin's superscription
through hard use. This image, furthermore, suggests the
sceptical, shrewd side of Penelope, which has made her wary
of strangers for a long time.

Chapman's ambiguities are also capable of an overt, sarcastic type of irony as in this reference to the wooers' final
and fatal banquet:

> But all were bid to come
> Exceeding early, and be rais'd to heaven
> With all the entertainment could be geven.
>
> (XX, 242-4, p. 312)

This piece of wit is entirely Chapman's. The original
merely says:

For the wooers will not be long absent from the hall but will
return early, for it is a feast-day for all men.[41]

The grim jest at the suitor's passionate epicureanism is in
tune with the sinister humour which darkens the mood of
the *Odyssey* just before the end.

One of the few ambiguities in the translation that has its

origin in Homer occurs in a reference to the weapons by
which the suitors are fated to die:

> In the quiver were
> Arrowes a number, sharpe and sighing gere.[42]

The original adjective, στονόεντες, means both 'full of sighs'
and 'grievous', and suggests both the sound of an arrow
in flight and the effect of its wound.

These passages illustrate the various uses of ambiguity in
Chapman's poem. In each case it creates, without any
laboured play on words, a special tone, a complex attitude,
or an insight into character that could not be achieved with
equal pith and force in any other way.

There is, however, a literary vice akin to ambiguity, to
which Chapman is also devoted, the popular Elizabethan
trick of style which Puttenham calls *antanaclasis*, a rather
pointless juggling with homonyms.[43] Any reader can readily
add to such examples as these:

> For on the marine shore, the people there
> To *Neptune*, that the azure lockes doth weare,
> Beeves that were wholy blacke gave holy flame.
>
> (III, 9-11, p. 31)

> But when aires rosie birth (the Morne) arose.
>
> (XVII, 1, p. 257)

> Besides, a graver thought
> *Jove* graves within you.
>
> (XIX, 19-20, p. 289)

The device is at worst a minor irritation.

Between ambiguity and paradox, as Chapman uses them,
it is hard to draw a strict line. Often the distinction depends
on whether one feels the double meaning of a word or
phrase as more important than the contradictions in meaning
or vice versa. A border-line case is the sardonic description

of one of Penelope's promiscuous maids:

> But she was great
> With great *Eurymachus*, and her loves heat
> In his bed quenched. And this cholericke thing
> Bestow'd this railing language on the King.
>
> (XVIII, 471-4, p. 285)

[But she loved Eurymachus and used to sleep with him. She then rated Odysseus with reviling words.]

(XVIII, 325-6)

The second 'great' is ambiguous in force: She is 'great' with Eurymachus' bastard, and therefore Eurymachus' 'greatness' may be no more impressive than her own. The first 'great' is paradoxical: The hussy 'great' with child is anything but great in any real sense. The passage does a neat job of reducing Eurymachus' swollen reputation to absurdity. The jest is extended further in the juxtaposition of 'loves heat' with both the psychological and physiological meanings of 'cholericke'. This places the girl's love on the same level with her bad humour.

In the following passage a stricter paradox revives a dead figure of speech:

> Blew-ey'd *Minerva* sent
> A fore-right gale, tumultuous, vehement,
> Along the aire, that her waies utmost yeeld
> The ship might make and plough the brackish field.
>
> (XV, 378-81, p. 235)

[Then flashing-eyed Athene sent them a favourable wind, blowing strongly through the sky, that speeding swiftly the ship might complete her course over the salt water of the sea.][44]

By itself 'plough the brackish field' is a piece of stock poetic diction hoary with age, already implicit in Homer's familiar phrase 'the unfruitful sea'. But here the paradox of ploughing a salt field or a sea, where nothing can grow, is recognized. Chapman rehabilitates the cliché by pursuing the impli-

cations of the paradox and making the barren field 'yeeld'
a swift passage to the ship. This is not an idle play on words,
for this image reflects the peculiar attitude of the *Odyssey*
toward seafaring. The oceans are regarded as waste places to
be ventured on only under a compelling need to be some-
where else. Thus an image which sees a ship as a plough and
the ocean as a field is distinctly appropriate.

The paradox is not, however, confined to such elaborate
examples as this. It is a feature of Chapman's style that gives
vitality to what would otherwise be rather commonplace
passages, as in Ulysses' reference to a former act of liberality
in entertaining one of the armies bound for Troy:

> [I] allow'd them meale and heat-exciting wine,
> And oxen for their slaughter, to confine
> In my free hand the utmost of their need.
>
> (XIX, 279-81, p. 295)

[So I took him [the leader] to the house and entertained him
and welcomed him kindly to use the rich store that was in the
house, and to the rest of his comrades who accompanied him I
gave out of the public store barley meal and flaming wine and
sacrificial bulls, that their hearts might be satisfied.][45]

The apparent conflict between 'confine' on one hand and
'free' and 'utmost need' on the other gives a lively sense of
the king's inexhaustible bounty. The same device also
serves to invigorate a somewhat flat piece of gnomic wisdom:

> But none can live without the death of sleepe.
>
> (XIX, 802, p. 306)

[It is impossible for men to be forever sleepless.][46]

This line is metaphysical, like many of Chapman's images,
in the sense that it leads the imagination through an apparent
inconsistency to a philosophical reflection. The inner idea
can only be communicated through the conflict of terms in
the image.

A technique related to paradox, which points out an

inconsistency by echoing a key word, is sometimes used for rhetorical emphasis. Penelope employs it to reveal a discrepancy between the wooers' concern for their reputations and their vicious behaviour:

> The fame of men, I see,
> Beares much price in your great suppos'd degree;
> Yet who can prove amongst the people great,
> That of one so esteem'd of them the seat
> Doth so defame and ruine?[47]

The repetition of 'fame' in 'defame' emphasizes the point of the question.

VI

Chapman's skilful use of ambiguity and paradox is indicative of his sensitivity to the connotations of words. There are innumerable instances in the *Odyssey* where a word that is used suggestively animates a whole passage, a word whose metaphorical roots would be moribund in the language of lesser writers. As Chapman uses them these words seem to grow filaments of association in the context. They can bear a great burden of meaning for this reason. One often feels that there is an indispensable rightness about them, as in Antinous' rebuke to the servants who are weeping as they think of their lost master and of the approaching marriage of Penelope:

> Why weepe ye, wretches, and the widdowes eyes
> Tempt with renew'd thought, that would otherwise
> Depose her sorrowes, since her lord is dead,
> And teares are idle?
>
> (XXI, 123-6, p. 323)

[Wretched pair, why do you weep and trouble the soul in the breast of this lady, whose heart as it is lies low in pain, seeing that she has lost her dear husband?][48]

'Depose' fuses the whole speech brilliantly. In that one

158

word Antinous unwittingly reveals the ignoble nature of his ambition and unconsciously acknowledges the propriety of Penelope's reluctance to wed again. Her grief is also related thereby to an order of values which Antinous and the other suitors are trying to 'depose'.

Key words like this have the power to convey a sense of seeing things anew, as does the apparently commonplace adjective in

> those pure clouds that (above
> The *breathing* aire) in bright Olympus move.[49]

This bit of descriptive detail occurs just after Ulysses' prayer to Zeus for relief from the misery which the suitors are inflicting upon him. 'Breathing' lifts the phrase above the level of simple statement by suggesting an implied contrast between the precarious and limited state of human life and the eternal serenity of Olympus, where there is no air to breathe nor any need of it. Here, perhaps, is an example of 'the direct sensuous apprehension of thought' which T. S. Eliot finds typical of Chapman.[50] The same sort of highly suggestive language gives a mystical dimension to Chapman's account of the last stage in the slaughter of the suitors:

> So (in their flight) *Ulysses* with his heire
> Did stoope and cuffe the wooers, that the aire
> Broke in vaste sighes, whose heads they shot and cleft;
> The pavement boyling with the soules they reft.
>
> (XXII, 401-4, p. 341)

[Even so did they set upon the wooers and smite them right and left through the hall. And from them rose a hideous groaning as their heads were struck, and all the floor swam with blood.][51]

Chapman achieves an effect of peculiar terror by substituting 'soules' for 'blood' in the last line. The breath of the harried suitors, breaking 'in vaste sighes', justifies the union of abstract and concrete in

> The pavement boyling with the soules they reft,

if one remembers that in Greek ψυχή, as in Latin *anima*, 'breath' and 'spirit' are represented by the same word and were felt among certain ancient writers to be indistinguishable.

There are passages in Chapman's poem where deep feeling is compressed into a small compass in a way that almost defies analysis. In them we find an irreducible simplicity and perfect tone. Here should be mentioned Penelope's complaint to a servant who has waked her in great excitement about the slaughter of the suitors:

> Why hast thou wak't me to more teares, when *Mone* [Moan]
> Hath turn'd my minde with teares into her owne?
> (XXIII, 23-4, p. 347)

[Why dost thou mock me, who have a heart full of sorrow, to tell me this wild tale, and rouse me from sweet slumber?][52]

The alliteration of 'm's in 'me', 'more', 'Mone' and 'my minde' dramatizes Penelope's identification of herself with sorrow. Later in the same Book she explains poignantly her hesitation in welcoming the stranger who has slain her suitors and claims to be her husband:

> For what is all to me
> If not my husband?
> (XXIII, 263-4, p. 354)

This is Chapman's interpolation, and there is no single phrase in his entire translation that summarizes better the essence of Penelope's character. A sort of symbolical ellipsis gives us a similar glimpse of intense and highly characteristic feeling in Laertes' remark to the disguised Ulysses who claims to have entertained his son in times past:

> but the gifts you gave
> Were given (alas) to the ungratefull grave.
> (XXIV, 378-9, p. 369)

[In vain did you give those gifts, those countless gifts.][53]

VII

Chapman, like Milton, is unusually aware of the Latin meanings of English words derived from Latin, although, unlike Milton, he does not make a practice of coining English words freely. Often this awareness bestows on his language considerable precision and distinction, and it unquestionably helps to heighten his epic language just as his Latinate syntax does. Peculiarly enough, Chapman's impulse to create his own vocabulary for his *Odyssey* by this means was evidently accompanied by an excessive respect for authority. In the hundreds of Latinate words he uses, I have found next to none with any flavour of distinctiveness about them that could not be traced to the Latin translation in Spondanus. While most of the words he does borrow testify to his discrimination and show anything but a slavish dependence on the 'trot', their great number suggests that he was anything but a bold innovator.

This widespread influence on the language of Chapman's *Odyssey* of the Latin version printed in Spondanus' edition deserves more study than it has received. Schoell, in my opinion, underestimates its importance and overestimates Chapman's reliance on the *Lexicon* of Johannes Scapula when he says: 'On peut affirmer que Chapman n'a, pour ainsi dire, pas traduit un seul vers grec sans vérifier le sens d'un ou de plusieurs mots dans son dictionnaire'.[54] Schoell probably exaggerates here to make a point, for while it is plain that many of Chapman's most important words and phrases can be traced to Scapula, the Latinisms borrowed from Spondanus are at least as numerous and bear an important relation to the style. Wherever one finds a conspicuously Latin word in Chapman's translation the odds are that one will find the same word in Spondanus, although, as the *O.E.D.* will show, at least one sense of the word was usually current in Chapman's time. These Latinisms widen the range of tone, and, as is the case with other successful techniques used in this poem, permit an unusual conciseness and precision of expression. Despite the fact that most were authentic English words in 1600, they are far from colloquial. The Latin sense is often present beside the English sense, and there is for this reason a distinctly bilingual quality about the language of the poem. In conjunction with the high proportion of Anglo-Saxon words used these Latinisms make Chapman's vocabulary extremely flexible. That Chapman would have himself considered an innovator in language is shown by the way he defends his 'beyond sea manner of writing' in some delightful remarks which preface his first published translation from Homer, *Achilles Shield*:

Why, alas, will my young mayster the reader affect nothing common, and yet like nothing extraordinarie? Swaggering is a new worde amongst them, and rounde headed custome gives it priviledge with much imitation, being created as it were by a naturall *Prosopopoeia* without etimologie or derivation; and why may not an elegancie authentically derived, & as I may say of the upper house, bee entertayned as well in their lower consultation with authoritie of Arte as their owne forgeries lickt up by nature? All tongues have inricht themselves from their originall . . . with good neighbourly borrowing, and as with infusion of fresh ayre and nourishment of newe blood in their still growing bodies, & why may not ours? *Chaucer* (by whom we will needes authorise our true english) had more newe wordes for his time than any man needes to devise now. And therefore for currant wits to crie from standing braines, like a broode of Frogs from a ditch, to have the ceaselesse flowing river of our tongue turnde into their Frogpoole, is a song farre from their arrogation of sweetnes, & a sin wold soone bring the plague of barbarisme amongst us.[55]

Thus unless the language is constantly invigorated by foreign words it becomes stagnant like the frog-pool, or it becomes barbarous. The passage itself, in its mixture of

idiomatic and somewhat esoteric words—'Prosopopoeia'
and 'forgeries lickt up by nature' for example—suggests the
range of Chapman's vocabulary.

It is not surprising that in some cases Chapman's borrowings from the Latin are unfortunate, as in Telemachus'
ponderously expressed amazement at the splendour of
Menelaus' palace:

> What gold and amber, silver, ivorie round
> Is wrought about it! Out of doubt the hall
> Of Jupiter Olympius hath of all
> This state the like. How many *infinities*
> Take up to *admiration* all mens sights!
>
> (IV, 90-4, p. 48)

[Mark the gleaming of bronze throughout the echoing halls, of
electrum, silver, and ivory! Such, I suppose, is the court of
Zeus on Olympus, there is such countless wealth; wonder holds
me as I look.][56]

In his last sentence Chapman alters the Latin construction
for the worse, while borrowing from it two words, 'in-
finites' and 'admiration', that are extremely pompous in the
context:

> Iovis nimirum talis est Olympii intus aula,
> Quanta haec *infinita* multa, *admiratio* capit inspicientem.[57]

In another case he takes an awkward periphrastic construction directly from the Latin. This is Theoclymenus'
remark to the suitors:

> Impieties ye commit,
> And every man *affect* with formes unfit.
>
> (XX, 551-2, p. 318)

[You who insult men and contrive wickedness and folly in the
house of godlike Odysseus.][58]

It is patterned on the Latin, 'viros iniuriis *afficientes*',[59] but
'formes unfit' is a weak substitute for 'iniuriis'. It is typical

of the prevailing moral tone of the translation that ὑβρίζοντες should be translated by 'Impieties ye commit'.

With a few exceptions of this sort the borrowings from the Latin are very valuable additions. They often achieve a more graphic and original effect than other possible English equivalents. This is true, for instance, of a passage which describes the dilemma of the Trojans caused by the gift of the wooden horse. One question they debate is whether to 'drag it up a peak and hurl it down from the rocks'—

> Aut de rupe *deicere* protractum in summitatem.[60]

Chapman brings the Latin verb into his version:

> Or, from the battlements (drawne higher yet)
> *Deject* it headlong.
>
> (VIII, 684-5, p. 123)

Such a word, because it is unusual, contributes a certain distinction to the passage.

Chapman's awareness of their Latin meanings gives these words the same sort of precision that we have found in his alertness to connotations of language. The precise Latin meaning is carried over into English, and we get that pleasure from recognizing the exact sense of the word that we get from Milton's 'wondrous Art pontifical' or from a Shakespearean neologism like 'knot *intrinsicate*'. Such words stimulate the imagination and make one read creatively. This is the case where Ulysses is shown fidgeting through the final ceremonies prior to his departure for home from Phaeacia:

> Yet through this choice
> Of cheere and musicke, had Ulysses still
> An eye directed to the easterne hill,
> To see him rising that *illustrates* all.
>
> (XIII, 48-51, p. 196)

> [At Ulysses
> Multum ad Solem caput vertebat omnia *illustrantem*.][61]

164

One of Chapman's favourite Latinisms, which we have encountered in various places, is 'dissolve', which is generally employed in some radical Latin sense archaic in English, as in this description of the judicious Arete:

> . . . for all affaires
> Wrapt in contention she *dissolves* to' men.
>
> (VII, 98-9, p. 100)

[Quibus bene vult, etiam viris lites *solvit*.][62]

It is likely to occur wherever the Latin uses 'solvo'. Chapman uses it principally in the sense 'to loosen, untie, unbind'. Hence:

> sleepe
> All juncture of her joynts and nerves did steepe
> In his *dissolving* humor.
>
> (IV, 1070-2, p. 68)

and

> quite *dissolv'd*
> Were all her lineaments.
>
> (XVIII, 276-7, p. 281)

Compare Spondanus:

> *solutae* sunt ei compages omnes.[63]

and

> *soluta* sunt autem ei membra omnia.[64]

In the first example from Chapman there is an interesting bilingual redundancy which shows how he uses Latin words to illuminate fundamental English meanings and vice versa. The interplay of 'juncture' and 'joynts' prepares us to accept 'dissolving' in its more literal archaic sense of 'loosening', as well as in the more figurative sense of 'melting'.

Sometimes a Latinism derived from Spondanus will convey two distinct meanings both of which are appropriate. In the description of Ulysses' plight on Calypso's island—

> For he had neither ship *instruct* with oares,
> Nor men to fetch him from those stranger shores—
>
> (IV, 755-6, p. 62)

the participle 'instruct' carries something of the modern English sense of 'guided' as well as the now obsolete sense of 'equipped', which is the Latin sense:

Non enim ei adsunt naves remigio instructae et sociis.[65]

Similarly when Ulysses complains to the suitors of

> Food devor'd
> Idely and rudely, wine *exhaust*, and pour'd
> Through throats prophane,
>
> (XVI, 145-7, p. 246)

'exhaust' carries both the original Latin sense of 'drawn off'—vinum exhaustum[66]—current in Chapman's time, and also the sense of 'used up completely'. A more striking double meaning occurs in Menelaus' contemptuous outburst at the suitors:

> O deed of most abhor'd indecency!
> A sort of *impotents* attempt his bed
> Whose strength of minde hath cities levelled!
>
> (XVII, 152-4, p. 260)

The literal meaning of the Greek is

Verily they wish to lie in the bed of a valiant man, although they themselves are cowards.[67]

Spondanus' translation is faithful:

> O pape, certe iam fortis viri in lecto
> Voluerunt dormire *impotentes* ipsi cum sint.[68]

'Impotents' catches the sarcastic note in Menelaus' speech very nicely. Likewise 'popular' in two rare senses of 'belonging to the public' and 'populous' is used to good effect to describe Ulysses' resentment of the mob that throngs his palace:

> he would not see
> His court made *populare*.
>
> (XX, 401-2, p. 315)

[. . . for this is no public resort, but the house of Odysseus.][69]

Here the Latin is

> quoniam non *popularis* est
> Domus haec, sed Ulyssis. . . .[70]

Many of the personifications in Chapman's *Odyssey* are derived from the text in Spondanus. Their chief function seems to be to give personal, dramatic force to a passage. Polyphemus' curse,

> but if it is his fate to see his friends and to reach his well-built house and his native land, may he arrive late and in evil plight, after losing all his comrades, in a ship that is another's; and may he find sorrow in his house,[71]

is reduced by Chapman to

> And when, at last, the day
> Of his sole-landing shall his dwelling show,
> Let *Detriment* prepare him wrongs enow.
>
> (IX, 725-7, p. 142)

The personification in the last line, developed from the Latin, solemnizes the Cyclops' prayer.[72] Chapman elsewhere uses personification to suggest the abstract, unfeeling aspect of war, when Demodocus sings how the warriors from the wooden horse

> made *Depopulation* tred
> Beneath her feete so high a cities head.
>
> (VIII, 696-7, p. 124)

Chapman has borrowed the Latin word, but altered the construction:

> Cecinit etiam ut urbem *depopulati* sunt filii Graecorum.[73]

There are many more of these Latin borrowings in the poem, but there is no need to add to the present examples, which are typical. There are, surprisingly, no similar borrowings from the Greek. On the whole these Latinisms testify to the discriminating manner in which Chapman has used this source to help make the language of his translation a more flexible and sensitive instrument.

VIII

The *Odyssey*, Chapman's greatest translation, marks the fulfilment of his development as an epic poet. The nature of this development may be defined by reference to two of his earlier translations from Homer. Few readers have had an opportunity to see his first attempt at Homer in pentameter couplets, *Achilles Shield* (1598), which appeared in the same year as his version in fourteeners of *Seaven Bookes of the Iliades of Homer*, for this little book is extremely rare and has never been reprinted. This early version of Homer in the metre which Chapman was to use again, many years later, enables us to see the relative merits of his two versions of the *Iliad* and, more important, to define the development of his epic pentameter verse.

The pentameter couplets of *Achilles Shield* are totally unlike those of the *Odyssey*, for they are closed, with lines strongly end-stopped, and with a high degree of metrical regularity. The rhetoric is far simpler, for there is little syntactical inversion. The sentences tend to be shorter, as well as simpler than those of the *Odyssey*. While this style has certain virtues, it lacks the range which the translation of a whole epic would have required, and it lacks the continuity of movement which syntactical inversion, enjambment, and metrical variations in the verse of the *Odyssey* make possible.

Chapman was probably thinking of these limitations in the pentameter couplet in its early stage of development when he decided on fourteener couplets for the *Iliad* and defended his choice on the grounds that

> this long Poeme askes this length of verse,
> Which I my selfe ingenuously maintaine
> Too long our shorter Authors to reherse.

In these longer lines he experimented, and indeed was

forced to experiment, with ways of gaining continuity, especially by running the lines over, lengthening the sentences, and using metrical substitutions. The experiment was not, on the whole, successful, chiefly because in trying to avoid the inherent monotony of the fourteener's regular seven-foot line, he often fell into the opposite danger, which is formlessness.

These characteristics are sooner demonstrated than described. Let us therefore examine two versions of a scene on the shield of Achilles in the eighteenth Book of the *Iliad* and then compare with them a similar passage from Chapman's *Odyssey*, Book XI. This scene from the *Iliad* presents in emblematic fashion the destruction of the community through war, just as the companion scene depicts the preservation of the community through law. Here is Chapman's version, in *Achilles Shield*, of the outbreak of the war:

When they had found a valley most select,
To couch their ambush (at a rivers brinke
Where all their herds had usuall place to drinke)
There (clad in shining steele) they close did lie,
And set farre off two sentinels to spie,
When all their flocks and crook-hancht heards came neere
Which soone succeeded, and they followed were
By two poore heardsman that on the bagpipes plaid,
Doubtlesse of any ambuscadoes laid:
The sentinels gave word, and in they flew,
Tooke heards and flockes, and both their keepers slew.
The enemie hearing such a strange uprore
About their cattell, being set before
In solemne counsell, instantly tooke horse,
Pursude and at the flood with mutual force,
The conflict joynd. Betwixt them flew Debate,
Disorderd Tumult, and exitial Fate.
Here was one taken with wounds bleeding greene,
And here one pale and yeelding, no wound seene:

Another slaine, drawne by the strengthles heeles
From the red slaughter of the ruthles steeles.
And he that slew him on his shoulders wearing
His bloodie weedes as trophies of his daring.[74]

The realistic narrative of the unsuspecting herdsmen entering
the ambush gives place to a more abstract treatment of the
battle which follows, with its *personae* of Tumult, Debate,
and Fate and its type-figures of warriors—one wounded and
captive, one pale with fear and giving himself up, and a
third being dragged dead along the battlefield, while his
slayer exults in the bloody trophies of his clothes. The
passage, following Homer in these details, moves, accordingly, from immediate and highly particularized action to
a series of vignettes which freeze the action in a number of
typical attitudes. The sculptural effect thus gained is clearly
appropriate to the medium of the shield on which this is all
pictured, and it also harmonized with Homer's universalizing
perspective on these events. Chapman, following Homer,
is depicting not a particular battle, but war. This is seen
most clearly if we compare the highly individualized herdsmen playing their bagpipes as they follow their flocks un-
warily into the ambush with the relatively impersonal
figures of the warriors, caught in the various poses of terror,
exultation, or death. The individuality of the herdsmen
gives the event its pathos; the typicality of the warriors
gives it general truth. While the verse is somewhat wooden,
it is adapted to the prevalently stylized quality of the
passage, which tends to modulate and distance the particular
emotion in the broader vision.

The verse of Chapman's final version in fourteeners is as
irregular as this is regular, but the irregularity makes for less
freedom, rather than more, in expressing a variety of effects.
While the earlier version is clear and forceful, this one has
lost rhetorical control, and having lost it, cannot dis-
criminate the typical from the individual:

When they came where that was to be urg'd
For which they went, within a vale close to a flood, whose
    stream
Usde to give all their cattell drinke, they there enambusht
    them,
And sent two scouts out to descrie when th'enemies herds and
    sheepe
Were setting out. They strait came forth with two that usde to
    keepe
Their passage alwayes; both which pip't and went on merrily,
Nor dream'd of ambuscadoes there. The ambush then let
    flie,
Slue all their white fleec't sheepe and neate, and by them laid
    their guard.
When those in siege before the towne so strange an uprore
    heard,
Behind, amongst their flocks and herds (being then in counsell
    set)
They then start up, tooke horse, and soone their subtle enimie
    met,
Fought with them on the river shore where both gave mutuall
    blowes
With well-pil'd darts. Amongst them all, perverse *Contention*
    rose,
Amongst them *Tumult* was enrag'd, amongst them ruinous *Fate*
Had her red-finger; some they tooke in an unhurt estate,
Some hurt yet living, some quite slaine, and those they tug'd to
    them
By both the feete, strip't off and tooke their weedes, with all
    the streame
Of blood upon them that their steeles had manfully let out.
(XVIII, 473-90)

For all its technical 'freedom', this is far less expressive than
the stricter couplet version. The run-over lines and metrical
variations do not result in strong rhetorical emphasis, but
rather in a rambling, prosy quality. The discrimination of

tone and mood has also been lost in a welter of periphrastic and parenthetical constructions and in an extraordinary profusion of particles, connectives, and auxiliaries. Chapman's fourteeners are characteristically diffuse. It is a form which seems to encourage *Flickwörter*. Compare especially

> When they had found a valley most select,
> To couch their ambush (at a rivers brinke
> Where all their herds had usuall place to drinke)

with

> When they had come where that was to be urg'd
> For which they went, within a vale close to a flood, whose stream
> Usde to give all their cattell drinke;

and

> Here was one taken with wounds bleeding greene,
> And here one pale and yeelding, no wound seene,

with

> some they tooke in an unhurt estate,
> Some hurt yet living.

The later version is both more wordy and more abstract. The appropriate swiftness of movement in

> Betwixt them flew Debate,
> Disorderd Tumult, and exitial Fate

is lost in these halting and clumsy lines:

> Amongst them all, perverse *Contention* rose,
> Amongst them *Tumult* was enrag'd, amongst them ruinous *Fate*
> Had her red-finger.

The false elegance which mars too much of Chapman's *Iliad* seems to be inseparable from the form which he unfortunately chose for it. Despite its limitations, the verse of *Achilles Shield* suggests very strongly that Chapman's experiment in fourteeners was in many ways a backward step in the development of his epic style. While this passage

represents the chief characteristics of his fourteener verse, it
is only fair to remind the reader that it occasionally rises to
greater heights of vigour and eloquence, especially in
passages of violent action or in speeches of vehement
emotion. Such passages, though good in themselves, depart
so widely from the verse norm that they place impossible
demands on the reader's attention and interrupt the flow of
the poem, so the lines I have used seem more representative
of the general effect of the *Iliad*.

Turning now to a similar scene in the *Odyssey*, the Pageant
of the Dead in Book XI, we find the freedom of the verse
which the poet struggled to realize in his fourteeners completely attained, as though he had wedded to the balanced
movement of the *Shield's* pentameter couplet the varied
rhythms which the domineering metre of his *Iliad* forced
him to attempt. The passage I have chosen, like the one we
have been discussing, has a visionary quality about it. If the
first is an anatomy of the experience of war, this is an
anatomy of the experience of death. Here, however, we find
the individual and the typical united in single figures—the
youth, the virgin, the warrior, the old man. This spectacle,
furthermore, is seen through the eyes of Ulysses, and his
reactions of amazement, pity, and horror make the whole
immediate and highly dramatic, especially because, in spite
of the compassion he feels, he must sternly ward off these
creatures from the pit of sacrificial blood, and in spite of the
dread he feels, he cannot flee until Teiresias has revealed his
future course to him.

> When to the powres beneath,
> The sacred nation that survive with Death,
> My prayrs and vowes had done devotions fit,
> I tooke the offrings, and upon the pit
> Bereft their lives. Out gusht the sable blood,
> And round about me fled out of the flood
> The soules of the deceast. There cluster'd then

Youths and their wives, much-suffering aged men,
Soft tender virgins that but new came there
By timelesse death, and greene their sorrowes were.
There men at armes, with armors all embrew'd,
Wounded with lances and with faulchions hew'd
In numbers up and downe the ditch did stalke,
And threw unmeasur'd cries about their walke,
So horrid that a bloodlesse feare surprisde
My daunted spirits. Straight then I advisde
My friends to flay the slaughter'd sacrifice,
Put them in fire, and to the Deities,
Sterne *Pluto* and *Persephone*, apply
Excitefull prayrs. Then drew I from my thigh
My well-edg'd sword, stept in, and firmely stood
Betwixt the prease of shadowes and the blood,
And would not suffer any one to dip
Within our offring his unsolid lip,
Before *Tiresias* that did all controule.[75]

Here the essential character of the original comes through.
Whatever emotions arise from the various details—loathing,
pity, rebelliousness—are all absorbed in one complex and
stable attitude of acceptance. Here death is not *primarily*
pitiable or revolting: more important is the sense of its
reality—it exists and this is a revelation of it in all its forms.
It testifies to Chapman's discrimination that he does not try
to palliate this pagan reality with a Christian gloss.

The situation here presented is extremely complex. Here
is a human witness relating his impressions of fellow creatures
who, though dead, retain enough characteristics of the
living to strike our pity and are yet alien or ghoulish enough
to evoke our horror. Being neither alive nor dead their
state is a paradox. They are human essences, but they drink
raw blood. Chapman renders the basic paradox by translating 'the tribes of the dead' by

The sacred nation that survive with Death.

These are the souls that live with death; when they die, they live on, yet they are the dead. A similar paradox centres on the

> Soft tender virgins that but new came there
> By timelesse death, and greene their sorrowes were.

Eternity and human time clash in this association of a recent event with timelessness, so that one perhaps feels that the virgins so lately arrived have always been here, just as the young lover on Keats's urn has been on the point of kissing his girl for thousands of years. At any rate, they will always be here, and this is what makes their 'greene' sorrows so poignant. For their sorrows will forever be intense, forever green, caught alive in the eternity of death. The mood is much like that of Dis's 'gathering' of Proserpina in *Paradise Lost*. The unresolvable tension between physical and metaphysical realities in such an insight exemplifies the way in which Chapman, by concentrating on a single perfect detail, can evoke a sense of mystery. His characteristic precision of language appears everywhere in the passage. The dead are said to have 'cluster'd', a verb which indicates their dispassionate gregariousness, yet suggests also the clustering of bees or flies drawn by the fresh blood which Ulysses has just poured. It appears also in a brilliant oxymoron where he

> would not suffer any one to dip
> Within our offring his unsolid lip. . . .

The concentration of the passage contrasts markedly with the diffuseness of the *Iliad* and recalls the earlier style of *Achilles Shield*. Its range of tone is utterly beyond the capacity of 'ballad-metre', while its movement is much more flexible and natural than that of the *Shield*. The extraordinary development in Chapman's epic verse is apparent in a comparison of these two scenes:

> Here was one taken with wounds bleeding greene,
> And here one pale and yeelding, no wound seene:

175

Another slaine, drawne by the strengthles heeles
From the red slaughter of the ruthles steeles.
And he that slew him on his shoulders wearing
His bloodie weedes as trophies of his daring.

There cluster'd then
Youths and their wives, much-suffering aged men,
Soft tender virgins that but new came there
By timelesse death, and greene their sorrowes were.
There men at armes, with armors all embrew'd,
Wounded with lances and with faulchions hew'd,
In numbers up and downe the ditch did stalke,
And threw unmeasur'd cries about their walke.

IX

Having finished examining the direct relationships between Chapman's *Odyssey* and Homer's, what conclusions
can we make about the style? In the first place the evidence
abundantly confirms the principal judgments of those critics
quoted early in this chapter about the unevenness of Chapman's performance—of vigour and clarity sometimes
marred by quaintness or diffuseness. In the second place, we
have seen how distinctive a style Chapman forged for his
Odyssey, a style markedly individual in vocabulary, in verse-
form, and in rhetoric. We have seen how, in the main, this
style served him well, chiefly because of its range: in diction
from the vernacular to the Latinate; in verse from the closed
to the wide-open couplet; in rhetoric from the most colloquial to the most inverted structures. In all these respects
we found his attitude toward Homer's style independent,
with a corresponding determination to exploit all means
appropriate to English poetry in rendering his great original.
Originality necessarily runs the risk of eccentricity, and in
Chapman's case this risk was aggravated by a too independent attitude toward the poetic achievements of his greatest

contemporaries, from whom he might have learned much, especially Spenser, Jonson, and Shakespeare. Finally, in its style as in its interpretation of Homer, Chapman's *Odyssey* is difficult and presents a real challenge to readers. Some of the difficulty we have seen is simple obscurity, but much of it arises from Chapman's depth, from an essentially clear and concise expression of complex ideas, feelings, and situations.

The combination of penetration with conciseness was the goal Chapman pursued from the beginning of his career, and he himself was entirely aware that many readers would find his style obscure. In the preface 'To the Understander' which accompanied an early instalment of the *Iliad* in 1598 Chapman defends his difficult style and varied vocabulary in much the same terms which he used in prefaces to his first published work, *The Shadow of Night* (1594), and to his second, *Ovids Banquet of Sence* (1595). In this preface Chapman tells his 'understander' that he is writing for a minority of wise souls who can penetrate the mysteries of his Homer:

You are not every bodie: to you (as to one of my very few friends) I may be bold to utter my minde; nor is it more empaire to an honest and absolute mans sufficiencie to have few friendes then to an Homericall Poeme to have few commenders, for neyther doe common dispositions keepe fitte or plausible consort with judiciall and simple honestie, nor are idle capacities comprehensible of an elaborate Poeme.[76]

He goes on to demand the same attention from readers for his translation that he thinks they bestow so willingly on foreign literatures:

. . . the truth is, my desire & strange disposition in all thinges I write is to set downe uncommon and most profitable coherents for the time, yet further removed from abhorde affectation then from the most popular and cold disgestion. And I ever imagine that as Italian & French Poems to our studious linguistes win much of their discountryed affection, as well because the understanding of forreigne tongues is sweete to their apprehension as that matter & invention is pleasing, so my farre fetcht and, as is were, beyond sea manner of writing, if they would take as much paines for their poore countrimen as for a proud stranger when they once understand it, should be much more gracious to their choice conceiptes then a discourse that fals naked before them, and hath nothing but what mixeth itself with ordinarie table talke.[77]

The familiar plea of Renaissance poets of every country in defence of the vernacular acquires unusual force here, as Chapman argues with a touch of sarcasm that his translation should appeal to the 'discountryed affection' of English intellectual snobs because its language is as strange as that of any of the Italian or French poems that they love. The main point, however, is the relation which Chapman repeatedly stresses in such utterances between difficulty and profundity. In line with the assertion that he shuns not only the chaotic and superficial ('the most popular and cold disgestion') but the pedantic or wilfully obscure ('abhorde affectation') as well, he proceeds to deny the imputation that his language is inkhorn:

For my varietie of new wordes, I have none Inckepot I am sure you know, but such as I give pasport with such authoritie, so significant and not ill sounding, that if my countrey language were an usurer, or a man of this age speaking it, hee would thanke mee for enriching him.[78]

There are, as we have seen, almost no 'inckepot' words in his *Odyssey*. Even its frequent Latinisms did not, for the most part, originate with Chapman, although their radical Latin meanings are now in most cases archaic or obsolete. What he meant by his 'farre fetcht and beyond sea manner of writing', or rather, what his *Odyssey* suggests that he meant, may be in part such Latinisms and in part the famous —or notorious—multiple epithets. The phrase applies more generally, however, to the complex stylistic texture in all his poems. In the 'Justification of Andromeda Liberata', as we have seen, he defends difficulty of a certain sort as a time-honoured means of concealing 'Learning . . . from the base and prophane *Vulgare*'.[79] This motive also appears in his defence of allegory in the *Odyssey*. Here, however, he appears to be talking of a much more general aspect of his poetry which is probably best defined in the letter to Matthew Royden which accompanies *Ovids Banquet of Sence*:

That *Enargia*, or cleerenes of representation, required in absolute Poems is not the perspicuous delivery of a lowe invention; but high and harty invention exprest in most significant and un-affected phrase. . . .[80]

In other words Chapman is insisting that in the finest poetry 'cleereness'—radiance, perhaps, as well as 'clarity'—is not the product of facility but profundity. In this sense Chapman's *Odyssey*, at its best, is both difficult and 'clear'. It communicates profound experiences with precision and intensity. But the poet himself is often his own best critic, and there is no need to paraphrase what he himself presents so succinctly:

Obscuritie in affection of words, & indigested conceits, is pedanticall and childish; but where it shroudeth it selfe in the hart of his subject, utterd with fitnes of figure, and expressive Epithetes; with that darknes will I still labour to be shaddowed: rich Minerals are digd out of the bowels of the earth, not found in the superficies and dust of it. . . .[81]

The manner of the *Odyssey* is affected only when the language becomes needlessly difficult or profuse. When this happens one feels that such momentary obscurities and pedantries are lapses from that profound *Enargia* which 'shroudeth it selfe in the hart of his subject'.

In the light of the characteristic virtues of Chapman's *Odyssey*, the faults, which I perhaps have belaboured, appear in their proper perspective. What Smith says about obscurity in Chapman is equally true of the turgid or verbose or confused passages which occur from time to time; because they are bodies 'foreign to the substance of the poem' they are not fatal defects, but blemishes that do not spoil its fundamental organic beauty. Of the good passages we have considered, on the other hand, it can be fairly said that they not only illuminate the characters, feelings, or events with which they are immediately concerned, but that they extend beyond the local to reveal some facet of the great themes which lie at the heart of the *Odyssey*.

The literal translations from Homer which have accompanied the passages from Chapman have had, it is hoped, a cumulative effect in defining the technique of the English poem. With few exceptions the various devices of imagery and wit which have been commented upon have originated with Chapman. This fact does not, of course, impugn the fidelity of his version. The utmost fidelity to the literal meaning of the original poem can never reproduce its spirit, since that literal meaning is only a small portion of the total meaning it contains. What the good translation can and must do is to create in the words and devices proper to its own language and literature a poem that represents the ideas, the values, and the emotions of the original, a poem which approximates, in its own way, the total experience of the original. A translation is therefore, in a very important sense, an exegesis of its original, since it must constantly interpret and evaluate the complex of events and speeches and attitudes which make up the other poem. Chapman's translation, with its searching and organic presentation of the meaning of the *Odyssey*, is an outstanding interpretation.

NOTES TO CHAPTER IV

1. *The Works of Charles and Mary Lamb*, ed. E. V. Lucas (London, Methuen, 1903–5), 4, 83 n.
2. *On Translating Homer* (London, 1861), pp. 24, 22.

THE STYLE

3. *George Chapman: a Critical Essay* (London, 1875), p. 2.

4. *Ibid.* p. 3.

5. 'George Chapman', *Scrutiny*, 3 (1935), 345.

6. *Ibid.* p. 345.

7. 'The Metaphysical Poets', *Selected Essays, 1917–1932* (New York, Harcourt Brace, 1932), p. 246.

8. *A History of English Prosody from the Twelfth Century to the Present Day* (London, Macmillan, 1906–10), 2, 161.

9. F. T. Prince, *The Italian Element in Milton's Verse* (Oxford, Clarendon Press, 1954), p. 122.

10.
ὦ μοι, τέκνον ἐμόν, περὶ πάντων κάμμορε φωτῶν,
οὔ τί σε Περσεφόνεια, Διὸς θυγάτηρ, ἀπαφίσκει,
ἀλλ᾽ αὕτη δίκη ἐστὶ βροτῶν, ὅτε τίς κε θάνῃσιν·
οὐ γὰρ ἔτι σάρκας τε καὶ ὀστέα ἶνες ἔχουσιν,
ἀλλὰ τὰ μέν τε πυρὸς κρατερὸν μένος αἰθομένοιο
δαμνᾷ, ἐπεί κε πρῶτα λίπῃ λεύκ᾽ ὀστέα θυμός,
ψυχὴ δ᾽ ἠΰτ᾽ ὄνειρος ἀποπταμένη πεπότηται. (XI, 216-22)

11. (Cambridge, Mass., Harvard University Press, 1944), pp. 130 ff., 224 ff.

12. *Paideia: the Ideals of Greek Culture*, tr. Gilbert Highet (New York, Oxford University Press, 1945), 1, 62 ff., 68 ff.

13. *History of English Prosody*, 2, 120.

14. *Ibid.* p. 121.

15.
Ζεὺς τό γ᾽ ἀλεξήσειε καὶ ἀθάνατοι θεοὶ ἄλλοι,
ὡς ὑμεῖς παρ᾽ ἐμεῖο θοὴν ἐπὶ νῆα κίοιτε
ὥς τέ τευ ἢ παρὰ πάμπαν ἀνείμονος ἠὲ πενιχροῦ,
ᾧ οὔ τι χλαῖναι καὶ ῥήγεα πόλλ᾽ ἐνὶ οἴκῳ,
οὔτ᾽ αὐτῷ μαλακῶς οὔτε ξείνοισιν ἐνεύδειν. (III, 346-50)

16.
λίην γὰρ ἀεικελίως ἐδαμάσθην
κύμασιν ἐν πολλοῖς, ἐπεὶ οὐ κομιδὴ κατὰ νῆα
ἦεν ἐπηετανός· τῷ μοι φίλα γυῖα λέλυνται. (VIII, 231-3)

17.
τοῦ γάρ τε ξεῖνος μιμνήσκεται ἤματα πάντα
ἀνδρὸς ξεινοδόκου, ὅς κεν φιλότητα παράσχῃ. (XV, 54-5)

18.
αὐτὰρ Ὀδυσσεὺς
ἷζεν ἐπ᾽ ἐσχαρόφιν, ποτὶ δὲ σκότον ἐτράπετ᾽ αἶψα·
αὐτίκα γὰρ κατὰ θυμὸν ὀίσατο, μή ἑ λαβοῦσα
οὐλὴν ἀμφράσσαιτο καὶ ἀμφαδὰ ἔργα γένοιτο. (XIX, 388-91)

19. *Notes and Lectures upon Shakespeare and Some of the Old Poets and Dramatists with Other Literary Remains of S. T. Coleridge* (London, 1849), 2, 231.

20. Ἐξαπίνης δ' Ὀδυσῆα ἴδον κύνες ὑλακόμωροι.
οἱ μὲν κεκλήγοντες ἐπέδραμον. . . .   (XIV, 29-30)

21. V. Scapula, 'Index'.

22. V. Liddell & Scott, p. 1600.

23. τὴν δ' ἄρα Φοίνικες πολυπαίπαλοι ἠπερόπευον.   (XV, 419)

24. Scapula, παλεύω, column 1238. Cf. Liddell & Scott, p. 1111.

25. *Odysses*, VIII, 632-5, p. 122. Italics mine. Cf. *Odyssey*, VIII, 471-2:
κῆρυξ δ' ἐγγύθεν ἦλθεν ἄγων ἐρίηρον ἀοιδόν,
Δημόδοκον λαοῖσι τετιμένον.

Then the herald approached, leading the good minstrel, Demodocus,
held in honour by the people.

Chapman's first hyphenated phrase translates the word ἐρίηρον. In his
note he modifies Scapula's definition on p. 204, which is 'sodales quorum
nobis apta est societas' into 'cuius hominibus digna est societas'. Also he
apparently associates the epithet with an unrelated word, ἐρίζω, 'to strive'.

26. *Odysses*, XX, 87-9, p. 309. Cf. *Odyssey*, XX, 56-7:
εὖτε τὸν ὕπνος ἔμαρπτε, λύων μελεδήματα θυμοῦ,
λυσιμελής, ἄλοχος δ' ἄρ' ἐπέγρετο κεδνὰ ἰδυῖα.

Now while sleep seized him, loosening the cares of his heart, sleep
that loosens the limbs of men, his true-hearted wife awoke.

27.   ἤ σέ γε μουνωθέντα παρ' οἴεσιν ἢ παρὰ βουσὶν
ἄνδρες δυσμενέες νηυσὶν λάβον ἠδ' ἐπίρασσαν
τοῦδ' ἀνδρὸς πρὸς δώμαθ'.   (XV, 386-8)

28.   οἱ δ' ἐπὶ χέρσου
Τηλεμάχου ἔταροι λύον ἱστία, κὰδ δ' ἕλον ἱστὸν
καρπαλίμως, τὴν δ' εἰς ὅρμον προέρεσσαν ἐρετμοῖς.
ἐκ δ' εὐνὰς ἔβαλον, κατὰ δὲ πρυμνῆσι' ἔδησαν·
ἐκ δὲ καὶ αὐτοὶ βαῖνον ἐπὶ ῥηγμῖνι θαλάσσης,
δεῖπνόν τ' ἐντύνοντο κερῶντό τε αἴθοπα οἶνον.   (XV, 495-500)

29. *Mimesis: the Representation of Reality in Western Literature*, tr.
Willard Trask (Princeton, Princeton University Press, 1953), pp. 6-7.

30. Ὣς εἰπὼν ξεῖνον ταλαπείριον ἦγεν ἐς οἶκον.
αὐτὰρ ἐπεί ῥ' ἵκοντο δόμους εὖ ναιετάοντας,
χλαίνας μὲν κατέθεντο κατὰ κλισμούς τε θρόνους τε,
ἐς δ' ἀσαμίνθους βάντες ἐϋξέστας λούσαντο.
τοὺς δ' ἐπεὶ οὖν δμωαὶ λοῦσαν καὶ χρῖσαν ἐλαίῳ,
ἀμφὶ δ' ἄρα χλαίνας οὔλας βάλον ἠδὲ χιτῶνας,
ἔκ ῥ' ἀσαμίνθων βάντες ἐπὶ κλισμοῖσι καθῖζον. (XVII, 84-90)

31. Εὐρύμαχ', εἰ γὰρ νῶϊν ἔρις ἔργοιο γένοιτο
ὥρῃ ἐν εἰαρινῇ, ὅτε τ' ἤματα μακρὰ πέλονται,
ἐν ποίῃ, δρέπανον μὲν ἐγὼν εὐκαμπὲς ἔχοιμι,

καὶ δὲ σὺ τοῖον ἔχοις, ἵνα πειρησαίμεθα ἔργου
νήστιες ἄχρι μάλα κνέφαος, ποίη δὲ παρείη.   (XVIII, 366-70)

32. *Odysses*, V, 129-31, p. 74. In this and the passages immediately
following I have italicized Chapman's changes. Cf. *Odyssey*, V, 99-101:

Ζεὺς ἐμέ γ᾽ ἠνώγει δεῦρ᾽ ἐλθέμεν οὐκ ἐθέλοντα·
τίς δ᾽ ἂν ἑκὼν τοσσόνδε διαδράμοι ἁλμυρὸν ὕδωρ
ἄσπετον;

33.   Ὤ μοι ἐγὼ δειλός, τί νύ μοι μήκιστα γένηται;
δείδω μὴ δὴ πάντα θεὰ νημερτέα εἶπεν,
ἥ μ᾽ ἔφατ᾽ ἐν πόντῳ, πρὶν πατρίδα γαῖαν ἱκέσθαι,
ἄλγε᾽ ἀναπλήσειν· τὰ δὲ δὴ νῦν πάντα τελεῖται,
οἵοισιν νεφέεσσι περιστέφει οὐρανὸν εὐρὺν
Ζεύς, ἐτάραξε δὲ πόντον, ἐπισπέρχουσι δ᾽ ἄελλαι
παντοίων ἀνέμων· νῦν μοι σῶς αἰπὺς ὄλεθρος.   (V, 299-305)

34.   τρισμάκαρες Δαναοὶ καὶ τετράκις οἳ τότ᾽ ὄλοντο
Τροίῃ ἐν εὐρείῃ, χάριν Ἀτρεΐδῃσι φέροντες.
ὡς δὴ ἐγώ γ᾽ ὄφελον θανέειν καὶ πότμον ἐπισπεῖν
ἤματι τῷ ὅτε μοι πλεῖστοι χαλκήρεα δοῦρα
Τρῶες ἐπέρριψαν περὶ Πηλεΐωνι θανόντι.   (V, 306-10)

35.   εἰ δ᾽ αὖ τις ῥαίῃσι θεῶν ἐνὶ οἴνοπι πόντῳ,
τλήσομαι ἐν στήθεσσιν ἔχων ταλαπενθέα θυμόν.   (V, 221-2)

36.   ὀψὲ δὲ δή ῥ᾽ ἀνέδυ, στόματος δ᾽ ἐξέπτυσεν ἅλμην
πικρήν, ἥ οἱ πολλὴ ἀπὸ κρατὸς κελάρυζεν.
ἀλλ᾽ οὐδ᾽ ὣς σχεδίης ἐπελήθετο, τειρόμενός περ,
ἀλλὰ μεθορμηθεὶς ἐνὶ κύμασιν ἐλλάβετ᾽ αὐτῆς,
ἐν μέσσῃ δὲ καθῖζε τέλος θανάτου ἀλεείνων.   (V, 322-6)

37.   ὄφρ᾽ ἂν μέν κεν δούρατ᾽ ἐν ἁρμονίῃσιν ἀρήρῃ,
τόφρ᾽ αὐτοῦ μενέω καὶ τλήσομαι ἄλγεα πάσχων·
αὐτὰρ ἐπὴν δή μοι σχεδίην διὰ κῦμα τινάξῃ,
νήξομ᾽, ἐπεὶ οὐ μέν τι πάρα προνοῆσαι ἄμεινον.   (V, 361-4)

38.   Οὕτω νῦν κακὰ πολλὰ παθὼν ἀλόω κατὰ πόντον,
εἰς ὅ κεν ἀνθρώποισι διοτρεφέεσσι μιγήῃς·
ἀλλ᾽ οὐδ᾽ ὣς σε ἔολπα ὀνόσσεσθαι κακότητος.   (V, 377-9)

39.   ξεῖν᾽, ἦ τοι μὲν ἐμὴν ἀρετὴν εἶδός τε δέμας τε
ὤλεσαν ἀθάνατοι, ὅτε Ἴλιον εἰσανέβαινον
Ἀργεῖοι, μετὰ τοῖσι δ᾽ ἐμὸς πόσις ἦεν Ὀδυσσεύς.
εἰ κεῖνός γ᾽ ἐλθὼν τὸν ἐμὸν βίον ἀμφιπολεύοι,
μεῖζόν κε κλέος εἴη ἐμὸν καὶ κάλλιον οὕτω.
νῦν δ᾽ ἄχομαι· τόσα γάρ μοι ἐπέσσευεν κακὰ δαίμων.
ὅσσοι γὰρ νήσοισιν ἐπικρατέουσιν ἄριστοι,
Δουλιχίῳ τε Σάμῃ τε καὶ ὑλήεντι Ζακύνθῳ,
οἵ τ᾽ αὐτὴν Ἰθάκην εὐδείελον ἀμφινέμονται,
οἵ μ᾽ ἀεκαζομένην μνῶνται, τρύχουσι δὲ οἶκον.   (XIX, 124-33)

40. ὄψει δ' ἄλλοτε μέν μιν ἐνωπαδίως ἐσίδεσκεν,
     ἄλλοτε δ' ἀγνώσασκε κακὰ χροΐ εἵματ' ἔχοντα. (XXIII, 94-5)

41. οὐ γὰρ δὴν μνηστῆρες ἀπέσσονται μεγάροιο,
     ἀλλὰ μάλ' ἦρι νέονται, ἐπεὶ καὶ πᾶσιν ἑορτή. (XX, 155-6)

42. Odysses, XXI, 14-15, p. 320. Cf. Odyssey, XXI, 12:
     πολλοὶ δ' ἔνεσαν στονόεντες ὀϊστοί. . . .
     And many arrows were in it, full of sighs.

43. George Puttenham, The Arte of English Poesie, ed. Willcock and
Walker (Cambridge, Cambridge University Press, 1936), p. 207. See
also Veré L. Rubel, Poetic Diction in the English Renaissance (New York,
MLA and London, Oxford University Press, 1941), pp. 206, 277.

44. τοῖσιν δ' ἵκμενον οὖρον ἵει γλαυκῶπις Ἀθήνη,
     λάβρον ἐπαιγίζοντα δι' αἰθέρος, ὄφρα τάχιστα
     νηῦς ἀνύσειε θέουσα θαλάσσης ἁλμυρὸν ὕδωρ. (XV, 292-4)

45. τὸν μὲν ἐγὼ πρὸς δώματ' ἄγων εὖ ἐξείνισσα,
     ἐνδυκέως φιλέων, πολλῶν κατὰ οἶκον ἐόντων·
     καί οἱ τοῖς ἄλλοις ἑτάροις, οἳ ἅμ' αὐτῷ ἕποντο,
     δημόθεν ἄλφιτα δῶκα καὶ αἴθοπα οἶνον ἀγείρας
     καὶ βοῦς ἱρεύσασθαι, ἵνα πλησαίατο θυμόν. (XIX, 194-8)

46. ἀλλ' οὐ γάρ πως ἔστιν ἀΰπνους ἔμμεναι αἰὲν
     ἀνθρώπους. . . . (XIX, 591-2)

47. Odysses, XXI, 439-43, p. 329. Cf. Odyssey, XXI, 331-3:
     οὔ πως ἔστιν ἐϋκλείας κατὰ δῆμον
     ἔμμεναι οἳ δὴ οἶκον ἀτιμάζοντες ἔδουσιν
     ἀνδρὸς ἀριστῆος.

Men who dishonour and consume the house of a prince cannot have
a good name throughout the land.

48. ἆ δειλώ, τί νυ δάκρυ κατείβετον ἠδὲ γυναικὶ
     θυμὸν ἐνὶ στήθεσσιν ὀρίνετον; ἦ τε καὶ ἄλλως
     κεῖται ἐν ἄλγεσι θυμός, ἐπεὶ φίλον ὤλεσ' ἀκοίτην. (XXI, 86-8)

49. Odysses, XX, 163-4, p. 310. Cf. Odyssey, XX, 103-4:
     ἀπ' αἰγλήεντος Ὀλύμπου
     ὑψόθεν ἐκ νεφέων.
     From gleaming Olympus, from the clouds high above.

50. Selected Essays, p. 246.

51. Cf. Odyssey, XXII, 307-9:
     ὣς ἄρα τοὶ μνηστῆρας ἐπεσσύμενοι κατὰ δῶμα
     τύπτον ἐπιστροφάδην· τῶν δὲ στόνος ὄρνυτ' ἀεικὴς
     κράτων τυπτομένων, δάπεδον δ' ἅπαν αἵματι θῦε.

52. τίπτε με λωβεύεις πολυπενθέα θυμὸν ἔχουσαν
τοῦτα παρὲξ ἐρέουσα καὶ ἐξ ὕπνου μ' ἀνεγείρεις
ἡδέος;   (XXIII, 15-17)

53. δῶρα δ' ἐτώσια ταῦτα χαρίζεο, μυρί' ὀπάζων.   (XXIV, 283)

54. *Études sur l'humanisme continental en Angleterre*, p. 157.

55. *Elizabethan Critical Essays*, ed. G. G. Smith (Oxford, Clarendon Press, 1904), II, 305.

56. Φράζεο . . .
χαλκοῦ τε στεροπὴν κὰδ δώματα ἠχήεντα,
χρυσοῦ τ' ἠλέκτρου τε καὶ ἀργύρου ἠδ' ἐλέφαντος.
Ζηνός που τοιήδε γ' 'Ολυμπίου ἔνδοθεν αὐλή,
ὅσσα τάδ' ἄσπετα πολλά· σέβας μ' ἔχει εἰσορόωντα.   (IV, 71-5)

57. Spondanus, p. 42.

58.   οἳ δῶμα κατ' ἀντιθέου 'Οδυσῆος
ἀνέρας ὑβρίζοντες ἀτάσθαλα μηχανάασθε.   (XX, 369-70)

59. Spondanus, p. 296.

60. *Ibid.* p. 112.

61. *Ibid.* p. 183. Cf. *Odyssey*, XIII, 28-9:
                               αὐτὰρ 'Οδυσσεὺς
πολλὰ πρὸς ἠέλιον κεφαλὴν τρέπε παμφανόωντα.

But Odysseus turned his head continually to the blazing sun.

62. *Ibid.* p. 89. Cf. *Odyssey*, VII, 74:
οἷσίν τ' εὖ φρονέῃσι καὶ ἀνδράσι νείκεα λύει.

She settles the disputes of those she favours, even if they be men.

63. *Ibid.* p. 63, Cf. *Odyssey*, IV, 794:
                        λύθεν δέ οἱ ἅψεα πάντα.

And all her joints relaxed.

64. *Ibid.* p. 263. Cf. *Odyssey*, XVIII, 189:
                        λύθεν δέ οἱ ἅψεα πάντα.

And all her joints relaxed.

65. *Ibid.* p. 55. Cf. *Odyssey*, IV, 559:
οὐ γάρ οἱ πάρα νῆες ἐπήρετμοι καὶ ἑταῖροι.

For he has neither ships with oars, nor companions.

66. *Ibid.* p. 231. Cf. *Odyssey*, XVI, 110-11:
καὶ οἶνον διαφυσσόμενον, καὶ σῖτον ἔδοντας
μάψ αὔτως, ἀτέλεστον, ἀνηνύστῳ ἐπὶ ἔργῳ.

Wine drawn to waste, and food eaten recklessly, without limit, with no end to the business.

67. ὦ πόποι, ἦ μάλα δὴ κρατερόφρονος ἀνδρὸς ἐν εὐνῇ
ἤθελον εὐνηθῆναι, ἀνάλκιδες αὐτοὶ ἐόντες.   (XVII, 124-5)

68. Spondanus, p. 246.

69.   ἐπεὶ οὔ τοι δήμιός ἐστιν
οἶκος ὅδ᾽, ἀλλ᾽ Ὀδυσῆος.   (XX, 264-5)

70. Spondanus, p. 294.

71.   ἀλλ᾽ εἴ οἱ μοῖρ᾽ ἐστὶ φίλους ἰδέειν καὶ ἱκέσθαι
οἶκον ἐϋκτίμενον καὶ ἑὴν ἐς πατρίδα γαῖαν,
ὀψὲ κακῶς ἔλθοι, ὀλέσας ἄπο πάντας ἑταίρους,
νηὸς ἐπ᾽ ἀλλοτρίης, εὕροι δ᾽ ἐν πήματα οἴκῳ.   (IX, 532-5)

72. Spondanus, p. 128: 'inueniat autem detrimentum domi'.

73. Ibid. p. 112. Cf. Odyssey, VIII, 514:

ἤειδεν δ᾽ ὡς ἄστυ διέπραθον υἷες Ἀχαιῶν.

And he sang how the sons of the Achaeans sacked the city.

74. Achilles Shield, p. 8. Cf. Iliad, XVIII, 520-40:

οἱ δ᾽ ὅτε δή ῥ᾽ ἵκανον ὅθι σφίσιν εἶκε λοχῆσαι,
ἐν ποταμῷ, ὅθι τ᾽ ἀρδμὸς ἔην πάντεσσι βοτοῖσιν
ἔνθ᾽ ἄρα τοί γ᾽ ἵζοντ᾽ εἰλυμένοι αἴθοπι χαλκῷ.
τοῖσι δ᾽ ἔπειτ᾽ ἀπάνευθε δύω σκοποὶ ἥατο λαῶν,
δέγμενοι ὁππότε μῆλα ἰδοίατο καὶ ἕλικας βοῦς.
οἱ δὲ τάχα προγένοντο, δύω δ᾽ ἅμ᾽ ἕποντο νομῆες
τερπόμενοι σύριγξι. δόλον δ᾽ οὔ τι προνόησαν.
οἱ μὲν τὰ προϊδόντες ἐπέδραμον, ὦκα δ᾽ ἔπειτα
τάμνοντ᾽ ἀμφὶ βοῶν ἀγέλας καὶ πώεα καλὰ
ἀργεννέων οἰῶν, κτεῖνον δ᾽ ἐπὶ μηλοβοτῆρας.
οἱ δ᾽ ὡς οὖν ἐπύθοντο πολὺν κέλαδον παρὰ βουσὶν
εἰράων προπάροιθε καθήμενοι, αὐτίκ᾽ ἐφ᾽ ἵππων
βάντες ἀερσιπόδων μετεκίαθον, αἶψα δ᾽ ἵκοντο.
στησάμενοι δ᾽ ἐμάχοντο μάχην ποταμοῖο παρ᾽ ὄχθας
βάλλον δ᾽ ἀλλήλους χαλκήρεσιν ἐγχείῃσιν.
ἐν δ᾽ Ἔρις ἐν δὲ Κυδοιμὸς ὁμίλεον, ἐν δ᾽ ὀλοὴ Κήρ,
ἄλλον ζωὸν ἔχουσα νεούτατον, ἄλλον ἄουτον,
ἄλλον τεθνηῶτα κατὰ μόθον ἕλκε ποδοῖιν.
εἶμα δ᾽ ἔχ᾽ ἀμφ᾽ ὤμοισι δαφοινεὸν αἵματι φωτῶν.
ὡμίλευν δ᾽ ὥς τε ζωοὶ βροτοὶ ἠδ᾽ ἐμάχοντο,
νεκρούς τ᾽ ἀλλήλων ἔρυον κατατεθνηῶτας.

But when they came to the place which seemed fit for an ambush, a
river bed where there was a water-hole for all the herds, they sat down
there accoutred in flaming bronze. And there were two scouts set apart
from the armies, waiting to see the sheep and sleek cattle. And these
came presently, and two herdsmen followed, playing on their pipes, and
they knew nothing of the treachery. But those who lay in wait, when
they saw these approaching, rushed forth and speedily cut out the herds
of cattle and fair flocks of white sheep, and slew the herdsmen. But
the besiegers, as they sat in the meeting place, and heard the tumult

among the cattle, mounted behind their high-stepping horses, and set out and quickly came upon them. Then they set the battle in array and fought beside the river banks, and struck one another with bronze-tipped spears. In their midst Strife and Tumult joined the fray, and deadly Fate, grasping one man alive, freshly-wounded, another without a wound, and another she dragged dead through the mêlée by the feet; and the clothing that she wore about her shoulders was red with the blood of men. Just like living men they joined in the battle and fought, and they were dragging away the bodies of each others' dead.

75. *Odysses*, XI, 37-61, p. 161. Cf. *Odyssey*, XI, 34-50:

τοὺς δ' ἐπεὶ εὐχωλῇσι λιτῇσί τε, ἔθνεα νεκρῶν,
ἐλλισάμην, τὰ δὲ μῆλα λαβὼν ἀπεδειροτόμησα
ἐς βόθρον, ῥέε δ' αἷμα κελαινεφές· αἱ δ' ἀγέροντο
ψυχαὶ ὑπὲξ Ἐρέβευς νεκύων κατατεθνηώτων.
νύμφαι τ' ἠΐθεοί τε πολύτλητοί τε γέροντες
παρθενικαί τ' ἀταλαὶ νεοπενθέα θυμὸν ἔχουσαι·
πολλοὶ δ' οὐτάμενοι χαλκήρεσιν ἐγχείῃσιν,
ἄνδρες ἀρηΐφατοι βεβροτωμένα τεύχε' ἔχοντες·
οἳ πολλοὶ περὶ βόθρον ἐφοίτων ἄλλοθεν ἄλλος
θεσπεσίῃ ἰαχῇ· ἐμὲ δὲ χλωρὸν δέος ᾕρει.
δὴ τότ' ἔπειθ' ἑτάροισιν ἐποτρύνας ἐκέλευσα
μῆλα, τὰ δὴ κατέκειτ' ἐσφαγμένα νηλέϊ χαλκῷ,
δείραντας κατακῆαι, ἐπεύξασθαι δὲ θεοῖσιν,
ἰφθίμῳ τ' Ἀΐδῃ καὶ ἐπαινῇ Περσεφονείῃ·
αὐτὸς δὲ ξίφος ὀξὺ ἐρυσσάμενος παρὰ μηροῦ
ἥμην, οὐδ' εἴων νεκύων ἀμενηνὰ κάρηνα
αἵματος ἆσσον ἴμεν, πρὶν Τειρεσίαο πυθέσθαι.

But when with vows and prayers I had made supplication to the tribes of the dead, I took the sheep and cut their throats over the pit, and the dark blood ran forth. Then there gathered out of Erebus the spirits of those that are dead, brides and unwedded youths, toil-worn old men, and tender virgins with hearts yet new to sorrow, and many, too, that had been wounded with bronze-tipped spears, men slain in battle, wearing their blood-stained armour. These came thronging in crowds about the pit from every side with dreadful cries, and pale fear seized me. Then I called my comrades and bade them flay and burn the sheep that lay there slain with the pitiless bronze, and to pray to the gods, to mighty Hades and dread Persephone. And I myself drew my sharp sword from beside my thigh and sat there and would not permit the powerless heads of the dead to approach the blood until I had inquired of Teiresias.

76. *Elizabethan Critical Essays*, ed. G. G. Smith, 2, 304.

77. *Ibid.* pp. 304-5.
78. *Ibid.* p. 305.
79. *Poems*, ed. Bartlett, p. 327.
80. *Ibid.* p. 49.
81. *Ibid.* p. 49.

CHAPTER V

Style as Interpretation: Chapman's 'Odyssey' and Pope's

I BEGAN this book by quoting a classical scholar, who has recently edited the *Odyssey*, on the extraordinary complexity of Homer's Odysseus. Chapman, as I have tried to show, appreciated this complexity and was able to restore, through his allegorical approach and his sensitive style, a large measure of Odysseus' many-faceted character. No translator has matched Homer in subtlety and richness, but Chapman's vision is so bold and comprehensive that it shows the inadequacy of all interpretations made from a more limited point of view.

The adaptability of Odysseus, as we have seen, ultimately transcends such categories as resourcefulness, intelligence, intuitiveness, and the like, to attain a wisdom above all these at the moment when he finally recognizes their limitations in dealing with life's problems. In the second half of the poem this wisdom is dramatized when Odysseus enacts a rôle as remote as any we can imagine from the one he reassumes at the climax of the poem—the rôle of a starving and homeless beggar. This is the ultimate test not only of his adaptability, but also of what we might call his social conscience. In the latter respect his assumption of the beggar's part resembles Lear's sympathetic recognition of the 'poor naked wretches', although in the *Odyssey's* fundamentally comic vision the hero attains, or rediscovers, this saving grace in time to forestall a tragic conclusion.

For several obvious reasons it is necessary for Odysseus to act the beggar's part convincingly, just as the *Odyssey's* broad, humane vision requires that the humble characters

like Eumaeus or Eurycleia should command our belief in
their authenticity. In a translation it is equally important that
the style should adapt itself to these humbler characters.
Odysseus has to convince not only the murderous suitors
and those who have known him most intimately, but he
must convey to us his compassionate intuition of the meaning
of poverty, hunger, humiliation, and homelessness. I shall
conclude this evaluation of Chapman's translation, therefore, by showing how the adaptability of its style can
represent varieties of human experience which Homer's
other leading English translator was unable to cope with.
The comparison may help us to appreciate how time and
circumstances conspired with Chapman's particular genius
to render a poem which, by the nature of its vision, lay
almost inevitably beyond the range of the great Augustan.
Personality and the concrete qualities of phenomena are
essential parts of the *Odyssey's* vision, but Pope, for all his
virtues, was unable to do them justice.

The striking difference between Chapman's *Odyssey* and
Pope's shows how little similarity a common original im-
poses on translations made in periods as different in manner
and outlook as the Elizabethan and Jacobean, on one hand,
and the Augustan, on the other. A comparison of these two
poems should suggest some of the ways in which English
epic changed in the period between them and reveal the
characteristic strengths and weaknesses of each. The su-
periority of Chapman's *Odyssey* to his *Iliad* and that of Pope's
Iliad to his *Odyssey* unfortunately prevent us from making
any final conclusions about their respective merits as translators of Homer.[1] Some of the absurdities in the Augustan
Odyssey which offended nineteenth-century critics who
thought Homer was primitive and simple—and which still
offend us—such as the designation of 'barren heifer' by 'a
steer ungrateful to the bull's embrace'[2] originated with Pope
himself. The majority of them, however, were the work of
Fenton or Broome, and should only be charged to Pope

insofar as his supervisory responsibilities extended to the whole poem.

In general the virtues and limitations of Pope's *Odyssey* will best reveal themselves in terms of such a definition of the Augustan temper as Maynard Mack's:

The subject of Augustan literature is predominantly man in his public aspects—general human nature—the permanent relations of human beings in society. Concerned with such matters, it would have occurred to no Augustan writer to give an account of the growth of a poet's mind, as Wordsworth does in *The Prelude*, since it would never have occurred to him that a poet's mind was a fit object for public contemplation. It is significant that the Augustan works which roughly—very roughly—correspond to *The Prelude* have generic titles like *An Essay on Man* and *The Pleasures of Imagination*. For the same reasons, Augustan literature is never intimate. When it turns to subjects like religion, or any of the great sources of human emotion, it tends to treat them in their public aspects: philosophical, social, moral; it does not record, like Donne's or Herbert's religious poems, the devotional act itself; or like much romantic poetry, the contours of individual feeling.[3]

The primary concern with 'man in his public aspects' is reflected in the Augustan *Odyssey* as well as in the original poetry of the period. We will find the Augustan interest in the generic displayed in Pope's characters as they reveal themselves in speeches and also in his treatment of narrative and descriptive passages. In the earlier *Odyssey*, except for a few passages of general moral observation interpolated by Chapman or developed from Homer, the balance is in favour of the specific, although, as we have seen, general truths emerge not only in these explicit expressions but through the symbolism, allegory, and the less obtrusive undercurrents of metaphor. Chapman's characters, episodes, and settings are both individual and typical. In them 'the contours of individual feeling' *are* recorded, but they transcend the merely personal or local. Ulysses, for example, is so closely identified with Man that the representation of his at times highly individual emotions does not limit his general significance. In a sense his very individuality makes him typical, especially in the earlier phases of his experience when he is racked by conflicting desires and behaves in a manner so inconsistent with reason. The fluctuation of his spirits between arrogance or self-confidence and servility or meekness, especially evident in his dealings with Polyphemus and in his conduct during the final tempest off the coast of Scheria, are as typical of human nature as the heroic self-control which he finally attains. The variety of rôles and disguises which he so cunningly assumes in the course of the poem, changing his appearance, manner, and life history to suit each one, is a further indication of his universal status. This combination of the individual with the typical is evident in most of Chapman's characters, and it is revealed on the very surface of the poem by the distinguishing idioms of their speech, and, in the hero, by noticeable shifts in style. It is revealed also in the varied texture and changing tempo of narrative and description.

The texture of Pope's *Odyssey* is more regular. Its couplets present greater neatness and finish, and its idiom is quite uniform by comparison with Chapman's. Its metaphor is more subdued than Chapman's with its striking moral symbolism and metaphysical wit. Mack defines its essential character in another article in which he discusses Pope's poetry as 'a poetry of statement':

We regard imagery to-day, especially metaphor, as the most essential of the means by which language achieves poetic character. . . . If we are right in this assumption about metaphor, it implies that a poetry of statement will be signalized not by the absence of metaphorical effects but by their use in such a way that they do not disturb a logical surface of statement.[4]

The more prominent elements of Chapman's imagery are,

192

as was noted in Chapter IV, supported and confirmed by ubiquitous undercurrents of metaphor which are completely assimilated into his poem. These, like Pope's images, 'do not disturb the logical surface of statement'. But Chapman's idiom and verse, as well as his philosophical reflections and moral symbols, frequently do disturb it, so that the reader's imagination must amalgamate and absorb their complexities before it can comprehend the statement. That combination of profundity and clarity, which Chapman called *Enargia*, is often incompatible with perspicuity of surface. His 'unconquerable quaintnesses' also disturb it, although when one grows accustomed to them, his *Odyssey* moves almost as fluently as Pope's.

The difference in surfaces is due in large measure to radical differences in the treatment of the pentameter couplet. Chapman constantly weakens the couplet's distinctiveness as a rhetorical unit by enjambment, imperfect rhymes, internal rhymes, and alliterative suites that extend through many lines, so that, as we have seen, his real unit tends to be a verse-paragraph. Pope's couplet normally is closed, his rhymes perfect, but the syntactical and rhetorical variations within the two-line unit are greater than Chapman's. The effect of these differences is clearly illustrated in the two versions of Nestor's remarks to Telemachus on the subject of Agamemnon's murder. The original may be rendered literally as follows:

Indeed thou thyself may guess how this matter would have turned out if the son of Atreus, fair-haired Menelaus, on his return from Troy, had found Aegisthus alive in his halls. Then not even in death would they have piled the mounded earth for him, but the dogs and birds would have torn him as he lay on the plain far from the city, nor would any of the Achaean women have lamented him, for it was a monstrous deed that he plotted. For our part we stayed there in Troy, completing our great task, but he, at ease in a corner of horse-pasturing Argos, sought continually to seduce with speeches Agamemnon's wife.[5]

Chapman's version of this passage is a unit:

> If *Menelaus* in his brothers house
> Had found the idle liver with his spouse,
> (Arriv'd from *Troy*) he had not liv'd, nor dead,
> Had the digg'd heape powrd on his lustfull head,
> But fowles and dogs had torne him in the fields
> Far off of *Argos*; not a dame it yeelds
> Had given him any teare, so foule his fact
> Shewd even to women. Us *Troys* warres had rackt
> To every sinewes sufferance, while he
> In *Argos* uplands liv'd, from those workes free,
> And *Agamemnons* wife with force of word
> Flatterd and softn'd, who, at first, abhord
> A fact so infamous.
>
> (III, 352–64, p. 39)

The first two couplets are about as close to Pope's couplets as Chapman ever gets. The rhyme words are important, they rhyme exactly, and they are monosyllables. Except for the fourth line the metre is regular. Within these couplets, as is normally the case in Pope, each line has its own rhetorical autonomy. Beginning with the fifth line, however, the passage moves into what might be called rhymed blank verse. The stress on 'fields' is diminished by the phrase 'far off of *Argos*', with which it belongs and which has slipped over into the beginning of the next line, while the repetition of 'f's in that phrase helps to lead one swiftly past the pause at the end of the line. From there on line-endings become less and less emphatic as the sense-units begin and end near the middle of each succeeding line. The effect of this development from the controlled couplets into a series of asymmetrical lines, coupled with the vehemence of language, is to suggest the breaking of normal rhythms under stress of great anger. The accentual possibilities of the language are increased, because the key words at the end of each sense-unit, 'teare', 'women', 'sufferance', 'liv'd', 'wife', 'softn'd', and 'infamous', are emphasized as much as the rhyme-words. The alliteration tends to distinguish these rhetorical patterns from the normal metrical patterns: one pattern is imposed on the other, but turned, as it were, ninety degrees. The first of these patterns,

> Us *Troys* warres had rackt
> To every sinewes sufferance,

is distinguished by the alliteration of 'r's and 's's; the second,

> while he
> In *Argos* uplands liv'd,

by 'l's; and the last three sense-units of two pairs of two half-lines, because of their greater homogeneity, by one predominating motif of 'f's and 'r's:

> from those workes free,
> And *Agamemnons* wife with force of word
> Flatterd and softn'd, who, at first, abhord
> A fact so infamous.

Even within these last lines there are distinguishable alliterative systems, although the distinctions are somewhat softened by the extension of the alliteration characteristic of one unit into the next.

Pope's passage, in contrast to this one, makes the couplet the basic sense-unit and confines the alliterative patterns within each unit. When sense coincides with the couplet or with the single line, alliteration is vulnerable to the danger of over-emphasis and hence monotony, so we will find that Pope generally uses it more sparingly than Chapman.

> For had the martial *Menelaus* found
> The ruffian breathing yet on *Argive* ground,
> Nor earth had hid his carcase from the skies,
> Nor *Grecian* virgins shriek'd his obsequies,
> But fowls obscene dismember'd his remains,
> And dogs had torn him on the naked plains.

While us the works of bloody *Mars* employ'd,
The wanton youth inglorious peace enjoy'd;
He, stretch'd at ease in *Argos*' calm recess,
(Whose stately steeds luxurious pastures bless)
With flattery's insinuating art
Sooth'd the frail Queen, and poyson'd all her heart.

(III, 318-29)

Within these couplets a rhetorical unit coincides with each line, and one feels these end-stopped lines and strongly-rhymed couplets as much more distinct elements than Chapman's lines and couplets. Although Pope's alliterative patterns, for example the pre-vocalic 'r's (as in 'ruffian', 'breathing', 'ground', and so on), are not limited to single lines and couplets, they do not modify the normal metrical balance of the lines as much as Chapman's do. For this purpose Pope relies chiefly on subtle rhetorical variations to avoid monotony. A factor which does great service in binding the whole speech and in controlling the separatist tendencies of the couplets is the very strong pattern of internal and final rhyme in 'martial', 'Argive', 'carcase', 'Mars', 'art', and 'heart', a device which also links and emphasizes key words in the speech.

In tone the two speeches are about as different as two speeches could be. The impetuous movement of Chapman's reflects Nestor's vengefulness. One feels that he is labouring under the stress of great anger, just as the verse strains under the impact of emphatic alliteration, cacophony, and such muscular language as 'digg'd heape', 'torne', and 'rackt | To every sinewes sufferance'. In his fierce indignation he seems to identify himself with the fowls and dogs that would have torn the murderer's corpse. In Pope the emotion is distanced, and Nestor seems to see the crime in a wider perspective. His anger is tempered by the reasoned judgment of one too old and civilized to become emotionally embroiled in the situation. Nestor, as transformed by Pope, evaluates the situation: his reflective, intellectual attitude is created principally by the high proportion of adjectives (thirteen to Chapman's six) that assess the elements in the drama—'martial *Menelaus*', 'fowls obscene', 'bloody Mars', 'wanton youth', 'inglorious peace', 'insinuating art', and 'frail Queen'. Instead of identifying himself with the predatory dogs and birds, Pope's Nestor holds these details fastidiously at a distance by calling them 'obscene' and by making them 'dismember' rather than 'tear' the body. Then, too, Chapman's scavengers tear 'him', Aegisthus, while Pope's 'dismember' only his 'remains'.

One feels from Pope's version of the speech that Nestor, the oldest and wisest hero in Homer, is suggesting all the time that, horrible and contemptible as Aegisthus' crime was, this was not the first time that such a *crime passionnel* had been committed. To this reflective quality is added a somewhat impersonal treatment of the situation: not only is Nestor in full control of his feelings, but the actors in the drama are types—'martial *Menelaus*', 'the wanton youth', and 'the frail Queen'. One result of this treatment is that the reader may feel he has met the situation before, and, of course, he has, for the types in this triangle apply equally well to the earlier triangle of Menelaus, Paris, and Helen, and it also suggests the dangerous possibility that the drama will again repeat itself with Ulysses, one of the suitors, and Penelope playing the key rôles.

In its own way each speech is excellent. In terms of the different styles it is as appropriate for Chapman's Nestor to lose his poise temporarily as it is for Pope's to retain his. Chapman's prevailing interest in the particular details of the experience is reflected in the wide rhetorical and metrical variations and in the immediate impact of detail; while Pope's prevailing interest in the generic is reflected in modulated rhetoric, more balanced movement, and in the distancing of detail. Josephine Miles' statement of the main concerns of neo-classical poetry is true, I think, of Pope's *Odyssey*: 'The odd, the excessive, the actively fictive, the fanciful, the far-fetched, the last ramifications are bad for poetry, as they are minute and particular, not grand and general. The values of the universe reside in its large basic central structures, both natural and human; the human, by this value, are natural too, as all are part of a natural and divine order. General human nature, then, the likenesses between men, is important; and general general nature, the likenesses between man and the external world, between objects and feelings, is important too. Poetry, like thought, becomes a matter of generalizing, instancing by normal forms, and similitudinizing.'[6]

II

Some of the main differences between the two poems are most apparent in passages describing commonplace details of daily life and in the speeches of the unheroic characters of the *Odyssey*—swineherds, beggars, and old serving-women. Chapman constantly endeavours to make his style conform to the subject or to the character of the speaker; Pope's style tends to elevate the subject-matter and to ennoble these humbler characters. Homer's own style has a flexibility which makes it equally at home in treating of heroic deeds and magnificent rituals or in presenting the earthiest details of ordinary life. Chapman tries to imitate this flexibility and is often at his very best in handling passages of the latter kind.

Ulysses' transformation into an old and miserable beggar provides a good introduction to the different approaches of Chapman and Pope to passages of this type:

So saying Athene touched him with her wand. She withered the fair flesh on his supple limbs, and destroyed the flaxen hair on his head and covered his whole body with the wrinkles of old age. And she dimmed his two beautiful eyes and dressed him in other clothes—a vile, ragged cloak, foul and tattered garments, begrimed with filthy smoke. And she cast about him the great skin of a swift hind, the hair of which was worn off, and she gave him a staff and a wretched wallet, full of holes, slung by a twisted cord.[7]

The disguise is complete. Since one purpose of it is to enable Ulysses to discover the attitude of the wooers toward poor strangers, who are under the special protection of Jove, he must look miserable and repulsive enough really to test their charity.

In Pope's version the disguised king has little of his original loathesomeness:

> A swift old-age o'er all his members spread;
> A sudden frost was sprinkled on his head;
> Nor longer in the heavy eye-ball shin'd
> The glance divine, forth-beaming from the mind.
> His robe, which spots indelible besmear,
> In rags dishonest flutters with the air:
> A stag's torn hide is lapt atound his reins;
> A rugged staff his trembling hand sustains;
> And at his side a wretched scrip was hung,
> Wide patch'd, and knotted to a twisted thong.
>
> (XIII, 498-507)

'Wrinkles of old age' becomes the abstract 'swift old age'. The head rather attractively 'sprinkled' with 'frost' suggests a type of personified 'Old Age' rather than one particularly dirty old man. The passage tends to dwell on what Ulysses usually is like rather than on his present appearance, hence the interpolated reference to 'The glance divine, forth-beaming from the mind'. The repulsive details of his clothes are omitted in favour of another generalization, 'rags dishonest', while 'spots indelible' is less graphic than 'be-grimed with filthy smoke'. The added detail about his 'trembling hand' supported by 'a *rugged* staff' completes the picture of a typical old man, whose fluttering rags are a sort of badge of office. Each detail is subordinated to the general truth of the picture.

Chapman, on the other hand, makes much of the particularity of the original with its sensuous apprehension of texture and odour:

> She toucht him with her rod, and every lim
> Was hid all over with a wither'd skin:
> His bright eyes blear'd, his brow curles white and thin,
> And all things did an aged man present.
> Then (for his owne weeds) shirt and coat all rent
> Tann'd and all sootied with noisome smoke,
> She put him on, and over all a cloke
> Made of a stags huge hide, of which was worne
> The haire quite off. A scrip, all patcht and torne,
> Hung by a cord, oft broke and knit againe;
> And with a staffe did his old limbes sustaine.

(XIII, 630-40, pp. 208-9)

This has less of the sense of magic and speed found in Pope's version, but the details make Ulysses a filthy beggar and not a sort of impoverished but picturesque type. We see the bleared eyes, the wrinkles, the worn hide, and we smell the smoky reek of his rags, a detail which Pope omits.

The differences in these two descriptions are reflected in the two styles of speech. Just before they enter the palace Eumaeus warns Ulysses of the harsh and arrogant treatment he can expect from the wooers, and the disguised king replies:

Your advice is given to one who understands. But go ahead, and I will wait here, for I am not at all unused to blows and beatings. My heart is staunch, for I have suffered much amid the waves and in the war; let this too be added to what has gone before. But no man can hide a hungry belly, that cursed plague that brings so many evils to men. Because of it the benched ships are made ready, that carry evil to enemies over the unresting sea.[8]

In Homer Odysseus talks as one man who has suffered much

and expects no favours to another of the same background.
In Pope he talks like a distressed prince:

> Just is, oh friend! thy caution, and address
> (Reply'd the Chief) to no unheedful breast;
> The wrongs and injuries of base mankind
> Fresh to my sense, and always in my mind.
> The bravely-patient to no fortune yields:
> On rolling oceans, and in fighting fields,
> Storms have I past, and many a stern debate;
> And now in humbler scene submit to Fate.
> What cannot *Want*? the best she will expose,
> And I am learn'd in all her train of woes;
> She fills with navies, hosts, and loud alarms
> The sea, the land, and shakes the world with arms!
> (XVII, 332-43)

The elaborate rhetorical pattern of inversion, apostrophe,
and double negative in the first couplet proclaims the noble
and cultivated background of the speaker. One might
attempt to justify the elevation of the speech on the grounds
that swineherd and beggar had already confided to each
other their patrician origins. But Eumaeus, after all, was an
infant when he was sold into slavery, and his prime function
in the *Odyssey* is not to prove 'once a prince always a
prince', but to show that the epic values of this poem, in
contrast to those of the *Iliad*, are not the exclusive property
of an aristocratic caste. Anything which emphasizes the
importance of his noble birth obscures this point, but Pope's
treatment of his speeches, as well as of Ulysses', is uniformly
elegant.[9] Here the effect of the diction is to give everything
a reflective, philosophical perspective. 'Blows and beatings'
becomes 'the wrongs and injuries of base mankind'; the
'hungry belly', which Homer is not ashamed to mention,
becomes the female personification, 'Want'. These abstractions are a means of giving a universal scope to the
truisms which Ulysses is enunciating, but since these ideas

201

are so widely implied in the whole poem, it seems unnecessary to present them in this way.

In Chapman the speaker is made a much more humble
person whose sufferings have given him a special earthy
wisdom. He speaks in a way calculated to appeal particularly
to the swineherd as a kindred spirit:

> You speake to one that comprehends (said he);
> Go you before and heere adventure me.
> I have of old bene usde to cuffes and blowes;
> My minde is hardn'd, having borne the throwes
> Of many a soure event in waves and wars,
> Where knockes and buffets are no Forreinars.
> And this same harmefull belly by no meane
> The greatest Abstinent can ever weane.
> *Men suffer much bane by the bellies rage,*
> For whose sake ships in all their equipage
> Are arm'd and set out to th'untamed seas,
> Their bulkes full fraught with ils to enemies.
> (XVII, 374-85, p. 265)

The speaker here is not expressing philosophical generalities
but certain primitive facts of life which he is peculiarly well
qualified to understand. This version of the speech, much
closer in spirit to Homer's, is far better calculated than Pope's
to explain Ulysses' intrepid persistence in begging from the
wooers.

As a general practice Chapman follows Homer's sense a
good deal more closely than Pope does, and this is partly
responsible for the greater 'realism' of his translation. The
humbler people in his poem are characterized by their
language in a way that Pope's are not. In the twentieth
Book there is a poor old woman who has been forced
interminably to grind meal day and night for the luxurious
suitors. Her prayer for divine vengeance on her oppressors
coincides with that of her disguised master, and may be
translated as follows:

202

Father Jove, lord of gods and men, truly it is thou who hast thundered from the starry sky, yet nowhere is there a cloud: surely this is a sign thou makest to some man. Fulfil now, even for my wretched self, the word I now speak. May the wooers this day, for the last and latest time, hold their glad feast in the halls of Odysseus. May those who have loosened my knees with the painful labour of grinding meal now eat their last.[10]

Pope turns this into:

> Father of Gods and men! whose thunders rowl
> O'er the *Cerulean* Vault, and shake the Pole;
> Whoe'er from heav'n has gain'd this rare Ostent,
> (Of granted vows a certain signal sent)
> In this blest moment of accepted pray'r
> Piteous, regard a wretch consum'd with care!
> Instant, O *Jove!* confound the Suitor train,
> For whom o'er-toil'd I grind the golden grain:
> Far from this dome the lewd devourers cast,
> And be this festival decreed their last!
>
> (XX, 141-50)

While we can at least relate the elegance of Pope's version of Ulysses' speech just examined to the fact that his noble birth is known to Eumaeus, there is no contextual justification for the high-toned quality of this. What would an old peasant-woman know of 'Cerulean Vaults' and where would she have learned phrases like 'wretch consum'd with care'? Would this poor drudge, who slaves in the mill day and, night care whether the grain was 'golden' or any other colour? Would she be likely to pray, 'confound the Suitor train'? These and other items of Latinate and poetic diction overlay her curse with a poise that conceals the exasperation which she feels so deeply, and they obscure the main point of her presence in the *Odyssey*, which is to show the destruction of the suitors as a communal punishment for injustices committed against all ranks of the community and not the mere personal vengeance of Ulysses.

203

Chapman's version preserves the bitterness of the original appeal in language appropriate to the woman's character. There are, to be sure, a few Latinisms here, too—'ostent', (which Pope borrowed), and 'dissolv'd', but these do not alter the tone of the whole speech:

> O King of men and Gods, a mighty stroke
> Thy thundring hand laide on the cope of starres,
> No cloud in all the aire; and therefore warres
> Thou bidst to some men in thy sure ostent!
> Performe to me (poore wretch) the maine event,
> And make this day the last, and most extream,
> In which the wooers pride shall solace them
> With whoorish banquets in *Ulysses* roofe,
> That with sad toyle to grinde them meale enough,
> Have quite dissolv'd my knees. Vouchsafe, then, now
> Thy thunders may their latest feast foreshow.
>
> (XX, 180-90, p. 311)

This poor old woman knows what has been going on in the palace and expresses, in 'whoorish banquets', the righteous malice of the poor drudge for the easy-living harlot. This is a crucial speech in the *Odyssey*, since it marks the point at which the innate patience and decency of the commonalty have been outraged by the antics of a degenerate aristocratic clique to the point of rebellion.

Pope's manner is more successful with the sophisticated and ironical bitterness of the suitors, as in Antinous' rebuke to Eumaeus for bringing the beggarly Ulysses into the banquet hall:

> And is this present, swineherd! of thy hand?
> Bring'st thou these vagrants to infest the land?
> (Returns *Antinous* with retorted eye)
> Objects uncouth! to check the genial joy.
> Enough of these our court already grace,
> Of giant stomach, and of famish'd face.

Such guests *Eumaeus* to his country brings,
To share our feast and lead the life of Kings.

(XVII, 450-7)

These remarks are obviously addressed from a superior
person to a wayward underling. They imply a code of
manners in the light of which the beggar's introduction is
annoying but also ridiculous, an opportunity for supercilious
amusement. Antinous' superior sensibilities are offended—
'objects uncouth'—but the amused detachment he shows is
quite different from the passionate selfishness of his speech in
Homer where he seeks jealously to bar others from sharing
Odysseus' substance:

Notorious swineherd, why did you bring this man to the city?
Have we not enough vagabonds without him, beggarly nuisances
to spoil our feasts? Don't you think it enough that they gather
here and devour the substance of your master, that you invite this
fellow too?[11]

The comic anguish with which this glutton marks the
arrival of yet another mouth to feed at the trough is brought
out in Chapman's version:

O thou renowned Herdsman, why to us
Brought'st thou this begger? Serves it not our hands,
That other land-leapers and cormorands
(Prophane poor knaves) lye on us, unconducted,
But you must bring them? So amisse instructed
Art thou in course of thrift, as not to know
Thy Lords goods wrackt in this their over-flow?

(XVII, 506-12, p. 268)

The irony here lies in the situation and not in the speech, and
it points up the truly base and ungenerous nature of
Antinous for which he is properly punished: in the midst of
abundance which costs him nothing he begrudges those who
are truly distressed the slightest share.

Similar distinctions are found in the two translations of

Odysseus' rebuke to Antinous for his lack of generosity:

Now it seems thou hast no brains to match thy beauty. Out of thine own substance thou wouldest give thy suppliant not even a grain of salt, thou who now, sitting at another's table hadst not the heart to take the bread and give me a little. And yet there is plenty here.[12]

The language of Pope's beggar is elevated, smooth and majestic:

> The Chief, retiring, Souls, like that in thee,
> Ill suit such forms of grace and dignity.
> Nor will that hand to utmost need afford
> The smallest portion of a wasteful board,
> Whose luxury whole patrimonies sweeps,
> Yet starving Want, amidst the riot, weeps.
>
> XVII, 537-42)

One can scarcely blame Antinous for throwing a foot-stool! In the speech we find that the specific elements of the original have been, characteristically, reduced to generalities. Ulysses' resentment is recast into a personification that recalls the mournful, stylized figures put on tombs. This personified Want, weeping 'amidst the riot', is embarrassing, since it makes Ulysses rather overdramatize himself.

Chapman finds drama enough in the details of the original:

> O Gods (replied Ulysses) I see now
> You beare no soule in this your goodly show.
> Beggars at your boord, I perceive, should get
> Scarse salt from your hands, if themselves broght meat;
> Since, sitting where anothers boord is spread,
> That flowes with feast, not to the broken bread
> Will your allowance reach.
>
> (XVII, 608-14, p. 270)

Here Ulysses the beggar speaks as one whose knowledge of want is too intimate and too pressing to allow leisure for generalities and personifications. The bitter jest about the salt, which Chapman has made more acrid than in the original, focuses on the immediate need, as 'The smallest portion of a wasteful board' does not, while the broken rhythms and simple words imply a strong personal emotion in the speaker. All this better suits the disguise which the king has assumed than the magniloquence of the Augustan version.

The bias of Pope's style in the *Odyssey* tends always to raise the poem above the level of ordinary experience. Whatever is accidental, local, individual, or mean is eliminated in the process. The idiosyncrasies which distinguish Homer's characters are largely abandoned in favour of a more uniform manner which has the effect of making them all speak alike. Some of the charm of the original which comes from the interaction of familiar and 'low' incidents with heroic or mythical ones is lost in the generalizing and elevating style of narration, which is perhaps better suited to the grander material of the *Iliad*. As Pope showed in the postscript to his *Odyssey*, he was profoundly aware of the challenge presented by the mixed style of this epic: 'Let it be remembered, that the same genius that soared the highest, and from whom the greatest models of the *sublime* are derived, was also he who stooped the lowest, and gave to the simple *narrative* its utmost perfection. Which of these was the harder task to Homer himself, I cannot pretend to determine; but to his translator I can affirm (however unequal all his imitations must be) that of the latter has been much more difficult.'[13] For this candid self-criticism the great Augustan deserves much credit. He recognized that Homer had shown Odysseus 'not in that full light of glory', as in the *Iliad*, 'but in the shade of common life, with a mixture of such qualities as are requisite to all the lowest accidents of it',[14] but he was unable to give full expression to these accidents and to the fascinating details of private and domestic life in which the poem abounds. The Augustan assumptions about the proper subject of poetry would probably have predisposed him in favour of Ulysses as the warrior-statesman at Troy rather than Ulysses as father, husband, and householder.

III

In translating more formal or elevated speeches Pope is usually Chapman's superior. He is more at ease than Chapman in enunciating the feelings of Telemachus on Orestes' act of vengeance, or Calypso's criticism of her fellow deities, or Ulysses' farewell to the Prince Alcinous, or in most of the other speeches on public topics or public occasions. In the examples which follow personal feelings have a public dimension as well, because the speakers and those they address and the subjects they speak on have a more than merely personal importance. Their language is therefore, rightly, oratorical. In such passages Pope's interest in general truths and broad similitudes finds its perfect expression in the most strikingly rhetorical capabilities of the closed couplet. Chapman's looser verse, on the other hand, tends to be disorderly in such speeches, principally because he habitually attempts to heighten his style with rambling circumlocutions. His genius for particularity which was evident in the humbler speeches of men and women speaking as individuals forsakes him often when he has to deal with princes talking to princes or gods to gods. Curiously enough, his language in such cases tends to be much more abstract than Pope's.

The speech of Telemachus to Nestor in which he compares his situation with that of Orestes is a tribute to a great public hero and an opportunity for him to express to Ulysses' old friend the earnest desire to avenge his own father which he feels and which he is expected to feel:

Nestor, great glory of the Achaeans, that son indeed took his revenge, and the Achaeans shall spread his fame abroad that men may yet hear of it. Would the gods might clothe me in such strength, that I might take vengeance on the suitors for their injurious and evil conduct, who wantonly plot evil against me.[15]

Eloquence and clarity are paramount in such a speech, but Chapman's Telemachus is neither eloquent nor clear:

> O thou the greatest grace of *Greece*,
> *Orestes* made that wreake his master peece,
> And him the Greeks will give a master praise,
> Verse finding him to last all after daies.
> And would to God the Gods would favour me
> With his performance, that my injurie,
> Done by my mothers wooers (being so foule)
> I might revenge upon their every soule;
> Who (pressing me with contumelies) dare
> Such things as past the powere of utterance are.
>
> (III, 268-77, p. 37)

This speech has little coherence and almost no rhetorical control. It is really a collection of clauses thrown haphazardly together, with a tentative use of alliteration here, of inversion there, of anaphora in another place.

Pope's version is clear, emphatic and alive:

> O thou the grace
> And lasting glory of the *Grecian* race!
> Just was the vengeance, and to latest days
> Shall long posterity resound the praise.
> Some God this arm with equal prowess bless!
> And the proud Suitors shall its force confess:
> Injurious men! who while my soul is sore
> Of fresh Affronts, are meditating more.
>
> (III, 246-53)

Here Telemachus' voice resounds with that conviction and resolution which he feels *and which he must show*. The rhetorical subtleties contribute to this effect, instead of detracting from it, as they do in Chapman.

We found earlier that Pope's shepherds and beggars affected a somewhat forensic style, so let us look now at a corresponding fault in Chapman illustrated by his treatment of a goddess's speech. The speaker is Calypso, who is complaining to Hermes of unjust behaviour at the hands of her fellow deities. Here is a close translation of the Homeric passage:

Cruel are ye gods, and above all others quick to envy, seeing that ye begrudge our love affairs with men, even if they are open. So when rosy-fingered Dawn took Orion, you easy-living gods envied her until in Ortygia chaste, golden-throned Artemis struck him with her gentle shafts and killed him.[16]

In Chapman the angry woman obscures the goddess:

> Insatiate are ye Gods, past all that live,
> In all things you affect; which still converts
> Your powres to envies. It afflicts your hearts
> That any Goddesse should (as you obtaine
> The use of earthly dames) enjoy the men,
> And most in open mariage. So ye far'd
> When the delicious-fingered Morning shar'd
> *Orions* bed; you easie-living States
> Could never satisfie your emulous hates,
> Till in Ortygia the precise-liv'd Dame
> (Gold-thron'd Diana) on him rudely came,
> And with her swift shafts slue him.
>
> (V, 155-66, p. 75)

The cynicism of 'the use of earthly dames' and the sarcastic allusion to Diana as 'the precise-liv'd Dame' are touches of personal rancour, but they are hardly in keeping with Calypso's character as the unsophisticated, innocently-amorous goddess of this naturalistic paradise.

Pope's Calypso is dignified in her anger:

> Ungracious Gods! with spite and envy curst!
> Still to your own aetherial race the worst!

Ye envy mortal and immortal joy,
And love, the only sweet of life, destroy.
Did ever Goddess by her charms ingage
A favour'd mortal, and not feel your rage?
So when *Aurora* sought *Orion's* love,
Her joys disturb'd your blissful hours above,
Till in *Ortygia, Dian's* winged dart
Had pierc'd the hapless hunter to the heart.

(V, 149-58)

The generalizing and depersonalizing tendency of Pope's translation is here perfectly appropriate. It raises the speech above the level of vilification to dignified rebuke, and Calypso speaks like a goddess.

Too often Chapman's attempts at grandeur evaporate in an effusion of words. This is especially true in the speeches of Alcinous, where it might be argued with some reason that the translator is trying to characterize a king who is dwarfed in every respect by his queen. But towards the end of his visit in the Phaeacian court Ulysses begins to suffer from the same defect. The hero's farewell speech is a case in point. It is literally rendered thus:

Lord Alcinous, famed above all men, pour libations now, and send me on my way in peace. Fare you well! For now whatever my heart desired has been fulfilled: a convoy and gifts of friendship. On my return may I find my blameless wife at home with my friends unscathed.[17]

Chapman mishandles this simple formula:

Alcinous, of all men most renown'd,
Dismisse me with as safe passe as you vow
(Your offering past) and may the Gods to you
In all contentment use as full a hand;
For now my landing heere and stay shall stand
In all perfection with my hearts desire,
Both my so safe deduction to aspire,

211

> And loving gifts, which may the Gods to me
> As blest in use make as your acts are free,
> Even to the finding firme in love, and life,
> With all desir'd event, my friends, and wife.
>
> (XIII, 66-76, p. 197)

The diffuseness of this need hardly be pointed out, but there are other faults worth noting. The prevailing looseness of the expression contrasts with the pinched-in reference to the pouring of libations in the parenthesis, 'your offering past'. Without the original as a guide one cannot be sure what the offering is or whether it has already been made or is about to be made. Yet this rite is important enough to deserve some rhetorical emphasis. Another fault is the colourless and abstract nature of the key words—'passe', 'full', 'stand', 'deduction', and 'event'. Then the transitive infinitive, 'to aspire', bears a very vague grammatical relation to the two lines which precede it, while the apposition, 'and loving gifts', following the long appositional clause in which the infinitive occurs, is a rhetorical anticlimax. The whole suggests a complexity of meaning which is simply not there.

One turns with relief to Pope's well-articulated version:

> O thou, the first in merit and command!
> And you the Peers and Princes of the land!
> May ev'ry joy be yours! nor this the least,
> When due libation shall have crown'd the feast,
> Safe to my home to send your happy guest.
> Compleat are now the bounties you have giv'n,
> Be all those bounties but confirm'd by Heav'n!
> So may I find, when all my wand'rings cease,
> My consort blameless, and my friends in peace.
>
> (XIII, 47-55)

There are both firmness and grace in this. On such an occasion, where the manner of expression is just as important as the ideas expressed, it is essential that each sentiment be spoken with the proper emphasis and in the right order: compliment to the king, kind wishes to the nobles, a pious and well-mannered regard for the customary rituals, a declaration of gratitude, and a hope for the future. Pope has no master in handling this kind of formal, occasional speech.

IV

While faults quite often mar Chapman's high style in the formal speeches of the *Odyssey*, his handling of the vivid descriptive passages is excellent. One of the best instances, as a final illustration, is his version of the following account of Hermes' flight from Olympus to Calypso's island:

With this [his wand] in his hand the mighty Argeiphontes flew. Onto Pieria he stepped from the upper air and swooped down upon the sea, and then sped over the wave like a cormorant, which in quest of fish over the dread gulf of the untiring sea wets its thick plumage in the brine.[18]

> This took, he stoopt *Pierea*, and thence
> Glid through the aire, and *Neptunes* confluence
> Kist as he flew, and checkt the waves as light
> As any sea-mew in her fishing flight,
> Her thicke wings soucing in the savorie seas.
>
> (V, 69-73, p. 73)

The delightful *élan* of this comes partly from the sense of free and joyful flight which is conveyed by the corresponding phrases 'glid through the aire' and 'kist as he flew', where the trochaic inversions give lilting motion and a feeling of ease and nimbleness. The simile, especially in the last line, contributes even more. Here the sea-mew sousing its thick wings seems to saturate itself in delight. 'Savorie seas' is a particularly good detail. It has the shock of an original perception which realizes the harmony of the seabird with its environment, in Homer a 'dread gulf' from the human viewpoint, but in Chapman, from the bird's view, an inexhaustible source of food. So richly sensuous is the image that the last two lines can support the extremely heavy alliteration of nine 's's. Chapman's whole passage expresses the carefree god's freedom from human limitations.

Where Chapman animates the passage by focusing on such details, Pope generalizes it into a set-piece:

> He grasps the wand that causes sleep to fly,
> Or in soft slumber seals the wakeful eye:
> Then shoots from heav'n to high *Pieria's* steep
> And stoops incumbent on the rolling deep.
> So wat'ry fowl, that seek their fishy food,
> With wings expanded o'er the foaming flood,
> Now sailing smooth the level surface sweep,
> Now dip their pinions in the briny deep.
>
> (V, 60-7)

'Stoops incumbent on the rolling deep' is appropriate to Satan lying on the asphaltic pool, but it suggests something much more ponderous than a sea-bird skimming over the waves. The difference between Chapman's sea-mew and Pope's 'wat'ry fowl' is indicative of fundamental differences between the two translations. The latter tries to give us the universal truth about these birds by normalizing all their actions: it shows more interest in genus than in the particular bird, while the former makes us feel the peculiar satisfactions of being a sea-gull—feelings which Pope, no doubt, would have considered no proper part of man's experience. These two small fragments represent, therefore, two totally different concepts: Chapman's is one where the texture of man's daily experience and of his immediate environment is considered valuable, and Pope's another where the general outlines and basic truths of man's world are considered most important. This distinction is reflected in the verse. Chapman's freer cadences help to convey a sense of relish and spontaneity. Pope's verse is managed as dexterously for its own purposes, which are to remind us of the majesty of the god in the bird rather than the joyous freedom of the bird in the god. Pope's 'surface' keeps us aware at all times of 'the permanent relations of human beings'—or of gods —'in society'—or the cosmos. These relations are repeatedly enunciated and continually implied in Chapman's poem, but its surface is much more variegated. The freedom of the Elizabethans and Jacobeans to be thus indirect, to 'imply immensely' and to state relatively little, is probably related to their intuitive, habitual response to the great truths which were beginning to be forgotten or challenged on a grand scale by the end of the seventeenth century, and which, by Pope's time, required more overt and more frequent emphasis lest they be overlooked.

My analysis of Chapman's *Odyssey* is finished, and now the reader will decide for himself how far Chapman was successful in 'reviving' his beloved original as an English epic poem. If I have represented Chapman's interpretation of Homer's meaning correctly, it is a profoundly original one. If Homer's poem supports this interpretation, as I think it does, then Chapman's version is a revelation in Homeric criticism. If, furthermore, Chapman has made his version live as an English epic, he has made a massive contribution to our literature which has not been fully appreciated.

NOTES TO CHAPTER V

1. Since Pope's *Odyssey* was a product of collaboration, examples will be drawn only from those Books attributed to Pope: III, V, VII, IX, X, XIII, XIV, XV, XVII, XX, XXI, and XXIV. See George Sherburn, *The Early Career of Alexander Pope* (Oxford, Oxford University Press, 1934), p. 260: 'Broome implies that he did three books of the translation, whereas from his correspondence with Pope and from his later statements it is clear that he did eight: II, VI, VIII, XI, XII, XVI, XVIII, and XXIII. To Fenton he ascribes two books, though Fenton actually did four: I, IV, XIX, XXII.'

2. *The Odyssey of Homer Translated from the Greek* (London, 1725–6), XX, 235.

3. *The Augustans*, ed. Maynard Mack (New York, Prentice Hall, 1950), p. 2. This is vol. V in *English Masterpieces—an Anthology of Imaginative Literature from Chaucer to T. S. Eliot*.

4. '"Wit and Poetry and Pope"': Some Observations on his Imagery', in *Pope and his Contemporaries, Essays presented to George Sherburn*, ed. Clifford and Landa (London, Oxford University Press, 1949), p. 21.

5.   ἦ τοι μὲν τόδε καυτὸς ὀίεαι, ὡς κεν ἐτύχθη,
εἰ ζωόν γ' Αἴγισθον ἐνὶ μεγάροισιν ἔτετμεν
Ἀτρεΐδης Τροίηθεν ἰών, ξανθὸς Μενέλαος·
τῶ κέ οἱ οὐδὲ θανόντι χυτὴν ἐπὶ γαῖαν ἔχευαν,
ἀλλ' ἄρα τόν γε κύνες τε καὶ οἰωνοὶ κατέδαψαν
κείμενον ἐν πεδίῳ ἑκὰς ἄστεος, οὐδέ κέ τίς μιν
κλαῦσεν Ἀχαιϊάδων· μάλα γὰρ μέγα μήσατο ἔργον.
ἡμεῖς μὲν γὰρ κεῖθι πολέας τελέοντες ἀέθλους
ἥμεθ'· ὁ δ' εὔκηλος μυχῷ Ἄργεος ἱπποβότοιο
πόλλ' Ἀγαμεμνονέην ἄλοχον θέλγεσκεν ἔπεσσιν.   (III, 255–64)

6. *The Primary Language of Poetry in the 1740's and 1840's* (Berkeley and Los Angeles, University of California Press, 1950), p. 234.

7.   Ὣς ἄρα μιν φαμένη ῥάβδῳ ἐπεμάσσατ' Ἀθήνη.
κάρψε μέν οἱ χρόα καλὸν ἐνὶ γναμπτοῖσι μέλεσσι,
ξανθὰς δ' ἐκ κεφαλῆς ὄλεσε τρίχας, ἀμφὶ δὲ δέρμα
πάντεσσιν μελέεσσι παλαιοῦ θῆκε γέροντος,
κνύζωσεν δέ οἱ ὄσσε πάρος περικαλλέ' ἐόντε·
ἀμφὶ δέ μιν ῥάκος ἄλλο κακὸν βάλεν ἠδὲ χιτῶνα,
ῥωγαλέα ῥυπόωντα, κακῷ μεμορυγμένα καπνῷ·
ἀμφὶ δέ μιν μέγα δέρμα ταχείης ἕσσ' ἐλάφοιο,
ψιλόν· δῶκε δέ οἱ σκῆπτρον καὶ ἀεικέα πήρην,
πυκνὰ ῥωγαλέην· ἐν δὲ στρόφος ἦεν ἀορτήρ.   (XIII, 429–38)

8.   Γιγνώσκω, φρονέω· τά γε δὴ νοέοντι κελεύεις.
ἀλλ' ἔρχευ προπάροιθεν, ἐγὼ δ' ὑπολείψομαι αὐτοῦ.
οὐ γάρ τι πληγέων ἀδαήμων οὐδὲ βολάων.
τολμήεις μοι θυμός, ἐπεὶ κακὰ πολλὰ πέπονθα
κύμασι καὶ πολέμῳ· μετὰ καὶ τόδε τοῖσι γενέσθω.
γαστέρα δ' οὔ πως ἔστιν ἀποκρύψαι μεμαυῖαν,
οὐλομένην, ἣ πολλὰ κάκ' ἀνθρώποισι δίδωσι,
τῆς ἕνεκεν καὶ νῆες ἐΰζυγοι ὁπλίζονται
πόντον ἐπ' ἀτρύγετον, κακὰ δυσμενέεσσι φέρουσαι.   (XVII, 281–9)

9. A typical example is Eumaeus' description of the suitors in XV, 350–6:

> Not such, my friend, the servants of their feast;
> A blooming train in rich embroid'ry drest,

With earth's whole tribute the bright table bends,
And smiling round celestial Youth attends.
Stay then: no eye askance beholds thee here;
Sweet is thy converse to each social ear;
Well pleas'd, and pleasing, in our cottage rest. . . .

10.   Ζεῦ πάτερ, ὅς τε θεοῖσι καὶ ἀνθρώποισιν ἀνάσσεις,
ἢ μεγάλ' ἐβρόντησας ἀπ' οὐρανοῦ ἀστερόεντος,
οὐδέ ποθι νέφος ἐστί· τέρας νύ τεῳ τόδε φαίνεις.
κρῆνον νῦν καὶ ἐμοὶ δειλῇ ἔπος, ὅττι κεν εἴπω·
μνηστῆρες πύματόν τε καὶ ὕστατον ἤματι τῷδε
ἐν μεγάροις Ὀδυσῆος ἐλοίατο δαῖτ' ἐρατεινήν,
οἱ δή μοι καμάτῳ θυμαλγέϊ γούνατ' ἔλυσαν·
ἄλφιτα τευχούσῃ· νῦν ὕστατα δειπνήσειαν.   (XX, 112-19)

11.   Ὦ ἀρίγνωτε συβῶτα, τίη δὲ σὺ τόνδε πόλινδε
ἤγαγες; ἢ οὐχ ἅλις ἧμιν ἀλήμονές εἰσι καὶ ἄλλοι,
πτωχοὶ ἀνιηροί, δαιτῶν ἀπολυμαντῆρες;
ἢ ὄνοσαι ὅτι τοι βίοτον κατέδουσιν ἄνακτος
ἐνθάδ' ἀγειρόμενοι, σὺ δὲ καὶ προτὶ τόνδ' ἐκάλεσσας;   (XVII, 375-9)

12.   οὐκ ἄρα σοί γ' ἐπὶ εἴδεϊ καὶ φρένες ἦσαν·
οὐ σύ γ' ἂν ἐξ οἴκου σῷ ἐπιστάτῃ οὐδ' ἅλα δοίης,
ὃς νῦν ἀλλοτρίοισι παρήμενος οὔ τί μοι ἔτλης
σίτου ἀποπροελὼν δόμεναι· τὰ δὲ πολλὰ πάρεστιν.   (XVII, 454-7)

13. Vol. V, p. 241.

14. *Ibid.* p. 237.

15.   Ὦ Νέστορ Νηληϊάδη, μέγα κῦδος Ἀχαιῶν,
καὶ λίην κεῖνος μὲν ἐτίσατο, καί οἱ Ἀχαιοὶ
οἴσουσι κλέος εὐρὺ καὶ ἐσσομένοισι ἀοιδήν.
αἲ γὰρ ἐμοὶ τοσσήνδε θεοὶ δύναμιν περιθεῖεν,
τίσασθαι μνηστῆρας ὑπερβασίης ἀλεγεινῆς,
οἵ τέ μοι ὑβρίζοντες ἀτάσθαλα μηχανόωνται.   (III, 202-7)

16.   Σχέτλιοί ἐστε, θεοί, ζηλήμονες ἔξοχον ἄλλων,
οἵ τε θεαῖς ἀγάασθε παρ' ἀνδράσιν εὐνάζεσθαι
ἀμφαδίην, ἤν τίς τε φίλον ποιήσετ' ἀκοίτην.
ὣς μὲν ὅτ' Ὠρίων' ἕλετο ῥοδοδάκτυλος Ἠώς,
τόφρα οἱ ἠγάασθε θεοὶ ῥεῖα ζώοντες,
ἧος ἐν Ὀρτυγίῃ χρυσόθρονος Ἄρτεμις ἁγνὴ
οἷς ἀγανοῖς βελέεσσιν ἐποιχομένη κατέπεφνεν.   (V, 118-24)

17.   Ἀλκίνοε κρεῖον, πάντων ἀριδείκετε λαῶν,
πέμπετέ με σπείσαντες ἀπήμονα, χαίρετε δ' αὐτοί·
ἤδη γὰρ τετέλεσται ἅ μοι φίλος ἤθελε θυμός,
πομπὴ καὶ φίλα δῶρα, τά μοι θεοὶ Οὐρανίωνες
ὄλβια ποιήσειαν. ἀμύμονα δ' οἴκοι ἄκοιτιν
νοστήσας εὕροιμι σὺν ἀρτεμέεσσι φίλοισιν.   (XIII, 38-43)

217

18.   τὴν μετὰ χερσὶν ἔχων πέτετο κρατὺς ἀργειφόντης.
Πιερίην δ' ἐπιβὰς ἐξ αἰθέρος ἔμπεσε πόντῳ·
σεύατ' ἔπειτ' ἐπὶ κῦμα λάρῳ ὄρνιθι ἐοικώς,
ὅς τε κατὰ δεινοὺς κόλπους ἁλὸς ἀτρυγέτοιο
ἰχθῦς ἀγρώσσων πυκινὰ πτερὰ δεύεται ἅλμῃ.   (V, 49-53)

SELECTED BIBLIOGRAPHY

THE first section of this bibliography includes the basic texts I have used in this study: editions of Homer and Chapman together with certain lexicons of the Greek language. In the second section I have listed items of three sorts: books and articles which I have found immediately and specifically relevant to my own subject, others to which I owe a more general debt, and finally, certain unpublished works which may have influenced my thinking in various ways. There are other books which I have found most useful which do not appear in this list—books which any student of seventeenth-century English literature, or the classics, or epic poetry would know, such as Basil Willey's *The Seventeenth-Century Background* or the Pauly-Wissowa *Real-Encyclopädie der classischen Altertumswissenschaft*. Books like these are as widely known as they are useful, but it would unnecessarily extend this bibliography to include them.

I have used the following abbreviations:

ELH: English Literary History.
MP: Modern Philology.
RES: Review of English Studies.
SP: Studies in Philology.

A. PRIMARY SOURCES

1. CHAPMAN

Achilles Shield. Translated as the other Seven Bookes of Homer, out of his eighteenth booke of Iliades. By George Chapman Gent (1598).
The Iliads of Homer Prince of Poets. Never before in any language truely translated. With a Comment upon some of his chiefe places; Donne according to the Greeke By Geo: Chapman (1611).
Homer's Odysses Translated according to yᵉ Greeke by Geo: Chapman (1615?).
The Whole Works of Homer; Prince of Poetts In his Iliads and Odysses. Translated according to the Greeke, By Geo: Chapman (1616).
Chapman's Iliad, ed. with notes and introduction by R. F. Hooper (2nd ed., London, 1865).

Chapman's Odyssey, ed. with notes and introduction by R. F. Hooper (2nd ed., London, 1897).

The Poems of George Chapman, ed. Phyllis Brooks Bartlett (New York, MLA; London, Oxford University Press, 1941).

Quotations from Chapman's poems are taken from this edition.

Elizabethan Critical Essays, ed. G. G. Smith (London, Oxford University Press, 1937).

Quotations from Chapman's critical prose are taken from this collection unless otherwise noted.

2. HOMER

Ilias, ed. D. B. Monro (3rd ed., Oxford, Clarendon Press, 1932).

Odyssea, ed. T. W. Allen (2nd ed., Oxford, Clarendon Press, 1917).

Quotations are from this text.

Odyssea, ed. W. B. Stanford (London, Macmillan, 1948–50).

I have made particular use of the notes in these three editions.

The Odyssey, ed. and tr. A. T. Murray (London, Heinemann, 1919).

B. SECONDARY SOURCES

Matthew Arnold, *On Translating Homer* (London, 1861).

On Translating Homer, ed. and int. W. H. D. Rouse (London, John Murray, 1905).

Roger Ascham, *The Scholemaster* (London, 1570).

J. W. H. Atkins, *Literary Criticism in Antiquity*, 2 vols. (Cambridge, Cambridge University Press, 1937).

English Literary Criticism: the Mediaeval Phase (Cambridge, Cambridge University Press, 1943).

English Literary Criticism: the Renaissance (London, Cambridge University Press, 1947).

Erich Auerbach, *Mimesis: the Representation of Reality in Western Literature*, tr. Willard Trask (Princeton, Princeton University Press, 1953).

Phyllis Bartlett, 'Chapman's Revisions in his *Iliads*', *ELH*, 2 (1935).

'The Heroes of Chapman's *Homer*', *RES*, 17 (1941).

Roy W. Battenhouse, 'Chapman and the Nature of Man', *ELH*, 12 (1945).

Margaret Bottrall, 'Chapman's Defence of Difficulty in Poetry', *Criterion*, 16 (1937).

SELECTED BIBLIOGRAPHY

C. M. Bowra, *From Virgil to Milton* (London, Oxford University Press, 1948).

Douglas Bush, *English Literature in the Earlier Seventeenth Century* (Oxford, Clarendon Press, 1945).

Mythology and the Renaissance Tradition in English Poetry (Minneapolis, University of Minnesota Press; London, Oxford University Press, 1932).

Archibald Y. Campbell, 'Homer and his Translators', *London Mercury*, 20 (1929).

S. T. Coleridge, *Notes and Lectures upon Shakespeare and Some of the Old Poets and Dramatists*, ed. Mrs. H. N. Coleridge (London, 1849).

Natalis Comes, *Mythologiae* (Paris, 1581).

Domenico Comparetti, *Vergil in the Middle Ages*, tr. E. F. M. Benecke (London and New York, 1895).

E. R. Dodds, *The Greeks and the Irrational* (Berkeley and Los Angeles, University of California Press, 1951).

Helen F. Dunbar, *Symbolism in Mediaeval Thought* (New Haven, Yale University Press, 1929).

T. S. Eliot, 'The Metaphysical Poets', *Selected Essays, 1917–1932* (New York, Harcourt Brace, 1932).

Havelock Ellis, *Chapman with Illustrative Passages* (Bloomsbury, The Nonesuch Press, 1934).

Epictetus, *Encheiridion. Item, Cebetis Thebani Tabula de vita humana prudenter instituenda. . . . Omnia H. Wolfie interprete* (Cologne, 1595).

Erasmus, *Adagiorum Chiliades quatuor cum sesquicenturia. . . . Henrici Stephani animadversiones* (Geneva, 1558).

H. C. Fay, *Chapman's Iliads of Homer*: a Critical Introduction, with a specimen edition of Book Eleven (London, 1954).

Marsilio Ficino, *Commentary on Plato's Symposium*, tr. and ed. Sears Reynolds Jayne (Columbia, University of Missouri Press, 1944).

William Frost, 'Dryden and the Art of Translation' (unpublished Yale PhD. thesis, 1946).

W. D. Geddes, *The Problem of the Homeric Poems* (London, 1878).

William Chase Greene, *Moira* (Cambridge, Harvard University Press, 1944).

Jane Harrison, *Themis: a Study of the Social Origins of Greek Religion* (Cambridge, Cambridge University Press, 1912).

Heracliti Quaestiones Homericae (Leipzig, Teubner, 1910).

Anne B. Hersman, *Studies in Greek Allegorical Interpretation* (Chicago, Blue Sky Press, 1906).

Roger Hinks, *Myth and Allegory in Ancient Art* (London, Warburg Institute, 1939).

Quintus Horatius Flaccus, *Epistulae*, ed. A. S. Wilkins (London and New York, 1899).

R. H. Horne, 'Remarks on Translation', *Classical Museum*, 1 (1844).

Werner Jaeger, *Paideia: the Ideals of Greek Culture*, tr. Gilbert Highet (New York, Oxford University Press, 1945).

Sears R. Jayne, 'Platonism in English Drama of the Renaissance, 1442–1642' (unpublished Yale PhD. thesis, 1949).

O. L. Jiriszek, *Specimens of Tudor Translations from the Classics* (Heidelberg, 1923).

Douglas M. Knight, *Pope and the Heroic Tradition: a Critical Study of his Iliad* (New Haven, Yale University Press; London, Oxford University Press, 1951).

The Works of Charles and Mary Lamb, ed. E. V. Lucas (London, Methuen, 1903–5).

H. B. Lathrop, *Translations from the Classics from Caxton to Chapman, 1477–1620* (Madison, University of Wisconsin Press, 1933).

C. S. Lewis, *The Allegory of Love: a Study in Medieval Tradition* (London, Oxford University Press, 1938).

George C. Loane, 'Chapman's *Homer*', *Cornhill Magazine*, 156 (1938).

George deF. Lord, 'The *Odyssey* and the Western World', *Sewanee Review*, 62 (1954).

The Augustans, ed. and int. Maynard Mack (New York, Prentice Hall, 1950).

Maynard Mack, '"Wit and Poetry and Pope"; some Observations on his Imagery', *Pope and his Contemporaries. Essays presented to George Sherburn*, ed. Clifford and Landa (London, Oxford University Press, 1949).

D. S. Margoliouth, *The Homer of Aristotle* (Oxford, Oxford University Press, 1923).

Josephine Miles, *The Primary Language of Poetry in the 1740's and 1840's* (Berkeley and Los Angeles, University of California Press, 1950).

Gilbert Murray, *The Rise of the Greek Epic* (3rd ed., Oxford, Clarendon Press, 1924).

Paul M. Pickrel, 'Religious Allegory in Mediaeval England: an Introductory Study based on the Vernacular Sermon before 1250' (unpublished Yale PhD. thesis, 1944).

Divini Platonis Opera omnia quae exstant. Marsilio Ficino interprete (Frankfort, 1602).

Plutarchi Chæronensis quae exstant omnia. Cum latina interpretatione Hermanni Cruserii; Gulielmi Xylandri, et doctorum virorum notis . . . (Frankfort, 1599).

L. A. Post, 'The Moral Pattern in Homer', *Transactions and Proceedings of the American Philological Association*, 70 (1939).

Ezra Pound, Letter to W. H. D. Rouse, *Hudson Review*, 3 (1950).

'Translators of Greek: Early Translators of Homer', *The Literary Essays of Ezra Pound* (New York, New Directions, 1954).

F. T. Prince, *The Italian Element in Milton's Verse* (Oxford, Clarendon Press, 1954).

George Puttenham, *The Arte of English Poesie*, ed. Willcock and Walker (Cambridge, Cambridge University Press, 1936).

H. M. Regel, 'Über George Chapman's Homerübersetzung', *Englische Studien*, 5 (1882).

Veré L. Rubel, *Poetic Diction in the English Renaissance* (New York, MLA; London, Oxford University Press, 1941).

Leslie A. Rutledge, 'George Chapman's Theory of the Soul and of Poetry' (unpublished Harvard PhD. thesis, 1938).

George Saintsbury, *A History of English Prosody from the Twelfth Century to the Present Day* (London, Macmillan, 1906–10).

Sir J. E. Sandys, *A History of Classical Scholarship* (3rd ed., Cambridge, Cambridge University Press, 1908–21).

J. Scapula, *Lexicon Græco-Latinum novum in quo ex primitivorum & simplicium fontibus derivata atque composita ordine non minus naturali, quam alphabetico, breuiter & dilucide deducuntur. Basileæ, MDCXV.*

F. L. Schoell, *Études sur l'humanisme continental en Angleterre* (Paris, Champion, 1926).

'Un Drame élisabéthain anonyme: "Charlemagne"', *Revue Germanique*, 9 (1913).

'George Chapman and the Italian Neo-Latinists of the Quattrocento', *MP*, 13 (1915).

'George Chapman's Commonplace Book', *MP*, 17 (1919).

George Sherburn, *The Early Career of Alexander Pope* (Oxford, Oxford University Press, 1934).

E. E. Sikes, *The Greek View of Poetry* (London, Methuen, 1931).

Donald Smalley, 'The Ethical Bias of Chapman's *Homer*', *SP*, 36 (1939).

Hallett Smith, *Elizabethan Poetry: a Study in Conventions, Meaning, and Expression* (Cambridge, Harvard University Press, 1952).

James Smith, 'George Chapman', *Scrutiny*, 3 (1934–5), 4 (1935–6).

Denton J. Snider, *Homer's Odyssey. A Commentary* (Chicago, 1895).

Janet Spens, 'Chapman's Ethical Thought', *Essays and Studies by Members of the English Association*, 11 (1925).

J. Spondanus (Jean de Sponde), *Homeri quæ extant omnia, Ilias, Odyssea, Batrachomyomachia, Hymni, poematia aliquot cum Latina versione omnium quæ circumferuntur emendatissim[a] aliquot locis iam castigatiore. perpetuis item iustisque in Iliada simul & Odysseam Io. Spondani . . . commentariis. Aureliæ Allobrogum Sumptibus Caldorianæ Societatis, MDCVI.*

A. C. Swinburne, *George Chapman: a Critical Essay* (London, 1875).

Allen Tate, 'Three Types of Poetry', *Reactionary Essays on Poetry and Ideas* (New York and London, Scribner, 1936).

J. Tate, 'Plato and Allegorical Interpretation', *Classical Quarterly*, 23 (1929).

'On the History of Allegorism', *Classical Quarterly*, 28 (1934).

J. A. K. Thomson, *Studies in the Odyssey* (Oxford, Clarendon Press, 1914).

W. B. C. Watkins, *Shakespeare and Spenser* (Princeton, Princeton University Press, 1950).

John William Wieler, *George Chapman: the Effect of Stoicism upon his Tragedies* (New York, King's Crown Press, 1949).